MW01028123

Impossible Women

IMPOSSIBLE WOMEN

*Lesbian Figures &
American Literature*

VALERIE ROHY

CORNELL UNIVERSITY PRESS *Ithaca & London*

First published 2000 by Cornell University Press
First printing, Cornell Paperbacks, 2000

Printed in the United States of America

Library of Congress Cataloging-in-Publication Data

Rohy, Valerie.
    Impossible women : lesbian figures and American literature / Valerie Rohy.
        p. cm
    Includes bibliographical references (p.) and index.
    ISBN 0-8014-3728-8 (cloth : acid-free paper)—ISBN 0-8014-8638-6
    (paper : acid-free paper)
        1. Lesbians' writings, American—History and criticism. 2. American
    literature—Women authors—History and criticism. 3. Homosexuality
    and literature—United States—History. 4. Women and literature—
    United States—History. 5. Lesbians in literature. I. Title.

PS153.L46 R64 2000
810.9'9206643—dc21
                                                                    99-087706

Cornell University Press strives to use environmentally responsible suppliers and materials to the fullest extent possible in the publishing of its books. Such materials include vegetable-based, low-VOC inks, and acid-free papers that are recycled, totally chlorine-free, or partly composed of nonwood fibers. Books that bear the logo of the FSC (Forest Stewardship Council) use paper taken from forests that have been inspected and certified as meeting the highest standards for environmental and social responsibility. For further information, visit our website at www.cornellpress.cornell.edu.

Cloth printing   10   9   8   7   6   5   4   3   2   1
Paperback printing   10   9   8   7   6   5   4   3   2   1

contents

Acknowledgments, *vii*

Introduction
Reading Impossibility, *1*

1 The Romance of the Real
The Blithedale Romance and *The Bostonians*, *13*

2 The Reproduction of Meaning
Language, Oedipality, and *The Awakening*, *42*

3 Modernist Perversity
The Repetition of Desire in *The Sun Also Rises*, *65*

4 Oral Narratives
"Race" and Sexuality in *Their Eyes Were Watching God*, *91*

5 Love's Substitutions
Elizabeth Bishop and the Lie of Language, *117*

Conclusion, *144*

Notes, *151*

Index, *185*

a c k n o w l e d g m e n t s

I have been very fortunate to have the assistance of a number of people while completing this book. It is a privilege to thank Lee Edelman, who helped to shape this study from its earliest pages and continues to represent for me what is most valuable and most compelling about the work of the academy. I am indebted to Linda Bamber both for her astute advice on these chapters and for her tireless encouragement. Other colleagues who read and commented on part or all of the manuscript include Elizabeth Ammons, Judith Brown, Bonnie Burns, Carol Flynn, Diana Fuss, John Fyler, Paul Morrison, and the members of the English Department "In Progress" group at Bowling Green State University; I thank all of them for their generous attention and invaluable suggestions. At Cornell University Press, Alison Shonkwiler, Catherine Rice, and Teresa Jesionowski guided the book's revision and production skillfully, and the Press's two readers provided insightful recommendations. Among the many others who followed this project's story, Annamaria Formichella, Meg Sempreora, Elliott McEldowney, and John Aberdeen have been faithful friends as well as sympathetic readers. Finally, I am grateful to my family for their steadfast love and support.

V. R.

Impossible Women

i n t r o d u c t i o n

Reading Impossibility

As its title suggests, this book finds its condition of possibility in a certain impossibility. The notion of lesbianism as impossible is, of course, common enough in contemporary heterosexual culture, which when not conjuring prurient images of lesbian sexuality can act incredulous about the very possibility of love between women. But the rhetoric of lesbian impossibility has a somewhat longer history and more complicated effects. From the 1880s to the 1920s, as Carroll Smith-Rosenberg suggests, masculinist sexology and literature used the figure of the "mannish lesbian" to designate "a freak of nature, a logical impossibility."[1] This "impossibility" becomes possible by being named as such; rather than suppressing the idea of lesbian desire, the homophobic discourse of impossibility promotes and structures its articulation. Terry Castle argues that lesbianism appeared in Western literature prior to 1900 "as an absence, as chimera or *amor impossibilia*—a kind of love that, by definition, cannot exist."[2] Her evocative phrase locates lesbian sexuality in the space of a contradiction, as a phantasm or "chimera" and also as a signifying "absence." The epistemological riddle of "*amor impossibilia*" hints at the paradoxical status of lesbian desire in dominant discourse: prohibited by language at the same time that it is produced by language, the desire that "by definition, cannot exist" comes into existence through the agency of the definition that names it as nonexistent.[3]

In patriarchal culture, as the following chapters explain, lesbian sexuality is construed as "impossible" in both senses of the word: it is supposedly nonexistent and at the same time intolerable. Taking "lesbian figures" as its focus, this book proposes that lesbianism and figurality bear a structural relation to one another in American literature and culture. *Impossible Women* examines representations of lesbian sexuality in American fiction from the mid-nineteenth century to the mid-twentieth century, elaborating a series of analogies between desire and discourse. The relation between representation and sexuality has informed some of the most important recent work in gay and lesbian criticism, which not only identifies the power of discursive practices to invent and police sexuality, but also recognizes the imbrication of sexuality in symbolic structures.[4] Lesbian theory in particular has profited from psychoanalytic readings of female sexuality by Judith Butler, Teresa de Lauretis, Diana Fuss, and Judith Roof, among others.[5] Building on the insights of such studies, this book suggests that understanding sexuality through theories of representation enables—indeed, requires—a literary criticism that examines representation, in turn, through the lens of sexuality. This book seeks to imagine how that critical project might take shape in the domain of nineteenth- and twentieth-century American literature and in relation to specific formations of lesbian sexuality in American culture.

Reading lesbian figures in American literature, I focus on the rhetorical and political consequences of lesbian "impossibility" as constructed by patriarchal discourse. In *Gender Trouble*, Butler suggests that gender is produced by a heterosexual discursive regime that refuses to recognize the existence of identities, including homosexuality, which it deems incoherent and unreadable. "The cultural matrix through which gender identity has become intelligible requires that certain kinds of 'identities' cannot 'exist'—that is, those in which gender does not follow from sex and those in which the practices of desire do not 'follow' from either sex or gender," Butler writes. Such identities consequently "appear only as developmental failures or logical impossibilities" within the realm of "norms of cultural intelligibility."[6] Yet as Butler notes, the institution of heterosexuality also demands that homosexuality exist and that it be culturally legible, for heterosexuality depends on the abjection of an "other" whose difference can never be defined with sufficient rigor to allay the paranoia of straight culture.[7] Discursively invented by the symbolic mechanisms it appears to precede, homosexuality becomes possible as a "logical impossibilit[y]." Gay and lesbian desires, that is, appear as simultaneously intelligible and unintelligible in straight culture; they become socially intelligible *as* the unintelligible. This paradoxical construction is especially resonant for lesbian figures, for as Judith Roof and Lynda Hart suggest, social and discursive prohibitions of lesbian desire are inextricably joined. Hart notes "the historical construction of the lesbian as a socially impossible identity" in sexology and psychoanalysis. Lesbianism, Roof suggests, figures a gap in patriarchal discourse, appearing only as a "representational impossibility: it can be there, but it cannot be seen in its own terms since such terms do not exist."[8] This view of lesbian sexuality recalls feminist theories of femininity itself as "impossible" or unrepresentable, notably Julia Kristeva's assertion that "woman" is "something that cannot be represented, something that is not said, something above and beyond nomenclatures and ideologies."[9] While lesbian sexuality, as this book will argue, is never exempt from hegemonic constructions of femininity, Roof's notion of lesbian desire as "representational impossibility" differs from Kristeva's theory of femininity in stressing the constructed, contingent nature of this formation. Lesbian impossibility is not essential but ideological.

Impossibility is also a privileged term in the vocabularies of deconstruction and psychoanalysis, designating a point of resistance inherent to the structures of symbolization and desire. For Paul de Man, language constitutes a *mise en abyme* founded on impossibility. The "impossibility of metaphor," as de Man puts it, and the "impossibility of theory" itself designate the impossibility of any meaning that is not compromised by the instability of signification, the unending slippages of figural language, and the fantasmatic bond between signifier and signified.[10] Framing this notion in psychoanalytic terms, Slavoj Žižek argues in *Looking Awry* that notions of "masculine" and "feminine" reflect the fact that "symbolization as such is by definition structured around a certain central impossibility, a deadlock that is nothing but a structuring of this impossibility."[11] This "fundamental impasse of symbolization," as Žižek calls it, these "paradoxes proper to language as such," inhere in the futile dream of secure meaning amid the unending displacements of the signifying chain, whose signs both exceed and fall short of what they signify. Yet the "paradoxes," the "deadlock," the "impasse" of symbolization also constitute the "fundamental" logic of its operation. In both deconstructive and psychoanalytic models, that is, the logic of representation not only contains but also depends on an immanent contradiction, the insistent recurrence of meaninglessness within structures of meaning.

I take impossibility, then, as a kind of vanishing point in both discourse and desire—not where these systems cease to exist but where they turn away from their own incoherence, where their success becomes their failure. As a name for an internal resistance, impossibility also describes the unacknowledged contradictions within hegemonic systems of sexuality, which patriarchal culture, in its will to meaning, displaces onto lesbian figures. The chapters that follow read lesbian sexuality as culturally framed by difference and negativity, impossibility and figurality, in an attempt to move beyond the register of presence and essentialism. But as de Man and Žižek make clear, the place of the "impossible" is far from nonexistent, empty, or insignificant. Rather, impossibility incites and enables desire and language; it is the very condition of their existence and of our existence as subjects. The aim of *Impossible Women*, therefore, is to examine the intersections of symbolic and sexual systems at the point of their mutual "impossibility" and to trace the construction of lesbian sexuality as a figure for a resistance on which sexual, national, and literary ideologies of normative reproduction depend.

Literary Desire

Reading texts by Hawthorne, James, Hemingway, Chopin, Hurston, and Bishop, *Impossible Women* examines the rhetoric of American literature that promotes its own analogies between desire and representation by equating female sexual perversity with linguistic perversity. How, this book asks, is lesbian sexuality inflected by the forms and conventions of American literature, and how does the representation of female perversity itself contribute to American literary traditions? What cultural work is performed by lesbian figures within heterosexual ideology? Why are lesbian figures made to symbolize a resistance to symbolization, and why do they also evoke a "corrupted" or improper symbolization? In order to address such questions, this study locates lesbian sexuality amid the discursive formations of American culture. I examine such tropes as transference and displacement, the disembodied voice, repetition-compulsion, and the uncanny—figures that, by representing a negation of or resistance to symbolic systems, make lesbian sexuality a repository for the failures of meaning inherent in figurality itself. *Impossible Women* endeavors to explain how lesbian sexuality is construed both as a resistance to signification and as an allegory of symbolic or figural language as such. It seeks to show how lesbianism is produced *in* and *as* language by cultural discourses that require it to symbolize, and be abjected in place of, the meaninglessness necessary to the positing of meaningful discourse. Tracing this construction of lesbian sexuality as a kind of enabling resistance within the symbolic order, it addresses the ways lesbian figures, in what Lauren Berlant has called the "national symbolic" of American ideology, take on distinctive forms when pressed to the service of national goals.[12]

Focusing on canonical American fiction, *Impossible Women* interrogates the tropes of familial relations and heterosexual coupling that undergird the American notion of the family as a privileged model for the nation.[13] Within this metaphorical landscape, I suggest, lesbianism is represented as a corruption not merely of fertility, the family, and patriarchal order, but also of meaningful language. Representing American literature itself as the product of a heterosexual union that holds out the promise of futurity, that is, this tropology aligns female perversion with the obverse of "natural" and socially useful discourse. And in a reciprocal gesture, what Emerson calls "perverted" and "barren" language is equated with the corrosive effects of a sterile and lifeless female sexuality that portends the failure of reproduction and the family.[14] Where dominant American ideologies sustain the promise of their own meaning by figuring proper representation as analogous to proper reproduction, they also conjure lesbian figures to allegorize the possibility of linguistic corruption. In this process, lesbian figures work to describe historical problems of difference; to differentiate American literature from a European heritage; to mediate tensions around such issues as gender and race; and to sustain the narratives through which American literature will imaginatively produce itself *as* "American literature."

The project of locating lesbian sexuality in the American literary tradition is by now well established. While valuable and prolific readings have emerged in the fields of contemporary literature and cultural studies, however, significantly less criticism has addressed the presence of lesbian figures in American literature from the early twentieth century and before. Moreover, the discussion of lesbian sexuality in American literature has tended to be author-centered, clustering around recognized lesbian writers such as Stein, Cather, Jewett, and Bishop, or proposing lesbian readings of female authors such as Dickinson. This approach has gone far toward outlining a recognizable lesbian tradition within American literature; but feminist scholarship has not fully addressed the multiple ways lesbian sexuality signifies throughout American literature, including texts and authors that do not, on their surface, seem engaged with lesbian desire. This book undertakes the task of identifying representations of lesbian sexuality in American writing that has, perhaps, seemed exempt from such concerns. Although works such as James's novel *The Bostonians* and authors such as Elizabeth Bishop are recognized as involved with lesbian issues, other works considered here—*The Blithedale Romance*, for example, or *The Sun Also Rises*—have generally been excluded from the purview of lesbian criticism. While each text participates in the work of articulating, and thus producing, notions of lesbian sexuality in American literature, however, I do not intend to present these texts as "representative" or synecdochal figures of a univocal tradition.[15] Indeed, the works of James, Hurston, Chopin, and the others engage with cultural discourses in strikingly different ways, sometimes resisting and sometimes replicating, but never escaping, the disciplinary and ideological machinery of American culture.

From the 1850s with *The Blithedale Romance* to the 1950s and 60s with Elizabeth Bishop's short stories, the texts considered here reflect a century during which the notion of lesbian sexuality appeared in public discourse. From the mid-nineteenth to the mid-twentieth century, American sexual ideology saw the fading of romantic friendship, the emergence of sexological and psychoanalytic theories, the creation of the masculinized "New Woman," and the earliest articulation of "out" lesbian identities and politics, while American literary history traveled from romance to realism, regionalism, modernist aesthetics, and the Harlem Renaissance. Although acknowledging historical and cultural contexts is a central concern, this book does not attempt to provide a comprehensive survey of American literature during the period, nor does it presuppose a teleological argument where either literature or sexuality is concerned. Instead, the following chapters constitute a series of variations on a theme, each of which responds to historical shifts in sexual ideologies, changes in American culture, and the evolution of literary genres in American writing. Pursuing thematic trends as well as rhetorical formations, they examine such topics as the female voice in *The Blithedale Romance*, *The Bostonians*, and *Their Eyes Were Watching God*; lesbian desire and mother-love in Hurston's novel and Bishop's stories; the notion of lesbian "morbidity" in *The Blithedale Romance* and *The Bostonians*; and the masculinized woman or "mannish lesbian" in *The Sun Also Rises*. These matters, in turn, give rise to such theoretical questions as the definitional impasse between lesbianism and femininity in *The Awakening*, *Their Eyes Were Watching God*, and Bishop's stories; sexuality and narrative form in *The Awakening* and *The Sun Also Rises*; and the notion of lesbian sexuality as "unrepresentable" in *The Blithedale Romance*, *The Bostonians*, and Bishop's stories.

Lesbian Figures

It may be useful at the outset to clarify my use of the term "lesbian," both to name the theoretical field this project inhabits and to describe various persons, desires, and effects within American culture. As historians of sexuality remind us, the language of "lesbian" and "homosexual" desires and identities is relatively new in European and American cultures. During the first half of the nineteenth century, relations among American women, particularly white women of the middle class, were largely governed by notions of romantic friendship. Influenced, as Nancy Cott argues, by the "general cultural valuation of 'the heart' and emphasis on women's superiority in sensibility," romantic friendship elaborated upon the ideology of the feminine separate sphere.[16] Intimacy between women, necessarily understood as nonsexual, was culturally validated and even idealized. As Smith-Rosenberg writes, in nineteenth-century America romantic friendship appeared as "a plausible and socially accepted form of human interaction."[17] By the 1880s, however, the ideology of romantic friendship began to yield to the language of sexual "inversion" and "lesbianism," prompted by the rise of sexology, women's increasing work outside the home, and concomitant cultural anxieties about the breakdown of gender roles.[18] The efforts of late-Victorian sexologists to define homosexuality effectively invented it as a sexual identity, prompting the ascendancy in the early twentieth century of the more rigid and pathologized notion of "lesbian" sexuality—a term first mentioned in an American medical journal in 1883.[19]

As a number of historians have noted, however, the separation between romantic friendship and the notion of lesbian perversion was by no means absolute. Martha Vicinus has called for a more complex understanding of romantic friendship and has persuasively argued that the anxieties surrounding female intimacy in the early nineteenth century indicate a cultural awareness that such relationships could be sexual, if only when pursued to an unhealthy extreme.[20] Marylynne Diggs corroborates this claim in the context of nineteenth-century American literature:

> Far from a presexological world in which women's intimacies were encouraged by a culture that perceived women to be innocent of sexuality, the nineteenth century was a period of contentious struggle over the definition and representation of a lesbian sexuality—a struggle in which writers of popular fiction were, by the 1850s, active participants.[21]

Nor did earlier notions of female perversion entirely vanish in the twentieth century. Although the historical shift to a discourse of lesbianism elevated object-choice to a defining role in sexual identity, the new notion of lesbianism also incorporated older understandings of female sexual propriety and impropriety. Smith-Rosenberg has argued that in early-nineteenth-century America the constitutive element of female perversity was a resistance to maternity: "American physicians through the 1870s talked of women's sexual deviance exclusively in terms of the rejection of motherhood—not of men."[22] While we may wish to question the exclusivity of this formulation, the discourse that defined normative female sexuality as committed to reproduction remained powerful at the close of the century, when—far from supplanting questions of motherhood—the notion of lesbianism was commonly conflated with the failure of reproduction and the rejection of appropriate feminine roles.[23]

In American culture, that is, lesbianism is not a reified concept. Taking shape, instead, in a loosely allied set of tropes, lesbian sexuality is never fully distinct from, if never wholly identical to, female sexuality as such. We need not imagine an undifferentiated "lesbian continuum" to recognize the interrelations among early notions of female perversity, the ideology of romantic friendship, and late-nineteenth-century views of lesbian sexuality.[24] For if the figure of the lesbian was unknown to Hawthorne, the notion of a deviant female sexuality, perverse in its resistance to marriage and motherhood, was all too familiar. I apply the term "lesbian" to texts and figures before the 1880s, then, as a strategic anachronism that can illuminate the continuities between nineteenth-century views of female deviance and twentieth-century notions of lesbian identity. Working through the problem of lesbian definition, this book attempts to explain how certain metaphors associated with lesbian sexuality have recurred in American literature, albeit differently inflected by historical circumstances, across the span of roughly a century. In my analysis of nineteenth- and twentieth-century texts, I take lesbianism not as an essential identity, morphology, or even, necessarily, object-choice, but as a name for the set of sexual and discursive effects that patriarchal culture displaces onto figures of perverse female desire. In patriarchal culture, that is, lesbianism can name any female sexuality that by refusing heterosexual object-choice, by failing to contribute to the work of reproduction, by alluding to a preoedipal bond with the mother, or by presenting a nongenital organization of desire, seems imbued with pathology or morbidity.[25]

My choice to consider a more complex and less literal notion of lesbian sexuality, then, responds not only to the discursive construction of sexuality as such, but also to the simultaneous articulation and collapse of "lesbian" particularity in the homophobic imagination. In her critique of utopian tendencies in lesbian criticism, Annamarie Jagose writes, "the category 'lesbian' is not essentially radical or subversive. Indeed, the category 'lesbian' is not essentially anything. It does not have a fixed valence, a signification that is proper to itself."[26] Arguing against the repressive hypothesis in lesbian theory, Jagose underscores a central presupposition of this study: that, as Foucault famously asserts, mechanisms of power do not merely suppress but also produce sexual identities. As Valerie Traub suggests, " 'lesbianism' is *constituted* by phallocentrism—or rather by the history that grants both phallocentrism and 'lesbianism' their embodied meanings."[27] This book presupposes that lesbian sexuality is discursively constructed, responding to the exigencies of specific historical events, actors, and ideologies. My intention in examining lesbian figures in American literature, in other words, is not to advance or reclaim some essential truth of lesbian identity, but to interrogate the notions of lesbianism elaborated and disseminated by hegemonic discourses of American culture. In describing patriarchal fantasies of lesbianism, I do not mean to endorse such views as inevitable "reality" but instead to analyze their cultural and political consequences. If there is no lesbianism before language, there is also no lesbianism before the law. This is not to say that the meaning of lesbian sexuality is solely constituted by homophobic culture, nor is it to deny the importance of lesbian-authored texts, politics, and literary criticism. But it is to recognize that the power of social discourses to produce sexuality extends to the identities, fantasies, and desires of individual subjects, as well as shaping the possibilities for identity-based communities and political engagement.

Locating the cultural construction of lesbian figures in two texts that address uncanny effects of the female voice, chapter 1 offers a reading of Nathaniel Hawthorne's novel *The Blithedale Romance* (1852) and Henry James's novel *The Bostonians* (1886). Responding to the disparate conventions of romance and realism in American literature, James and Hawthorne locate lesbian "morbidity" at the site of these genres' crossing and collapse. In each novel the celebration of the heterosexual romance as self-evident social reality requires the representation of lesbian figures on whom are projected the failures or impossibilities of both literary and sexual ideologies. The specter of a female sexuality not yoked to the Oedipal drama and the work of reproduction becomes, in these texts, a figure for the unassimilable resistance to signification that props up the operations of the heterosexual symbolic. Subject to both homophobic discipline and homophobic denial, lesbian sexuality becomes an allegorical figure for the trauma of the real, marked, as Žižek notes, by the prohibition of "something which is already in itself impossible."[28]

Chapter 2, continuing this inquiry into sexuality and rhetorical structures, examines relations between lesbianism and femininity in nineteenth-century America by reading Kate Chopin's novel *The Awakening* (1899) along with Emerson's and Fuller's formulations of American literature. The reproduction of the American tradition, Emerson and Fuller suggest, is emblematized by that of the Oedipal family and threatened by a morbidity and "corrupted" language that patriarchal culture attributes to lesbian sexuality. Tracing the articulation in *The Awakening* of *reproduction* as both representation and maternity, this chapter considers how lesbianism is constructed and repudiated as a token of the perverse displacements essential to both female Oedipality and signification. This gesture of disavowal sets a fantasy of a truly "creative writing" against a female sexuality imagined as an endless displacement, or in Lacan's words, as a "chain of dead desire."

Moving into the twentieth century, chapter 3 reads Ernest Hemingway's novel *The Sun Also Rises* (1926) along with his short story "The Sea Change" (1932) and the posthumously published novel *The Garden of Eden* (1986) to explore the place of lesbian sexuality in modernist culture. If Chopin traces the cultural association of a circular, objectless desire with lesbianism, Hemingway construes that resistance to meaning as an effect of return and repetition. In a male modernist aesthetic dedicated to originality, repetition comes to signify an abject form of literariness as well as a nonproductive form of sexual desire. Laboring to differentiate sterile repetition from salutary reproduction, Hemingway describes repetition as a perversion, consonant with that of lesbian sexuality, that is also both intolerable and ultimately inescapable.

Chapter 4 addresses another aspect of twentieth-century American culture, examining the rhetorical relations among dominant ideologies of race, gender, and sexuality through a reading of Zora Neale Hurston's *Their Eyes Were Watching God* (1937). This reading seeks to explain the representational logic through which white patriarchal culture imposes on certain subjects and bodies a burden of meaning, making those bodies bear the weight of materiality as such so that "whiteness," like the phallus, can claim the transcendent authority of the "pure sign." The endless slippage of these transcendental signifiers from "invisibility" to abased materiality suggests a failure of *form* that, like lesbianism in the homophobic imagination, poses a threat to the distinctions—oral and genital, speech and writing—upon which white and patriarchal hegemony relies.

Chapter 5 returns to several central issues of this study, using two of Elizabeth Bishop's short stories—"The Country Mouse" (1961) and "Gwendolyn" (1953)—to consider the problems of lesbian particularity inherent in relations between lesbianism and femininity, and between lesbianism and symbolization. Bishop's texts trace the discursive processes of gender formation that create the "little girl" and connect the question of femininity to the girl's negotiation of her mother's loss, raising questions of mourning and melancholia, the distinction between desire and identification, and the intersection of feminine propriety and perversion. Comparing lesbian love with the figural "lie of language," Bishop's stories complicate and challenge the patriarchal construction of lesbian sexuality as a resistance *to* symbolization, locating that desire, instead, within the structure of language and the logic of displacement.

c h a p t e r   o n e

The Romance of the Real

The Blithedale Romance
and *The Bostonians*

E
arly in *The Bostonians*, recording Basil Ransom's impressions of Olive Chancellor, Henry James asks a deliberate question: "Why was she morbid, and why was her morbidness typical? Ransom might have exulted if he had gone back far enough to explain that mystery." Although Basil fails to answer it, this question suggests a "mystery" with which the novel is itself concerned. Indeed, one project of the text is to chart the connection between "morbidness" and the "typical," between the lesbian pathology Olive is made to typify and the symbolic mechanism of representation. Such questions are not confined to *The Bostonians*; they also inform its literary predecessor, *The Blithedale Romance*, and the criticism that seeks to explain James's connection to Hawthorne.

Readers of *The Bostonians*, noting the similarities between James's novel and *The Blithedale Romance*, have frequently focused on form and genre, describing the relation of the two texts as that of realism to allegory.[1] In doing so, they follow the lead of James himself, who in his 1887 study of Hawthorne faults the author of *The Scarlet Letter* for relying too heavily on allegory and symbolism. Hawthorne's notebooks, in James's view, may have a tiresome literality, but his novels suffer from an overuse of "one of the lighter exercises of the imagination"—that is, allegory.[2] The resulting "want of reality" in Hawthorne's works, James argues, sets him apart from the realist "theory" of more contemporary writing, including James's own. This late-nineteenth-century realism, articulating its distance from romance precisely in order to establish itself *as* "theory," could not, it seems, overstress its difference from its predecessors: "It cannot be too often repeated," James writes, "that Hawthorne was not a realist."[3]

Why was her morbidness typical? The notion of the "typical" functions as a switchpoint between allegory and realism , denoting relations both of essence and of context. The *OED* defines "typical" first as a metaphoric substitution grounded in essential similarity ("Of the nature of, or serving as, a type or emblem . . . symbolical, emblematic"), then as a metonymic likeness based on contiguity with a larger group ("Having the qualities of a type or specimen; serving as a representative specimen of a class or kind"). This doubleness is reflected in American literature and culture, where the type, hallmark of Puritan symbolism, also informs realist aspirations to social and psychological accuracy.[4] In a notebook entry, for example, James recorded his realist intention to address, in *The Bostonians*, a "very national, very typical" subject: the "situation of women."[5] The same understanding of the type that sustains social taxonomy and scientific observation also enables the late-Victorian sexology, which, in the decades following Karl von Westphal's 1869 study of the female invert as a type, sought to describe what Havelock Ellis would call the "typical invert."[6] When *The Bostonians* appeared in 1886, the same year as Krafft-Ebing's *Psychopathia Sexualis* and a decade before Ellis's *Studies in the Psychology of Sex: Sexual Inversion* (1897), categories of lesbian pathology were already sufficiently familiar that, borrowing from the rhetoric of the case study, Basil could repudiate not only his cousin but "such a type as that"—which is to say, Olive's "kind of women."[7]

Generic distinctions like that of realism and romance are, of course, not exempt from systems of social discipline; they never escape the cultural law that would produce heterosexual "romance" not only as a "realistic" expectation but as the sum of sexual reality.

And while lesbianism is framed in American culture as an *effect of* discourse—whether rhetorical or scientific—American culture in turn attributes to lesbian sexuality a peculiar set of discursive effects. As James and Hawthorne suggest, the distinction between romance and realism is by no means absolute. When these categories collapse in *The Blithedale Romance* and *The Bostonians*, the resulting crisis in generic form signals a crisis in ideological form, a disruption of symbolic and social order that fixes upon figures of lesbian sexuality. Each text frames lesbianism as a sort of epistemological problem: in *The Blithedale Romance*, Coverdale is impelled to discover the "secrets" of Priscilla and Zenobia's relationship in much the same way that *The Bostonians'* Basil Ransom concerns himself with the "mystery" of Olive Chancellor. But each text also imagines lesbian "types" as capable of disrupting epistemology, interpretation, and linguistic order: in *The Blithedale Romance* lesbianism marks the point of conflict between realism and allegory, and in James's "very typical" novel lesbianism seems to undermine the coherence of realist narrative.

Reading *The Blithedale Romance* and *The Bostonians*, I want to consider the role played by lesbian sexuality in these negotiations of genre and literary form, as well as the place of lesbian figures in the symbolic order of patriarchal culture. Associated with the breakdown of narrative and generic conventions in the two texts, lesbianism is also imagined as a disruption in signification attributed to certain supernatural and uncanny effects of the female voice. Both in the Veiled Lady's "Sibylline" utterance and in the weirdly compelling public speeches of Verena Tarrant, this improper articulation assigns the possibility of lesbian desire to the place of symbolic "impossibility": to the place, as Slavoj Žižek puts it, "where 'the word fails'."[8] *The Bostonians* and *The Blithedale Romance*, that is, show how patriarchal culture construes lesbianism as a figure for the real, the stubborn node of resistance to representation that both threatens and sustains the symbolic order.[9] Lacan writes, "the real, or what is perceived as such, is what resists symbolization absolutely" and instead appears as "the pressing manifestation of an unreal, hallucinatory reality."[10] The connection between American realism and the real is a catachrestic one, to be sure, but it offers a productive way of reading the sexual mythologies of patriarchal culture as well as the place of lesbian figures in nineteenth-century American literature. If *The*

Blithedale Romance is, in the words of an early reviewer, "eminently an American book," and if *The Bostonians* fulfills James's desire, by crafting a novel "as local, as American, as possible . . . to show that I *can* write an American story," these texts have shaped both canonical American literature and American ideologies of sexuality and gender.[11] The notion of the real enables a reading of national and sexual rhetoric in Hawthorne and James, even as *The Bostonians* and *The Blithedale Romance* bring to our "arguments with the real" a deeper sense of how lesbian sexuality functions within symbolic structures.[12]

A Fine *Romance*

Among both nineteenth- and twentieth-century readers, *The Blithedale Romance* has elicited charges of "morbidity" and suggestions of homosexuality, objections that are often all the more vehement for their inability to identify the unsavory element in this otherwise, as James says, "very charming" novel.[13] In his review of *The Blithedale Romance*, E. P. Whipple of *Graham's Magazine* noted "a certain morbid tint"; the reviewer at *Blackwood's Magazine* found in it "less of a natural character and more of a diseased and morbid conventional life"; and *The American Whig Review* decried not only the characters' "evilness of nature" but also Hawthorne's own "morbid suspicion" and "melancholy craving for human curiosities."[14] "Morbidity" could be localized in Hawthorne's text, according to nineteenth-century readers, primarily where it assumed female form. A reviewer for the *Southern Quarterly Review*, for example, concluding that marriage was "the best remedy for such a case" as Zenobia, effectively rendered her character a case study.[15] Reopening the case on lesbian sexuality, more recent discussions of *The Blithedale Romance* suggest that if we recognize, as one reader does, Zenobia's trademark ornament as one of Baudelaire's *fleurs du mal*, we must also concede, in the words of another, that "Priscilla's affection for Zenobia seems a bit perverse."[16]

How is that perversity figured in the novel? The Blithedale community, as Coverdale sees it, seems "to authorize any individual, of either sex, to fall in love with any other, regardless of what would elsewhere be judged suitable and prudent."[17] Indeed, *The Blithedale*

Romance is remarkable for its proliferation of homosexual desire, both male and female. But in Hawthorne's effort to heterosexualize a community that is so emphatically and so diversely anything but, the burden of reform falls on figures of lesbian sexuality, which the novel must at all costs re-form in the shape of heterosexual femininity. That anxiety about feminine desire is articulated in Moodie's point-blank question, "Does she love her?" (81). What form of feeling, in other words, binds Zenobia and Priscilla? What *kind* of love might they share? The text eventually provides a heavily underscored answer to Moodie's question, which turns out to be no answer at all. "We are sisters!" Priscilla tells Zenobia near the end of the novel (202); yet the relationship between the two women, who have also acted the parts of mistress and "slave," rival and lover, cannot so easily be resolved. While Priscilla and Zenobia are, as Hawthorne puts it, "types" of womanhood, they are also evidence of the stubborn adhesion between femininity as such and women's "mysterious attraction" (46) to other women—an attraction that Hawthorne's text, like James's, will both analyze and mystify. Of Priscilla's love for Zenobia, Hawthorne writes,

> A brilliant woman is often an object of the devoted admiration—it might almost be termed worship, or idolatry—of some young girl, who beholds the cynosure only at an awful distance . . . Even a woman, of mature age, despises or laughs at such a passion. (30)

Outlining the relationship between the "mature" woman and the "young girl," this passage maps the conventional teleology in which women's adult heterosexuality must and will supersede juvenile homosexuality.[18] Tellingly, Hawthorne names that youthful love "idolatry." As a term for worship not only of a false god, but of a mere image in place of the transcendent deity, the notion of idolatry describes lesbian sexuality as a kind of misreading. A corrupt form of representation, idolatry confuses signifier with signified; it mistakes material form for sacred essence and enshrines the copy in the place of the original.

In naming Priscilla's passionate "admiration" for Zenobia "idolatry," Hawthorne condemns lesbianism as a bad copy of a more authentic, not to say more divine, organization of desire. And indeed,

The Blithedale Romance finds echoes of both male and female homosexuality in other bad copies, other ersatz identities. The dandified Westervelt—who, as his false teeth suggest, has "nothing genuine about him" (88)—and the "false glitter" (168) of Fauntleroy, the "man of show" (178), link artificiality with gay male sexuality. Lest there be any doubt about it, the rhetoric surrounding Moodie's (that is, Fauntleroy's) unspeakable crime announces, "It was just the sort of crime, growing out of its artificial state, which society . . . neither could nor ought to pardon. More safely might it pardon murder" (168).[19] As the most flamboyant figure for this unpardonable but unnameable perversion, Westervelt is, not coincidentally, the spokesman for the disreputable business of mesmerism, whose fakery he synecdochally represents. But the notion of artificiality is not restricted, in Hawthorne's novel, to male homosexuality. Zenobia's showy flower and the paradoxically uncanny and mechanical "supernatural machinery" (31) associated with the Veiled Lady's performance mark both women as unnatural, combining the patriarchal myth of feminine duplicity with the idolatrous implications of a more specific lesbian "passion."[20]

Coverdale himself is not exempt from the artificiality that signals sexual perversity in *The Blithedale Romance*. In chapters titled "The Hotel" and "The Boarding-House," he assumes the role of detective, subjecting Priscilla and Zenobia to his inquisitive gaze even as his own sexuality comes under suspicion. Having left Blithedale for Boston, Coverdale returns to "the effeminacy of past days," basking in the "artificial temperature" (135) of a hotel room whose window opens onto a "little portion of the backside of the universe" (137). He is drawn to that backward vista and quickly discovers the voyeuristic pleasures it affords. If "each characteristic sound was too suggestive to be passed over, unnoticed" (136), the sights afforded by this Hitchcockian rear window are even more compelling, enticing Coverdale to examine every detail of the garden and the houses across the courtyard. When his investigation reveals Zenobia, Priscilla, and Westervelt illuminated in the windows of the house opposite, Coverdale is drawn to investigate. And at that moment, not only is the watcher "transfixed" by what he terms "goblins of flesh and blood," but the novel is itself transfixed by a narrative crisis precipitated by these startling "figures" (145).

Discussions of literary form in *The Blithedale Romance* have sketched the role of "realities"—as opposed to allegory—in strikingly different and contradictory ways. A contemporary reviewer for *Blackwood's Magazine* complained of the novel's detachment from concrete reality: "we want more than thoughts and fancies—we want *things*."[21] And James, in his study of Hawthorne, concurred. Although the Blithedale community is "in no sense of the word" a realistic description of Brook Farm in Roxbury, where Hawthorne briefly lived, James argues that the novel is at its best while it remains at Blithedale early in the book, and before it moves, as if inevitably, "too much out of reality."[22] Hawthorne, however, takes pains to divorce the narrative from historical fact. Introducing its cast of characters as allegorical figures—"the self-concentrated Philanthropist," "the high-spirited Woman," and "the weakly Maiden"—the novel's preface explains that any resemblance to Brook Farm or its inhabitants is, if not purely coincidental, at least "altogether incidental to the main purpose of the Romance" (1). One may suspect that Hawthorne protests too much; yet the Blithedale setting, as promised, occasions an extended study of the characters *as types* in the first half of the novel. In "The Hotel" and "The Boarding-House," however, the allegorical "romance" of the novel's title gives way to realism, as Coverdale's scopophilic fixation on the "realities" of the adjoining buildings and their inhabitants plunges the text into minutely realistic description. Noting the oscillation between narrative modes in *The Blithedale Romance*, Richard Brodhead uses the back-window passage to epitomize Hawthorne's "realistic" rendering of a specific "view" in "very high resolution of detail"; other readers, however, identify this as the moment when, as Allan Lefcowitz and Barbara Lefcowitz write, "the strain finally does cause the whole vision to break down into near-allegory."[23] Both rightly note a rhetorical trauma that threatens the distinction between allegory and realism, suspending the narrative that has directed the novel thus far.

This narrative disruption evokes both an epistemological desire and a vision of epistemology's failure. As he muses on Zenobia and Priscilla's mysterious errand in the city, Coverdale begins to ponder the larger mysteries of Zenobia's "character" and the women's relation to one another. Dedicating himself, as he puts it, "by generous sympathies, by delicate intuitions, by taking note of things too slight for record . . . to learn the secret which was hidden even from themselves" (148), Coverdale takes up in earnest the novel's concern with lesbian sexuality. Just as, in *The Bostonians*, the question of Olive's "morbidness" constructs the text's project as an epistemological problem and its narrative as a detective story, Coverdale's endeavors to learn the women's "secret" cast him in the role of detective or psychoanalyst. Coverdale's interpellation as an investigating subject, and a subject as such, is enabled by the introduction of "realism," the medium of psychic interiority, in a text that, while it lingered in the realm of allegory, seemed to present its characters as mere surface.[24] But this subjectivization also depends on Coverdale's voyeuristic relation to homosexual figures. The back-window scene holds Coverdale mesmerized because it promises a way to overcome or transform, if only fantasmatically, his unsettling similarity to Westervelt, for whom Coverdale feels an "intuitive repugnance" (86) perhaps precisely because their positions are never fully distinct. Coverdale, as Hawthorne tells us, occupies the space of "effeminacy," the "artificial," and the "back-room" point of view (134–5) whose very backwardness must recall the role of anality as a governing trope of gay male sexuality. When he assumes the role of investigator in relation to Zenobia and Priscilla, Coverdale allies himself with cultural discipline, as if that identification could preclude his being the subject of another such investigation. His methodology, however, surely fails to absolve him of suspicion: for the axiomatic principle of Coverdale's investigation, "Realities keep in the rear" (138), itself reveals the impossibility of distinguishing between empirical "realities" and a homosexualized "rear" view, or between the epistemology of the law and the logic of outlaw sexuality.[25]

Lesbianism and the Real

Acting the part of the detective, then, despite or because of his own vexed relation to the law, Coverdale gazes through his back window determined to uncover the "realities" hidden behind the surface of things. Yet his view of Zenobia's apartment confronts the voyeuristic observer with another opaque and mysterious surface:

the glow of an astral lamp was penetrating mistily through the white curtain of Zenobia's drawing-room. The shadow of a passing figure was now-and-then cast upon this medium, but with too vague an outline for even my adventurous conjectures to read the hieroglyphic that it presented. (149)

The semitransparent "white curtain" in Zenobia's room appears as a kind of veil, alluding—as the pun on "medium" suggests—to the Veiled Lady's theatrical costume. The allusion also places this passage within a chain of reference linking the Veiled Lady to another Hawthorne text, "The Minister's Black Veil." And like that other famous veil, the gauzy curtain in *The Blithedale Romance* is, as Hawthorne writes, "a type and a symbol" that symbolizes symbolization itself.[26] Coverdale has been a watcher; now the watcher explicitly becomes a reader, or would-be reader, endeavoring "to read the hieroglyphic" that the shadowy forms present. Describing the relations between figure and ground, "passing figure" and "white curtain," Coverdale construes the curtain as a page and the "figure" as a kind of writing. But that unreadable "hieroglyphic" is entirely the product of reading; it is only through an act of interpretation that Coverdale can construe it as a text at all. The shadowy "figure," as Hawthorne makes clear, is both literally and figuratively a projection. It becomes a text *to be read* only through an effort of reading that projects meaning upon a meaningless form—an effort that nevertheless fails to recuperate the "hieroglyphic" to the symbolic order. Whatever secrets Priscilla and Zenobia keep remain outside representation.

The scene of Coverdale's "adventurous conjectures" at the back window describes the appearance within the symbolic field of a resistance to symbolization, a moment when the very mechanism of sense making comes to a halt. Psychoanalytic theory names this effect as *the real*. As Lacan explains, "the hole, the gap of being as such is hollowed out in the real."[27] A stubborn node of the inarticulable, it both resists and paradoxically enables the operations of symbolization. Žižek notes that the real is characterized by its inconsistency, its bad logic, appearing as both a "hard kernel" and a "gap" in the symbolic order, both an origin and a by-product of the symbolic, both a spur and an obstacle to the work of interpretation, both a mystifying absence and a source of horrifying confrontation.[28] Whereas Lacan emphasizes the function of the real as a fundamental negativity, a "missed encounter," so that psychoanalysis constitutes "an appointment to which we are always called with a real that eludes us," Žižek brings the real closer to the ontological, stressing the "hard kernel" over the "missed encounter."[29] Lacan underscores the function of the real as trauma, while Žižek is drawn to the notion of the real as a seductive marker of enjoyment. Judith Butler's broader, more historical reading relates the function of the real to the workings of hegemonic social systems and their political consequences. Arguing that the projection of the real outside the symbolic can be understood as a "strategy of social abjection," Butler suggests that "the real is always that which any account of 'reality' fails to include"—that is, what is unassimilable within social reality and individual experience as structured by the symbolic order.[30] In particular, Butler criticizes Žižek for naturalizing the notion of the real by failing to acknowledge its association with particular forms of social discipline and its construction *by* the symbolic order that it ostensibly resists. In Butler's view, the "impossible" ontological status of the real allows it to represent *both* the origin of the law and the repository of the socially unsymbolizable. While the law of castration, Butler suggests, appears as the real of patriarchal culture, and while resistance *to* the real "threatens to dissolve the heterosexual axis of desire" and "carries the fear of occupying a site of homosexual abjection," homosexuality can itself constitute the real of straight culture.[31]

The notion in late-nineteenth- and early-twentieth-century sexology of homosexuality as unwritable, unintelligible, but also needful of vigilant reading testifies to the equation of homosexuality with the real—that which, Žižek suggests, props up symbolic processes by mobilizing effects of meaningfulness and inciting hermeneutic desires. The "piece of the real" that means nothing in itself, Žižek writes, "triggers the endless work of interpretation" that seeks to connect a symbolic message with "real life."[32] In much the same way, the moving "shadow" in Zenobia's window serves Coverdale as an enticement to reading, an unsymbolizable effect misread as symbol, "figure," and "hieroglyphic." As the paranoid energy of straight culture's efforts to "read" and identify homosexual persons attests, the very unreadability of homosexuality, like the persistence of the real as "missed encounter," renders it both as the stubborn kernel of a traumatic confrontation and as the fantasmatic image of an impossible enjoyment or *jouissance*.[33] Žižek suggests that "the fundamental paradox which unfailingly attests to the presence of the Real" consists in "the fact of prohibiting something which is already in itself impossible" or, more to the point, the fact of barring from speech what is already supposed to be unspeakable—a formulation that also accurately describes the cultural policing of homosexuality.[34] Gay and lesbian sexualities often appear as the real of heterosexual culture, subject to disciplinary measures even though—indeed, *because*—they cannot, so we are told, properly exist in language. If the cultural nomination of sodomy as "the crime not fit to be named" suggests the suppression of the unspeakable, the evasion and elision of lesbian sexuality in patriarchal culture evinces this logic in a different sense.

Unlike male homosexuality, lesbianism is insistently framed in terms of impossibility, as a form of desire that is almost inconceivable yet wholly objectionable within the phallic sexual economy. During the 1921 debate over the British Criminal Law Amendment Act, as Terry Castle has noted, the argument against the inclusion of lesbianism in the vocabulary of law claimed that, although the threat of lesbianism warranted disciplinary attention, its public inscription could only promote a "noxious and horrible suspicion"—where homophobic "suspicion," interestingly, approximates homosexual desire—among women who had "never even heard a whisper" of lesbian desire.[35] In her essay "The Match in the Crocus," Judith Roof argues that straight culture represents lesbianism as the unrepresentable par excellence.[36] And if lesbian desire must *be* named as the unnameable, it replicates the logic by which the real is *produced* as the unsymbolizable by the symbolic order. In her valuable reading of the "queer real," Lynda Hart suggests that "in the psychoanalytic symbolic lesbians are only possible in / as the 'Real,' since they are foreclosed from the Symbolic order—they drop out of symbolization."[37] Indeed, in the symbolic order of straight culture lesbian figures, bearing the horror and fascination of an unspeakable desire, are fantasmatically constructed as a site of resistance to meaning.

Both lesbianism and the real, that is, represent fantasies within language of what lies beyond the pale of language. The real is always a kind of ghost or illusion: imagined as the limit of symbolization, the "rock" on which figurality founders, the real is visible only from the vantage point of the symbolic order, for it is produced in and by symbolization. The real is in this sense a kind of projection, not unlike the projection of the Veiled Lady's magical voice: an externalization of the resistance to, and within, representation through the displacement of difference within the symbolic onto the distinction between symbolic and real. The real, as Žižek elaborates it, is one name for the "internal self-impediment" or "immanent antagonism," the "inherent, internal 'excess' which impedes *from within* the 'smooth running' of the psychic apparatus."[38] While lesbianism, then, evokes the traumatic eruption of the real into the symbolic field, it can also function, like the real, as an enabling self-resistance or constitutive impossibility of the symbolic order. Hart writes,

> the "Real" gives us a concept that acknowledges what many feminists have been claiming in a number of discourses: that the symbolic order itself is what is "lacking," indeed it constructs itself as the illusion of a coherent system that nonetheless depends upon disguising the void in its center by displacing the "lack" onto an element that is posited as "outside" when it [is] always already *necessarily inside*.[39]

As Hart notes, the notion that lesbian sexuality shares the effects of the real resembles Monique Wittig's claim that in the straight mind lesbianism is an "impossibility." But this does not mean that straight culture simply denies the existence of lesbians; according to Hart, "phallocentrism / heterosexism does not merely secure its dominance through a simple negation. Rather, it needs lesbianism as a negative ontology. It needs its status as both radically real and impossible."[40]

Thus although lesbianism marks moments of trauma in the patriarchal imagination, such moments are not necessarily subversive; indeed, they can enable dominant systems to define and sustain themselves. Adduced in order to explain and cover over failures of representation, lesbian figures, like the real, can function to paradoxically support the very systems they would appear to endanger. Refocusing her earlier argument, Roof's longer study of lesbian sexuality and theory in *A Lure of Knowledge* recognizes lesbian figures as place-holders for an "impossibility" inherent in patriarchal structures. Lesbian sexuality, Roof writes, constitutes the phallocentric system's "own self-defiant space, defined by and within a phallocentric logic, but as the point where such logic is undone—where something is inaccessible."[41] As she points out, however, lesbian sexuality comes to inhabit "points of systemic failure" through the discursive machinery of phallocentric culture, not through any essential quality of its own. To identify the discursive construction of lesbianism as figure for the real is, crucially, not to claim that lesbianism *is* the real. The equation of lesbianism with the real is instead an ideological formation, which, though it fails to describe the "truth" of lesbian sexuality, nonetheless has powerful consequences. Reading the traumatic effects of the real and of lesbian figures in Hawthorne's text, therefore, means interrogating this fantasy *as a fantasy* in order to recognize the ways such formations, in Hawthorne's time and our own, delimit the possibilities for thinking about desire, shape the material conditions of life for women who identify as lesbians, and influence the formal concerns of American literature.

In *The Blithedale Romance*, the alignment of lesbian sexuality with the real centers on the figure of the Veiled Lady, locus of supernatural power, impossible enjoyment, and the obscene violation of heterosexual reality. Offering an account of her mesmeric performance, the "Village-Hall" chapter presents the Veiled Lady as token of the "miraculous power" through which "the maiden, with her lover's kiss still burning on her lips, would turn from him with icy indifference; the newly made widow would dig up her buried heart out of her young husband's grave, before the sods had taken root upon it; a mother, with her babe's milk in her bosom, would thrust away her child" (183). Scornful of both heterosexual union and the patriarchal family, this "power" perverts the woman's culturally celebrated roles as an object of heterosexual desire, as a wife within the legal institution of marriage, and as a mother who enables the reproduction of the Oedipal family. As such, the Veiled Lady inspires attempts at discipline and abjection that are all the more virulent for taking as their object something that, strictly speaking, may be mere "nothingness." In order to communicate with spirits as the Veiled Lady does, Coverdale says, we must stoop, and grovel in some element more vile than earthly dust. These goblins, if they exist at all, are but the shadows of past mortality, outcasts, mere refuse-stuff, adjudged unworthy of the eternal world, and, on the most favorable supposition, dwindling gradually into nothingness. (183–84)

These are not entirely the words of an unbeliever. Hardly consoled by the possibility that the "goblins" with whom the Veiled Lady keeps close company may not "exist at all," Coverdale rhetorically expels such spirits into the realm of the abject, from whose "vile" waste and "refuse-stuff" they seem to have issued.

As this passage suggests, and as *The Bostonians* will elaborate, the appearance of lesbianism in heterosexual culture is, like the real, characterized by the prohibition of something already considered impossible. In Žižek's view, the real is "an entity which, although it does not exist (in the sense of 'really existing,' taking place in reality), has a series of properties—it exercises a certain structural causality, it can produce a series of effects in the symbolic reality of subjects."[42] In *The Blithedale Romance*, the performer who is only briefly glimpsed, whose clairvoyant knowledge is never demonstrated, and whose powers are bracketed with all of Hawthorne's skeptical rationality functions as a nonexistent cause that, like the real, nevertheless generates effects. Even as Coverdale represents the Veiled Lady as an example of the most cynical deception and the most flimsy showmanship, he also sustains the idea of a true, uncanny clairvoyance, an arcane knowledge embedded in the unreadable traces of the real. His first account of the Veiled Lady as a popular phenomenon dismisses her "apparent miracle[s]" as "skilfully contrived circumstances of stage-effect," only to admit that at least one of her predictions about the Blithedale community "certainly accorded with the event" (5–6). Žižek notes the same effect of simultaneous belief and disbelief in his reading of "fortune-telling and horoscopes" as a manifestation of the real: "a totally contingent coincidence is sufficient for the effect of transference to take place; we become convinced 'there is something to it.' "[43] And in *The Blithedale Romance*, the crass promotion of the Veiled Lady does not prevent Coverdale from believing that "there is something to it." Suggesting a female resistance to normative heterosexuality and with it the possibility of lesbian sexuality, the Veiled

Lady's "miraculous power" occupies the position of the real as a "nothingness" that bears with it unsettling effects.

Voice Lessons

The same narrative that seeks to rescue Priscilla from the Veiled Lady—a narrative fueled by Coverdale's and Hollingsworth's anxious scorn for the performer—also enshrines the Veiled Lady as an object of desire who seduces Coverdale as she does her other auditors. Yet the Veiled Lady is more "a type and a symbol" than a presence or a person in *The Blithedale Romance*. Unlike *The Bostonians'* Verena Tarrant, with whom she shares a theatrical career and a fate of assimilation to heterosexual "romance," the Veiled Lady has very little to say. Despite her lecture-hall celebrity, we see her onstage for only a moment in the chapter titled "The Village-Hall" and hear her voice only as performed by Zenobia in the "Legend" that enlivens a Blithedale evening. Even in that story the speech of the Veiled Lady comes to us several times removed: "perhaps," Zenobia suggests, "in the intervals of the wild, breezy music which accompanied the exhibition, [Theodore] might hear the low voice of the Veiled Lady, conveying her Sibylline responses" (103). Still, the fantasy of the Veiled Lady—for fantasy it is, enabled by the projection of desire onto a white veil and a half-audible "low voice"—remains capable of inspiring the greatest pleasure, curiosity, and outrage.

The absence of the Veiled Lady's voice from Hawthorne's text in no way mitigates the disciplinary efforts directed against it; in fact the animus against the Veiled Lady, the force that inspires Coverdale to denounce her supernatural claims as "refuse-stuff" and impels Hollingsworth to remove Priscilla from the stage, seems motivated precisely by the absence of any real object. In *The Blithedale Romance*, that is, lesbianism is heard only as a whisper, albeit a stage whisper with resounding effects.[44] Both Zenobia and the Veiled Lady are characterized by a relation to speech, Zenobia defending with her own oratory the right of women to present "their natural utterance in public" (111). Yet Zenobia's eloquence only makes her, in Coverdale's eyes, a "stump-oratress" (41); it fails to match the fascination of the Veiled Lady's "supernatural" voice. While Zenobia claims, on behalf of women's speech, that "it is with the living voice, alone, that she can compel the world to recognize the light of her intellect" (112), the Veiled Lady suggests the more compelling power of a voice outside the province of the living, outside the ordinary logic of material embodiment. Combining the horror of what Coverdale calls "shadows of past mortality" with an unearthly allure, her voice seems always to be elsewhere, never fully fixed in a physical form.

In a well-known anecdote from *Three Essays on the Theory of Sexuality*, Freud addresses the relation of voice to embodiment, connecting the disembodied voice to an infantile organization of desire and a particular fantasy of maternal presence:

> For this explanation of the origin of infantile sexuality I have to thank a three-year-old boy whom I once heard calling out of a dark room: "Auntie, speak to me! I'm frightened because it's so dark." His aunt answered him: "What good would that do? You can't see me." "That doesn't matter," replied the child, "if anyone speaks, it gets light." Thus what he was afraid of was not the dark, but the absence of someone he loved; and he could feel sure of being soothed as soon as he had evidence of that person's presence.[45]

In Freud's story of what happens when someone speaks, the child puts the aunt in the place of the mother, the first loved one. When she responds to the child's call "out of a dark room," her voice conjures the absent mother's presence and with it the magical effect of "light." Simultaneously a simulacrum and a signifying "evidence," the aunt's disembodied speech replaces meaningful discourse with a voice imagined as *pure* voice, a voice that resists ordinary structures of representation.

Freud's anecdote describes the bodiless voice as a fantasmatic form of pure presence, a nostalgic reminder of a time before castration and entrance into the symbolic.[46] Although his notion of maternal presence does not depend upon disembodiment, the disembodied voice frequently conjures the uncanny effects of the maternal voice. In cinema, Michel Chion writes, "As long as the face and mouth have not been revealed, and the eye of the spectator has not 'verified' the coincidence of the voice with the mouth . . . the vocal embodiment is incomplete, and the voice conserves an aura of invulnerability and of magic power."[47] This "sound one hears without seeing what causes it" Chion elsewhere identifies as an "acousmatic voice."[48] Like the aunt's voice in Freud's anecdote, it is, as Žižek elaborates, "a voice without a bearer, without an assignable place, floating in an intermediate space, and as such all-pervasive."[49] In *The Blithedale Romance* we hear the acousmatic effect in the Veiled Lady's voice, a voice "floating" out from behind a long veil "so impalpable, so ethereal, so without substance" (103) as to make the form beneath it equally insubstantial. She appears, Hawthorne later writes, like a "disembodied spirit" (185). In Chion's account the acousmatic voice can be either masculine or feminine, but it is defined within a heterosexual tropology: "Embodiment is realized through the simultaneous assembly of a visible body and an audible voice . . . through a sort of marriage contract consecrating the reassuring fixation of the voice in the residence of the body." Under normal circumstances voice and body participate in a "marriage contract," becoming, like man and wife, "a conventional couple that one may wish to sunder." Yet the "conventional couple" of voice and body is also, Chion continues, an "impossible couple."[50] When such a union is "impossible," what is at stake in preserving it as an illusion? At the same time that the illusion of embodiment engenders a "reassuring fixation" of voice within body, it reassures us with the illusion of meaning, fortifying the symbolic order against the eruption of the real. Dividing the "conventional couple" of voice and body, then, the disembodied or acousmatic voice exemplified by Hawthorne's Veiled Lady represents a violation of this contract and the heterosexual coupling it implies. The effect of acousmatism can withstand, if not undermine, the heterosexual imperative, *The Blithedale Romance* suggests, even as it reveals the impossibility upon which the symbolic order is itself founded.

While the figure of the Veiled Lady evokes the trauma of the real, the acousmatic effect of her voice alludes to the imaginary, raising the specter of preoedipal relations. Reinforcing the mythology of lesbianism as developmentally stunted or regressive, psychoanalytic accounts often attribute lesbianism to incomplete or failed Oedipalization. Freud locates lesbianism in the space of the preoedipal, prior to the symbolic order; lesbian sexuality seems to allude to a time before lack and consequently before desire, remaining fixed in the register of infantile demand.[51] Samuel Weber adduces Freud's anecdote of "when someone speaks, it gets light" as one example of this logic of demand.[52] According to Lacan, demand is always a "demand for a presence or an absence"; in contrast to desire, it belongs to the preoedipal stage. Joining lesbian sexuality and maternal attachment, Lacan argues that the child demands from the mother's love "the gift of something which it does not have"; and he invokes the same phrase to explain lesbianism as "the love which gives what it does not have."[53] When confronted by the "demand for a presence or an absence," the mother and the lesbian each render what they do not have by magically bestowing a kind of presence that the law of castration would insist is not theirs to give. In *The Blithedale Romance* and in Freud's anecdote, each does so through the acousmatic voice. "Whatever is refused in the symbolic order," Lacan writes, "reappears in the real."[54] When, that is, the acousmatic effect that evokes the preoedipal stage appears within the symbolic order, it seems to bear with it the simultaneously traumatic and seductive effect of the real. While it can suggest the eerie effect of "spirit possession or ventriloquism," as Chion notes, such a voice also holds out the impossible promise of pure presence, the accomplishment of desire and the end of linguistic displacement.[55] Situated *within* the symbolic order and in relation to the "conventional couples" and structures of symbolic reality, the acousmatic voice is not imaginary, but appears as a kind of artifact of preoedipal relations, a form of speech that is simultaneously horrifying and erotically compelling.

In seeking to rescue Priscilla, in a sense, from the Veiled Lady, Coverdale hints at the Oedipal trajectory of Hawthorne's novel. If one concern of the novel is epistemological, reflected in Coverdale's determination "to learn the secret which was hidden" from Priscilla and Zenobia themselves, another aim is teleological, working to propel Priscilla beyond the province of such secrets. Positing the utopian community at Blithedale as an emblem of the nation, and both Blithedale and the nation as versions of the Oedipal family writ large, Hawthorne's narrative labors to recuperate heterosexual order. It is not enough that Zenobia must die and the Veiled Lady retire from the stage; the rehabilitation of a heterosexual *Romance* finally rests on Priscilla's transition from infantile homosexuality—the "idolatry" of young girls for older women—to adult female hetero-sexuality. But female Oedipality is only tenuously achieved in Hawthorne's text. Indeed, if *The Bostonians* demonstrates the high cost of that project's success, *The Blithedale Romance* seems to prove its impossibility. For Coverdale's belated confession of his love for Priscilla, Priscilla's renunciation of the stage and her marriage to Hollingsworth, and even Zenobia's death fail to persuade us that a polymorphously perverse "Golden Age" has aged gracefully into a more mature heterosexuality. Instead, the novel's conclusion makes Priscilla and Zenobia more clearly one another's doubles, more wholly at the crossroads of identification and desire, as Priscilla inherits the jeweled flower that was Zenobia's emblem and Zenobia, under death's "black veil" (210), herself becomes a Veiled Lady.

Henry James and the Lesbian Type

Like *The Blithedale Romance*, *The Bostonians* imagines lesbian sexuality in the place of the real, as a marker of the moment when language and the logic of patriarchal order turn against themselves. Taking Hawthorne's negotiation of allegory and realism a step further, James suggests that the realist depiction of heterosexual "romance" as social reality owes a debt to allegory and to the operations of figural language. In *The Bostonians*, that is, lesbianism signifies "morbidness" or deathliness precisely because it bears the burden of the "typical," which is to say, the burden of representation in all its inevitable failures. As Paul de Man writes, "Allegories are always allegories of metaphor and, as such, they are always allegories of the impossibility of reading."[56] The impossibility of reading lies in the failure of the chain of signification ever to end its own displacements—and the failure of allegory ever to coincide with realism. The heterosexual "romance" depends on allegory insofar as it requires a system of sexual difference founded on the notion of castration and the metaphorical equation of the penis with the phallus. As *The Bostonians* and *The Blithedale Romance* suggest, lesbian figures are then produced to represent the "immanent antagonisms" out of and against which the effect of heterosexual "reality" thus defines itself.

James's dedication of the novel to what he terms a "very national, very typical" subject connects such questions of realistic and allegorical representation to issues of American nationalism. Peopled by what one critic calls "examples of typological being," *The Bostonians* occupies the space of realism uneasily, as throughout the novel James simultaneously unfolds and undermines the seemingly lifelike portrait of his Bostonians.[57] When, for example, the author responds to William James's complaint that Miss Birdseye is too closely and unflatteringly modeled on the well-known reformer Elizabeth Peabody, it is difficult not to hear in his protests an echo of Hawthorne's introduction to *The Blithedale Romance*, which seeks to assure the former inhabitants of Brook Farm that the novel will not attempt "sketching any of their likenesses" (2). "I am quite appalled by your note," James writes, "in which you assault me on the subject of my having painted a 'portrait from life' of Miss Peabody! . . . Miss Birdseye was evolved entirely from my moral consciousness, like every other person I have ever drawn."[58] Describing the relationship between Olive and Verena in his notebook, however, James announces his realist intention to produce a novel that is "as local, as American, as possible" through "a study of one of those friendships between women which are so common in New England."[59]

Certainly readings of *The Bostonians* have produced a sort of reality effect, but what lesbian desire means in James's novel is no more simple than in Hawthorne's.[60] In Judith Fetterley's compendium of a century's critical responses to gender and sexuality in the novel, the claim that there is no lesbianism in *The Bostonians* becomes almost indistinguishable from the complaint that there is too much of it. Walter F. Wright notes that "without encumbering the story with Lesbianism, one can still recognize in Olive's obsession a serious evil."[61] Whether such critical responses call the women's relationship lesbianism or "obsession," or as another reader would have it, "unnatural friendship," they reenact the ways in which the novel both produces and evacuates the notion of lesbian sexuality. James examines sexual identity within a discourse of typology that, like one onlooker in *The Bostonians*, recognizes Olive and Verena as "of the same kind" (222), but perpetually sustains the slippage between the lesbian type and the pathology of femininity itself. Just as in *The Blithedale Romance* Zenobia and Priscilla embody feminine types—the "High-Spirited Woman" and "the Weakly Maiden"—in *The Bostonians*

Olive's vision of herself as a "representative woman" is never truly discredited (249).

The problematic distinction between femininity and lesbianism in both James and Hawthorne can be understood, in part, as an effect of American sexual ideology. From the nineteenth century through the present, women's political resistance has been construed as sexual resistance, and the impulse for reform, that linchpin of masculine "progress" in American myth, has been regarded, in women's hands, as a token of perversity. Contemplating women's "unnatural" influence over other women, *The Blithedale Romance* speaks to a long and anxious history of female authority in American culture and literature. As Joel Pfister has suggested, early accounts of Anne Hutchinson blame her corruption of impressionable women for an epidemic of "monster" births. One Edward Johnson, Pfister notes, "ascribes to Hutchinson the wish to displace the father and to impregnate her female followers ('the breeder') with her influence."[62] In an astute reading of "Rappacini's Daughter," Pfister considers Hawthorne's 1830 essay on Hutchinson, in which the young writer compares the historical threat of Hutchinson's heresy to the contemporary threat of women's growing public roles, and offers this gloss of Hawthorne: "The 'public women,' of which Hutchinson was a type in her own times, are on the loose, in the 'press,' and perhaps worst of all, will soon become 'fair orators.' "[63] Nineteenth-century accounts of Margaret Fuller, the supposed model for Hawthorne's Zenobia, reflect that anxiety about the transmission of dangerous ideas among women, whose overly intense friendships seemed a breeding ground for corrupt beliefs and whose ventures into public oratory threatened the demarcation of the separate spheres.[64]

The Bostonians takes shape within this rhetorical tradition, which, projecting the ruinous consequences of women becoming "fair orators," conflates perverse female sexuality, radical politics, and public speech. In James's America, of course, politics and public discourse remained a masculine arena, and the appearance of female orators was an occasion for profound anxiety. As Lynn Wardley has suggested, national welfare seemed to depend in the nineteenth century on the preservation of discursive gender codes: "if it is true that woman's speech and her physiology serve as the source of both cultural and biological regeneration in the democracy, it is also the case that voice and the maternal body represent the possibility of unregulated signification and reproduction."[65] In a formulation that goes far toward explaining Zenobia's fate, and that of the feminism she represents, Lauren Berlant notes that in *The Blithedale Romance* and other Hawthorne texts "the public prominence of a theorizing woman . . . is always scandalous and always provokes some kind of textual discipline."[66] And Claire Kahane has argued in a persuasive reading of *The Bostonians* that in nineteenth-century American culture women's public speech constituted a "radical gesture," a spectacle that seemed "particularly horrifying" to a male audience because it claimed both "the power of the maternal body as a figure of presence as well as the power of the father's language."[67]

I will return shortly to the relation between maternal body and paternal language in *The Bostonians*, for the terms of that gender binarism structure Verena's ability to inspire both desire and anxiety—if in fact the two can be separated. While women's public speech in *The Bostonians* and in nineteenth-century American culture surely implies the appropriation of the paternal voice, as Kahane suggests, Verena's role in the novel is more ambivalent. To insist, as Olive does at Miss Birdseye's home, that "a voice, a human voice, is what we want" is to acknowledge the way in which, as Brodhead notes in his reading of *The Bostonians*, that "oratory's effect is always the creation of desire."[68] And Verena's voice works, on Basil if not on the reader, less as a trauma than as a tease; its "horrifying" effects prove, in the end, all too assimilable to the heterosexual narrative. For Basil the lure of Verena's speech lies neither in the grace of its rhetoric nor in the structure of its logic, but instead, James tells us, in its magical sound. As Fetterley notes, "Verena's power is in her voice, not in her words."[69] At her first Boston appearance Verena begins "incoherently, almost inaudibly" and quickly achieves a degree of eloquence, but for Basil "it was not what she said; he didn't care for that, he scarcely understood it." Indeed, "the argument, the doctrine, had absolutely nothing to do with it" (51). To Basil, "the necessity of her nature was not to make converts to a ridiculous cause, but to emit those charming notes of her voice" (51–52). Those "charming notes" gradually draw Basil into Verena's orbit: after listening to her speech in New York he cannot "repeat a word she had said; he had not definitely heeded it, and yet he had not lost a vibration of her voice" (231).

Basil's dismissive notion of Verena's speech as mere sound, empty of sense and meaning, is not without precedent in nineteenth-century American culture. As Caroline Field Levander has documented, from the late eighteenth century through the turn of the twentieth century male commentators on language tried to "interpret the woman orator's speech in terms of her body." "In highlighting the tone of the female voice, as opposed to its content, and in linking that tone to the female body," Levander argues, "linguists tried to place woman's speech firmly in the private arena."[70] Such constructions of the female voice not only denied the possibility of a woman having anything to say, but also worked to define feminine speech as essentially different from masculine speech, following the conventional binarism: femininity as bodily form, masculinity as transcendent thought.

In Western philosophy the distinction between body and mind, form and content, is fundamental to the distinction between speech and writing. As Derrida explains in *Of Grammatology*, speech is privileged over writing as the original that material signs can only imitate.[71] In the logic of the philosophy that privileges original over copy, Derrida argues, writing is the essence of artifice, and "the perversion of artifice engenders monsters." That formulation suggests a resemblance not only between writing and the violation of proper reproduction but also, specifically, between writing and homosexuality. Out of an "intolerable and fascinating . . . intimacy," Derrida observes, writing generates "a mirroring, inverting, and perverting effect," which threatens to displace speech from its celebrated role.[72] And if, as Lee Edelman has argued, Western culture aligns male homosexuality with the artifice of writing, it identifies lesbianism with its own "inverting and perverting" effects.[73] According to the gendered division between spirit and matter, transcendence and materiality, the authentic discourse of speech would normatively belong to masculinity and the secondary mode of writing to femininity. Basil's distinction between the meaningful "word" and the "charming notes" of Verena's voice can therefore be seen as a rehearsal in another register of the philosophical distinction between speech and writing, and as a reaction to the problem of speech and writing in the world of *The Bostonians*. From the beginning, *The Bostonians* has signaled that the ascendancy of female public speech has significant effects on the relation of speech to writing as well as the negotiation of gender and sexuality. On the novel's first page Basil, in a characteristic gesture, picks up a book from Olive's drawing room and becomes instantly "absorbed" in reading (1). In contrast to Verena and the feminist movement, who are dedicated to oratory, Basil is aligned with textuality—so much so that it comes as no surprise when he finally turns to writing for the conservative *Rational Review*. James introduces Basil within a world of disorder, where the hierarchy of speech and writing has been emptied of meaning, where the prerogatives of public speech are claimed by feminine discourse and masculinity is relegated to the realm of writing.

One aim of the novel, then, is to reestablish the dominant regime of representation—to assign the power of speech to masculine heterosexuality and to subordinate the "perverse" possibilities of writing to that purer discourse—a project that will demand the rehabilitation of normative structures of sexuality as well as language.[74] For Basil, that task requires not only the removal of Verena from the stage to the properly feminine domestic sphere, but also the recovery of public speech as a masculine discourse and of speech as *logos*, the transcendent word. This is the goal to which Basil applies the nineteenth-century masculine rhetoric on female speech, representing Verena's voice as a sound evacuated of meaning. But while Basil prevails in James's narrative, ending Verena's public career, the insistence of his misogynist reading of the female voice indicates what his dismissive tone may not: that this response emerges in the face of a real threat, to which the anxious mechanisms of cultural containment may never be commensurate.

When in *The Bostonians*, as in *The Blithedale Romance*, the "intolerable and fascinating" effect of a perverse representation attaches to feminine speech rather than writing, the very category of speech becomes debased, absorbing the meaning of the female body as token of materiality and losing its authority as the privileged bearer of the word. Women's speech thus poses a double threat. While female orators violated the nineteenth-century American dictum of separate spheres, claiming access to the masculine register of public discourse, the feminine voice also implies the ruin of speech as such, corrupting the transcendent authority of that privileged discourse. In *The Bostonians*, Verena undermines the authority of speech by exposing the gap between word and voice, between meaning and sound, thus revealing the unbridgeable space between a fantasy of impossible presence and the endless displacements of differential articulation. De Man reads this schism between sound and meaning as an effect of "literariness," which is to say, evidence that "the convergence of sound and meaning" is "a mere *effect*," just as "the link, the relationship between word and thing, is not phenomenal but conventional."[75] Whereas Hawthorne's Veiled Lady's voice is disembodied, Verena's is overembodied. Yet each in its own way troubles the "marriage contract" between voice and body. The acousmatic voice in *The Blithedale Romance* contradicts the patriarchal distinction between masculine essence and feminine materiality, undermining the cultural logic that, as Chion suggests, posits the relation between voice and body as essentially heterosexual. If the Veiled Lady does so by dividing voice from body, Verena does so by presenting the relation of voice and body—sound and content, embodiment and meaning—not as a "conventional couple" but instead as a lesbian couple.

Basil, after all, is not the only one enticed by the "charm" of Verena's lovely voice. Olive too carries the "contagion" of that excitement, recognizing in Verena "what she had been looking for so long—a friend of her own sex with whom she might have a union of soul" (68). Accordingly, the relationship the two women will share is defined not only by the *project* of speaking on behalf of women's rights, but also by the *trope* of speech. When Verena's dedication to the work of speaking occasionally lapses, James writes, Olive must revivify her sense of purpose:

> after a short contact with the divine idea—Olive was always trying to flash it at her, like a jewel in an uncovered case—she kindled, flamed up, took the words from her friend's less persuasive lips, resolved herself into a magical voice, became again the pure sibyl. (137)

Although it is a word and not a kiss exchanged between women's lips, that substitution serves only to enlarge the erotic possibilities of rhetoric, not to diminish the brilliant perversity of the scene. Olive's "jewel in an uncovered case," predicting the reticule and "jewel-case" of Freud's Dora case, links the notion of speech to a fantasy of the female body fantasmatically invented as a site of lesbian desire, making "magical voice" and lesbian sexuality effects of one another in a circuit of endless renewal and return.

So although Basil's view of Verena unflatteringly attributes to her "a singular hollowness of character" (52), as James writes, that "hollowness" aptly suggests the capacity of her speeches to be filled with the arguments Olive provides. The rhetoric of "hollowness," of course, evokes the patriarchal myth of woman as a receptacle meant to carry children or masculine ideas, but it also accurately describes the function of the sign. As a vessel filled with meaning, the sign can eclipse its contents: the signifier can overtake the signified. Identifying the perverse possibilities of this timeworn trope, Olive presses it to the service of a quite different sexual relation, a sort of erotic ventriloquism in which one woman's bodily "form" is occupied by the spirit of another. In a passage that trenchantly connects what she will later call the "magical voice" and "divine idea," she tells Verena, "you are my form—my envelope" (136). "Form" here indicates the materiality of the body, but it also alludes to the structure of language. As such it designates what de Man has identified as the principle of grammar, whose meaning-making function orders civilization.[76] As Verena's relation to Olive demonstrates, however, the lesbian intervention in linguistic "form" bears with it a *de*formation—or rather, a demystification—that reveals the contingency of the relation between signifier and signified and the fragility of the effect we take to be meaningful language.

Impossible Desire

The Bostonians and *The Blithedale Romance* together suggest an answer to Basil's question: "Why was her morbidness typical?" The answer demands that we recognize, as Basil does not, the complex relations between lesbianism and language. If in *The Blithedale Romance* the allegorical association of lesbianism with the real inspires Coverdale's desire to conquer "goblins" of the supernatural realm even—or especially—when they do not "exist at all," in *The Bostonians* this logic recurs in efforts to suppress forms of female speech and sexuality that the culture has already deemed nonexistent. The "prohibition of the impossible," the axiomatic principle of the real, governs *The Bostonians'* final scene, which presents the obtrusion of a lesbian voice into the text through and *as* a spectacular occlusion. There is perhaps no more economical representation of the prohibition of the impossible than Basil's complaint to a policeman in the Music Hall: "If the door was locked, what was the good of your standing before it?" (385). If an act is impossible, that is, why must it be proscribed? Clearly this question emblematizes Basil's own anxious relation to Verena's speeches, and especially to what must seem, in his misogynist view, the already "impossible" or oxymoronic topic of "A Woman's Reason." But as a rhetorical question, like the question of Olive's "typical" morbidity, Basil's query also testifies to the text's own disavowed, conflicted investment in the female voice and lesbian erotics, an investment matched only by the law's obsessive returns to an entrance to desire that never seems securely enough locked.

In order to subordinate Verena to its heterosexual conclusion, *The Bostonians* will displace the trauma of her public voice from the symbolic order to the site of the real and transfer its disciplinary energies to another speech that, where the narrative is concerned, can never exist. When Verena renounces her career, the burden of her speech falls on Olive, for whom that effort may be literally impossible.[77] "I can't speak," she protests early on, "I have none of that sort of talent. I have no self-possession, no eloquence; I can't put three words together" (29–30). We cannot know whether, for all these disavowals *in* speech *of* speech itself, Olive will muster the "self-possession" to satisfy the audience at the Music Hall, for like Hawthorne's Veiled Lady she is never seen to speak in public. But although the narrative cuts, almost cinematically, to Basil and Verena at the moment when Olive will test her "eloquence," James remains fascinated by the anticipation of that impossible speech. The voice on which the novel pointedly turns its back is a voice from which, in the end, it can hardly tear itself away:

> In the outer labyrinth hasty groups, a little scared, were leaving the hall, giving up the game. Ransom, as he went, thrust the hood of Verena's long cloak over her head, to conceal her face and her identity. It quite prevented recognition, and as they mingled in the issuing crowd he perceived the quick, complete,

tremendous silence which, in the hall, had greeted Olive Chancellor's rush to the front. Every sound instantly dropped, the hush was respectful, the great public waited, and whatever she should say to them, (and he thought she might indeed be rather embarrassed), it was not apparent that they were likely to hurl the benches at her. (395)

Leaving Olive backstage as Mrs. Burrage asks, "Oh, are *you* going to speak?" the novel follows Verena and Basil, who exit the theater only to enter their own drama. As Basil hurries a tearful Verena into the street, the force of the novel's last prophetic—one is tempted to say, sibylline—line threatens to overshadow James's rather inconclusive account of Olive's public appearance: "But though she was glad, he presently discovered that, beneath her hood, she was in tears. It is to be feared that with the union, so far from brilliant, into which she was about to enter, these were not the last she was destined to shed" (395).

Yet the scene in which Olive takes Verena's place on the platform seems compelling to precisely the extent that it does not exist within the space of the narrative. In the passage that establishes both Olive's success and her failure, the text declines to make her form visible or her voice audible to us. Representing Olive's voice as the unrepresentable, as the gap of a "complete, tremendous silence," James grants her speech the status of "missed encounter" with the real, as what must go unsymbolized, in *The Bostonians*, as the precondition of narrative closure. As Joseph Litvak has observed in his reading of theatricality and embarrassment in *The Bostonians*, Olive is the "odd woman out" in the novel's heterosexual conclusion; "left out and left over," she functions as "an improbable, inert-looking semiotic residue in the narrative machinery."[78] Seemingly "inert" but actively inciting reading and (dis)identification in Basil, not to say James himself, Olive comes to mark a failure of the boundary between the real and the symbolic. She stands as a figure of excess in the novel's movement toward narrative closure and takes the place of the real as what must be foreclosed, "what must remain unsaid," Žižek writes, in the service of narrative closure and symbolic coherence.[79] As the "left over" residue that is also a necessary condition of signification, the real itself alludes to the "latent" homosexuality that, for Freud, is the precondition of "manifest" heterosexuality and the origin of the woman's teleological movement toward adult heterosexuality.[80] James's text, after all, does not merely aim to represent some credibly "Bostonian" characters; like *The Blithedale Romance*, it also strives to accomplish female Oedipalization by tracing Verena's progress toward adult heterosexuality. Verena is, as Kahane notes, "as yet uninscribed in the conventional oedipal narrative of culture" that sets the girl on the path toward her prescribed place in the social and symbolic orders.[81] Just as *The Blithedale Romance* propels Priscilla toward adult Oedipal relations, the narrative progress of *The Bostonians* requires that Verena's lesbian investments undergo a transference onto an appropriate heterosexual object. Yet when Olive, however painfully, takes Verena's place onstage, that reversal should alert us to the possibility of another: for if Olive can become Verena, Verena can also become Olive, at least in the cultural fantasy of a heterosexual femininity ever poised on the brink of regression.

Like *The Blithedale Romance*, *The Bostonians* fails to accomplish the Oedipal distinction between "woman" and "lesbian," and that failure leaves the relation between speech and writing equally uncertain. Within his household Basil may reign over both voice and book, relegating Verena's oratorical skills to the entertainment of dinner guests, but Olive's voice remains a disturbing excess in the text, like the "stain" of the real within the symbolic order. To the heterosexual world finally embodied by Basil and Verena, who sense the "hush" that precedes Olive's speech from an outer corridor, her voice must remain unheard and formless. But if the space of Olive's speech appears as a site of trauma, unassimilable to the narrative and to James's realist ambitions, it is also the site of a certain sublimity. As Basil and Verena leave the text and "every sound instantly drop[s]" away, the novel itself, like the hushed Music Hall, seems poised to take Verena's place as an envelope for Olive's voice—a voice that, resonant with the rhetorical "vibration" of a lesbian sexuality, names the embarrassment and the *jouissance* of every effort of speech.

chapter two

The Reproduction of Meaning
Language, Oedipality, and *The Awakening*

In 1899 Willa Cather, writing in the *Pittsburgh Leader*, named *The Awakening* "a Creole *Bovary*" and offered this criticism of Kate Chopin's novel:

> There was, indeed, no need that a second *Madame Bovary* should be written, but an author's choice of themes is frequently as inexplicable as his choice of a wife. . . . This is particularly so in women who write, and I shall not attempt to say why Miss Chopin has devoted so exquisite and sensitive, well-governed a style to so trite and sordid a theme.[1]

Along with the startling illogic of Cather's generalized masculine case, it is not difficult to recognize in these lines a normalizing regime of sexuality that promotes heterosexual marriage as the paradigm of narrative form. In this tropology, whose particular effects in American literature I will examine later, the failure of the romance narrative can be read only as another kind of courtship, the "choice" of an unworthy object of desire, or thematic material, that in Chopin's text perversely elevates "style" over substance. Cather's remarks indicate the impossible position of the woman writer, whose relation to her own "themes" can only, within these terms, constitute an act of imposture or lesbian desire. Her review, however, goes on to situate the problem of Chopin's text not in the "trite and sordid" subject—or bad object—of adultery, but in the indulgence of an "individual and self-limited passion." The perversity of *The Awakening*, for Cather, lies in feminine narcissism, in Edna Pontellier's solipsistic cathexis not of the love-object but of "love" itself *as* an object.[2]

For all its dilation on the pleasures and pains of heterosexual relations, *The Awakening*, as Cather rightly suggests, always returns to the inward-turning eroticism signaled in Chopin's original title, *A Solitary Soul*. The text, after all, ends with the detachment of Edna's love from any object, proper or improper, and with the fixation of her desire only in eternal restlessness: "There was no one thing in the world that she desired. There was no human being whom she wanted near her except Robert; and she even realized that the day would come when he, too, and the thought of him would melt out of her existence, leaving her alone."[3] In its negation of object-choice, this passage echoes Margaret Fuller, whose remarks on her own desire profoundly earn the title "A Solitary Soul." In an early letter, Fuller writes, "I was always to return to myself, to be my own priest, pupil, parent, child, husband, and wife." She continues, "I think I may say, I never loved . . . I have never really approached the close relations of life."[4] However acute her sense of isolation, Fuller's meditation on her relations with herself is not devoid of pleasure; yet in the discourse of the nineteenth century, the female solipsism she describes could be construed only in terms of morbidity. Literalizing the fatal implications of female solitude, Hawthorne would borrow from Fuller's own death by drowning to represent the suicide of Zenobia in *The Blithedale Romance*—a scene that Chopin, in turn, restages at the conclusion of *The Awakening*. In the masculine literary tradition, this narrative fashioning of female solipsism works to repudiate a female perversity whose danger is identified both with feminist politics and with resistance to the narrative of heterosexual reproduction, the *leitmotif* of patriarchal culture. Within this logic, the patriarchal ideology that celebrates masculine solipsism in the form of Emersonian "self-reliance" must—as Fuller's place in American literary history suggests—regard the woman's tendency "always to return to [her]self" as a mark of doomed or deviant subjectivity.

"Self-reliance," that famously American virtue, is not incidental here, for in Emerson the nineteenth century found an influential fantasy of American literature elaborated in tropes of sexual and familial relations. While questions of literary production, as Michael Warner has explained, were central to nationalist self-definition from the early days of the American republic, it was not until the early nineteenth century that the consolidation of national identity demanded a uniquely American literary aesthetic.[5] And in the nineteenth century the task of producing a national identity, literary or otherwise, depended on the rhetorical positing, revision, and repudiation of a familial connection between American culture and its European progenitors. The idea of "American literature" called upon the same narrative of resistance to parental authority that had informed the colonies' struggle for political independence from England. In 1836 Emerson invoked this Oedipal metaphor in the first lines of his essay "Nature": "Our age is retrospective. It builds the sepulchres of the fathers."[6] Positing retrospection and the ritual obligations of son to father as obstacles to the experience of an "original relation to the universe" and the emergence of a truly new American literature, Emerson locates American writing within the Freudian "family romance" that Harold Bloom has identified as a central trope of literary inheritance. And if, as Bloom has suggested, the Oedipal relation of son to father structures the drama of poetic influence, it does so in a particular way, equating heterosexual generativity with the very possibility of meaning.[7]

I call attention to the Oedipal geometry in Emerson's vision of American literature not only to acknowledge the ways in which it shapes our possibilities for imagining desire, representation, and literary history, but also in order to examine the consequences of its failure and the costs of its success. That family romance places a burden on the male writer, whose accomplishment of poetic originality, in Bloom's and Emerson's terms, depends on assuming the place of his literary fathers; but it also exacts a price from every subject within American patriarchal culture, not least the woman whose task it is to complete (or corrupt) the Oedipal triangle. For Emerson as for Freud, the succession of the son to the place of the father requires the figure of the woman, who must embody either the hope of the Oedipal family's perpetuation or the danger of its perversion. Before returning to *The Awakening*, therefore, I want briefly to consider Emerson's account of the relations among gender, sexuality, and language. Understanding how, in Emerson's view, masculine "self-reliance" enables a national literature through the narrative of Oedipal succession allows us to see how feminine "self-reliance," in contrast, appears to threaten that Oedipal order and familial—which is also to say, cultural—reproduction. This notion of female perversity informs Chopin's portrait of Edna Pontellier in *The Awakening*—a portrait that suggests how feminine solipsism evokes the possibility of lesbian desire in nineteenth-century American culture, and how notions of debased female sexuality are aligned with the debasement of language.

In Emerson's vision of American literature, the possibility of writing issues from intersecting narratives of Oedipal struggle, heterosexual reproduction, and patriarchal authority. One important strand presents the agonistic relation to cultural inheritance whose "retrospective" effects Emerson denounces. In an essay entitled "American Literature: Its Position in the Present Time, and Prospects for the Future" (1846), Margaret Fuller describes this familial metaphor in distinctly Bloomian terms: "there is often, between child and parent, a reaction from excessive influence having been exerted, and such a one we have experienced, in behalf of our country, against England."[8] At the same time, however, the Oedipal drama assumes the form of the marriage plot, taking "reproduction" as a trope of representation and imagining meaning as the product of feminine "nature" wedded to masculine thought. In "Nature," Emerson explains the complementary relation between the natural world and human cognition through a familiar metaphor of heterosexual coupling: "All the facts in natural history taken by themselves, have no value, but are barren like a single sex. But marry it to human history, and it is full of life" (19). The marriage of feminine nature and masculine intellectual "history" is a fruitful one, giving birth and "life" to a new discourse. Here is the promise of a national literature, the possibility of Emerson's "new lands, new men, new thoughts" to supplant those of "the foregoing generations" (7).

Underscoring the need for productive coupling to redeem those "facts," or persons, that "taken by themselves, have no value," Emerson offers a fine précis of the law of heterosexual ideology, under whose dictates "value" as such is cognate with "family values." Not confined to contemporary right-wing politics, "family values" structure the sexual ideology that, without pausing to acknowledge political dissent, installs heterosexual reproduction as the natural and inevitable goal of civilization. Associating sexual deviance with *rhetorical* deviance, Emerson reflects the nineteenth-century American ideology that commonly equated perversions of language with perversions of sexuality. From Emerson to the late-Victorian sexologists, as Jesse F. Battan has argued, the proper usage of words and the presence of an "essential link between words and the physical and spiritual realities they represented" were deemed fundamental to the preservation of "natural" hierarchies and the social order.[9] Accordingly, in Emerson's literary marriage plot the "corruption of language" (20) inheres in the feminine desire, the unnatural face of "nature," whose refusal to accede to Oedipality threatens the vitality of meaning, the fertility of the heterosexual family, and the reproduction of civilization itself. The "value" that Emerson invokes, synonymous with the procreative potential of "life," demands that a heterosexual model of language supplant those other forms of discourse that can only, he goes on to suggest, represent "falsehood" and "fraud" (20).

In her essay, "American Literature," Fuller returns to Emerson's marital trope, placing the question of literary production within the realm of familial relations. While not without its own perversity, the heterosexual model of literary reproduction lays claim to naturalness through the projected threat of the *truly* perverse—in Fuller's text, the threat of parthenogenic reproduction by what Emerson calls the "single sex." Without original "national ideas," Fuller writes, "all attempts to construct a national literature must end in abortions like the monster of Frankenstein, things with forms, and the instincts of forms, but soulless, and therefore revolting."[10] Inverting the terms of Mary Shelley's novel of reproduction without women, Fuller imagines a literary reproduction without men. Her vision of the "abortions" of a failed literature invokes an Emersonian vocabulary in order to assign the horror of pure materiality ("things with forms, and the instincts of forms, but soulless") to femininity, as distinct from the transcendent promise of masculine "national ideas." And like Emerson's "Nature," Fuller's "American Literature" adduces such monstrous births as proof that a national literature must issue from a heterosexual union of "ideas" and "things." Within the familiar terms of the mind / body binarism, female parthenogenesis constitutes not only a grotesque parody of normative reproduction but also, and more importantly, a fatal miscarriage of meaning.

Of course the full scope of Fuller's life and work as a woman writer complicates the matter by resisting the patriarchal framing of intellectual labor. Despite her depiction of the monstrous issue of nonheterosexual literary relations in "American Literature," Fuller would describe her Boston "Conversations"—weekly women's meetings devoted to the discussion of intellectual issues—as sites of "re-production."[11] Christina Zwarg has argued that Fuller locates in women's discourse "a type of feminist agency."[12] Suggesting the possibility of a vital, even valorized, female generativity, this other reproduction brings into relief the contradiction at the heart of Fuller's "American Literature," an essay that itself may enact the solitary female literary production Fuller seeks to repudiate. Her peculiar conservatism in "American Literature" suggests how powerful and how pervasive the heterosexual model of literary production was in nineteenth-century American culture. Read alongside Fuller's notion of feminine intellectual discourse, however, "American Literature" also suggests the centrality of the trope of reproduction, which, as a figure for representation, will prove as fundamental to Chopin's *Awakening* as it is to Emerson's remarks on literature.

Throughout the nineteenth century "reproduction" signified both procreation and representation—meanings whose intersection had significant consequences for women writers. Both are governed by Oedipal narratives: while procreation is required to perpetuate the patriarchal family, the notion of representation, specifically the *literary* elaboration of an American canon in the nineteenth century, takes shape within the Oedipal tropology Emerson describes. Further, these two reproductive systems share a structural similarity in their dependence on *displacement*. As the marker, for Freud, of the metonymic association of signs in the dreamwork; as the principle, for Lacan, of linguistic slippage or *glissement*; and as the name given by psychoanalysis to the transference of erotic meanings or cathexes from one object to another, displacement is a switchpoint between the reproductive systems of sexuality and of language. As such, the notion of displacement also suggests the nexus where these reproductive systems meet the perversion that must be relegated to the realm of what does not signify—a perversion simultaneously imagined as the lesbian difference within female Oedipality and as the endless deferral of meaning in language.[13]

Kate Chopin's novel *The Awakening* calls upon both senses of reproduction in its portrait of Edna Pontellier, a figure for the debased femininity that in Emerson's "Nature" and Fuller's "American Literature" constitutes the "corruption of language" and of desire. That Edna's "awakening," in the novel's central irony, should come to mean her death suggests a conflation of vitality and fatality not unlike the lesbian "morbidness" that, in the nineteenth century, promised the ruin of normative reproduction, both familial and figural. Grounded in the language of nineteenth-century sexology, this notion, as we have seen, informs such texts as James's *Bostonians*: having pointedly identified Olive Chancellor as "morbid," Basil Ransom imagines her proper place, and that of her feminist ideals, as "the land of vapours, of dead phrases."[14] The "dead phrase," as a phrase, evokes the notion of the dead metaphor and also bespeaks the deathliness of metaphor itself. The "morbid," for James, is figural language that can consist only of displacement, as opposed to language that promises literal meaning, aspiring to the status of truly, as they say, creative writing. Lesbianism is understood as morbidity or deathliness, in other words, because it is made to bear the burden of rhetoric as such, whose sterile reproduction and displacement of meaning become the hallmarks, in patriarchal culture, of lesbian desire. Thus what *The Awakening* knows about Edna—that "there was no one thing in the world she desired"—is enough to identify her with the system of endless displacement, the circuit of non-meaning that Lacan, writing on transference, calls a "chain of dead desire."[15]

Exceptions That Prove the Rule

It comes as little surprise when Chopin's heroine, determined to take up "a course of improving studies" (70), reads a few pages of

Emerson before bedtime, for the novel has consistently framed Edna Pontellier's "awakening" in Emersonian terms, as the problem of recognizing "her relations as an individual to the world" (14). Indeed, where Chopin relies on an Emersonian rhetoric of self-reliance to frame Edna's quest for "a language which nobody understood"—or a discourse outside the masculine symbolic—the novel threatens to lapse into cliché, and thus by definition to participate in a language that everybody understands only too well. In the end *The Awakening* demonstrates the failure of Emersonian individualism for women, for whom the solitude that enables male genius can only mean perversity or annihilation. In so doing, however, it betrays the sexual stakes of "self-reliance": how easily, for example, Emerson's vaunted "introversion" can be misread as "inversion," and how little besides misogyny separates heroic solitude from the unwholesome narcissism of Edna Pontellier.[16]

It is well known that when the novel was published in 1899, readers of *The Awakening* found its content distasteful and its heroine's motivations baffling. Chopin's novel was, in the words of one reviewer, "a morbid book"; it seemed, another wrote, as "unhealthily introspective" as its heroine.[17] In such contemporary reviews, the problem of Edna's sexuality was articulated as one of representativeness. Early readers, not unlike the feminist critics who would some eighty years later elevate the novel to canonical status, sought to determine whether Edna Pontellier was an exceptional woman or an exemplary one. Taking up the Emersonian relation of "an individual to the world," the one reading sees Edna's story as an isolated case, while the other claims *The Awakening* as feminist allegory and, taking a cue from Emerson's *Representative Men*, hails Edna Pontellier as a representative woman.[18] If late-twentieth-century feminist criticism largely endeavors to position Edna as typical of women's place in American culture and in patriarchal ideology (even as it seeks to disidentify from her suicide by reading Chopin's conclusion as the "solitary" instance of a unique pathology), Chopin's contemporaries, for the most part, labored to establish her heroine as exceptional (even as they noted how patently Edna displayed the peculiarities of "woman" as such). The possibility that Edna might *be* representative produced a visceral disgust in one early reviewer: the novel, she wrote, "makes one wonder, for the moment, with a little sick feeling, if all women are like the one." Another reader confidently identified Edna as a "feminine type," to wit: one of "that large section of femininity which may be classified as 'fool women.' "[19] Such questions are already present within the text, if in less contentious form. Edna herself, after all, wonders "what character of a woman I am." She tells Arobin, "By all the codes with which I am acquainted, I am a devilishly wicked specimen of the sex. But some way I can't convince myself that I am" (79). Economically suggesting the paradox of Edna's representativeness, Chopin juxtaposes the language of the "specimen," indicating Edna's representative status as "woman," with the language of "character" and wickedness, with its appeal to notions of individual morality.

Why is it so difficult, and so important, to determine whether Edna Pontellier is a typical or an exceptional woman? The question requires that we consider the relation between "lesbian" and "woman" at the turn of the twentieth century, when American sexual rhetoric began to reify the distinction between feminine heterosexuality—itself a very recent invention—and a rapidly disseminated notion of pathological lesbianism.[20] Within the dominant common sense of the particular and the general, the exception and the rule, that inevitably consigns lesbianism to the status of the exceptional, to see Edna as a "feminine type" is to accept her as representative of heterosexual femininity. In the critical commentary on the novel, this all too common sense has largely prevailed. Despite the tone of knowingness with which early reviewers greeted Edna Pontellier—in Cather's recognition, for example, of Edna's special "type" or "class" of women—readers have largely found in *The Awakening* a narrative of (failed) heterosexual love.[21] But if the novel's critics have been reluctant to read Edna's desire as lesbian, we might do well to ask why not. Having posed this question, let me signal my intention to take it seriously. I am not interested in adjudicating the question of Edna Pontellier's "real" sexual identity, for to search for essential identity in this context is merely to rehearse the Emersonian clichés of self-discovery. Instead, taking that question at its word, I want to untangle the working of the discursive network within which the "unhealthily introspective" Edna Pontellier can, and will, be understood as heterosexual.

The Awakening undertakes the epistemological project of differentiating between the general and the particular, between femininity and lesbianism, at a historical moment when women's romantic friendships were being redefined as pathologically "lesbian," due in part to the efforts of Victorian sexologists such as Havelock Ellis to define homosexuality and heterosexuality.[22] Although this shift in sexual discourses elevated notions of object-choice and identity to governing principles of female sexuality, the new notion of "lesbianism" also incorporated older understandings of female propriety and perversity. Jonathan Katz has argued that the emergence of "homosexuality," both male and female, corresponded to the development of "heterosexuality" as the dominant model of relations between the sexes; in each case, sexuality was newly defined as an identity based not on discrete acts but on a generalized sexual desire for the other.[23] One might say that the notion of object-choice, at least as the primary component of sexual identity, was born at this time; yet at the turn of the twentieth century, object-choice was not yet the preeminent definition of female sexuality. In her recent reading of *The Awakening*, Cynthia Griffin Wolff suggests that nineteenth-century American culture regarded female sexuality as perverse insofar as it exceeded or deviated from the desire for motherhood.[24] Unlike notions of male homosexuality, American concepts of lesbian sexuality foregrounded the question of reproduction, linking lesbianism to earlier formulations of female sexual perversity as a resistance to motherhood. Commonly construed as the failure of proper reproduction and a rejection of appropriate female roles, lesbianism appeared as a deviation from maternal aims as well as masculine objects. This ideology became more public and more explicit at the turn of the twentieth century, when the "New Woman" was condemned as a sexual deviant because, in an era of sharply declining birthrates among white middle-class women, she seemed to have forsaken her maternal duties.[25]

Published in 1899, Chopin's novel reflects the discomfort of its own positioning within changing sexual ideologies, presenting the notion of lesbianism both as a relational *effect* of desire, in Edna's friendship with Adele Ratignolle, and as a regime of sexual *identity*, in the spinster pianist Mademoiselle Reisz. While Adele's "excessive physical charm" (14) has a magnetic power for Edna, arousing in her "the subtle bond which we call sympathy, which we might well call love" (15), her "candor ... which every one might read" (14) remains exempt from the fantasy of bodily legibility to which Mademoiselle Reisz is subjected. Adele's appeal to the senses establishes her "charm" as a surface effect, not an essential quality, of lesbian desire, allowing Edna's "love" to merge into narcissism when, touching Adele, she becomes "intoxicated with the sound of her own voice" (19). In contrast, *The Awakening* describes Mademoiselle Reisz as a body obsessively written and read as the signifier of a lesbian desire that, to a homophobic culture, must be recognized and repudiated. Here the physiognomy of the lesbian "type," like that of the male homosexual, becomes the legible text of a perverse desire.[26] Chopin pauses to note, as token of Reisz's erotic overinvestment in Edna, the pianist's "strikingly homely" face (59) and the "weazened," "twisted" body (25) that gives her an "appearance of deformity" (61). And readers of the novel—abundantly demonstrating, as Kathryn Lee Seidel has noted, the legibility of Reisz's sexuality—have gone further, naming her, among other things, a "chimera," a "she-monster," and a "sorceress," a woman who is not only "unnatural" but also sexually "dead" and endowed with "a voyeur's appetite for vicarious pleasure."[27]

Yet to ask Mademoiselle Reisz, or even Adele Ratignolle, to bear the burden of representing "the lesbian" in the text is to accede to the rhetoric of sexual identity, by locating lesbianism—whether as "excessive charm" or "deformity," metonym or metaphor, effect or essence—and thereby strengthening the rhetorical *cordon sanitaire* that allows Edna's heterosexuality to seem utterly natural. In the patriarchal imagination, as we know, femininity is normatively construed as pathological. Misogynistically defined as incomplete and narcissistic, femininity is the embodiment of the lack that installs masculinity as the locus of presence. When, in *The Awakening*, Edna abandons her domestic responsibilities, causing her husband to wonder "if his wife were not growing a little unbalanced mentally" (55), Doctor Mandelet reassures Leonce in the language of masculine science, suggesting that a lack of balance is the nature of the "very peculiar and delicate organism" that is woman (64).[28] If femininity itself is a sort of perversity, how does lesbianism differ from Oedipal heterosexuality? The production of lesbianism as categorically distinct from femininity reifies difference in the body of the lesbian, the abjected version of a femininity that is thus rehabilitated to its pre-scribed place under phallic law. But in *The Awakening*, paradoxically, the exception proves *to be* the rule. Despite the differential produc-tion of Edna's heterosexuality as distinct from, for example, Made-moiselle Reisz's deviance, the force of Edna's desire can signify as "lesbian" in the discourse of patriarchy insofar as it resists female Oedipalization and exceeds the register of heterosexual object-choice. The pathology of femininity is never distinct from lesbianism in phallocentric discourse, which instead allows the fantasmatic ef-fect of their difference to flicker into and out of visibility. And this, in a sense, is the failure of heterosexual femininity: not merely its fail-ure, as in *The Awakening*, to sustain women as living subjects, but the incessant failures—and endless recuperations—of the cultural effort to sustain heterosexual meaning.

"A Solitary Soul"

However charmless we may find Emerson's assertion that nature is naturally, so to speak, "made to serve," the truth of femininity is perhaps more brutal (25). As Freud reminds us, women must *be* made to serve the reproduction of the Oedipal triangle—and of civiliza-tion—through the negotiation of the female Oedipal stage. In the Freudian narrative of female desire, heterosexual femininity is predi-cated on the displacement of the girl's erotic cathexis from mother to father, a process that is oblique, difficult, and often incomplete. Prompted by her recognition of women as castrated, the girl will re-nounce the "exclusive attachment to the mother" that characterizes the preoedipal phase and undergo the Oedipal transition to an adult realm of genital erotics and cultural reproductivity.[29] The female Oedipal stage seeks to fix desire in the register of heterosexuality— and thus to forestall, as Diana Fuss has argued, the possibility of the "fall" back into preoedipality—by reorienting female desire toward the phallus, the object par excellence, so that the woman's desire may eventually be satisfied by accepting a baby as token of the phallus.[30] In the Oedipal stage this displacement of desire from mother to phallus and finally to her own child secures the woman's submission to the ideal of futurity, casting her in the role of the "mother-women" to whom Edna Pontellier compares herself at Grand Isle (9). In Freud's account, the family romance is the structure on which "the whole progress of society rests"; by enabling the "propagation of the species," the Oedipal stage represents for both women and men "the victory of the race over the individual."[31] The rhetoric of the Oedipal transition, identifying individual "progress" as crucial to the "progress" of society, thus imagines Oedipality as a teleological project that redirects desire in the service of future generations.

If Oedipal relations are the *telos* or destination of female heterosexual development, forms of resistance to the Oedipal narrative—particularly the refusal of object-choice and the perpetuation of desire's displacement—bring with them the suggestion of lesbianism. While Edna's susceptibility to the "excessive charm" of Adele Ratignolle invokes the common twentieth-century understanding of lesbianism as the pursuit of an improper object, more disturbing to heterosexual ideology is her refusal to accede to the very logic of object-choice. Indeed, Edna's perpetual displacement of desire—from Robert to Adele to Reisz to Arobin, and finally to her own artistic ambitions—refuses the fixity of "choice." Remembering her girlhood, Edna notes as a "propensity which sometimes had inwardly disturbed her" (18) her passionate love for a series of men who, one after the other, "melted imperceptibly out of her existence": a cavalry officer, the young gentleman who came to court a neighbor, a "great tragedian" (18), and finally, if ambivalently, Leonce Pontellier. Edna's desire seems exclusively to reside in impossibility: at the most radiant moment of her dinner party, "There came over her the acute longing which always summoned into her spiritual vision the presence of the beloved one, overpowering her at once with a sense of the unattainable" (85). To be "beloved" is in this erotic economy always to be elsewhere and "unattainable," for as Edna recognizes, Robert and Arobin are only the figures on whom her desire is momentarily projected. Just as Robert is destined to "melt out of her existence," she says, "Today it is Arobin, tomorrow it will be someone else" (108).

This displacement of an unattainable desire is also elaborated in *The Awakening* as a form of narcissism reminiscent of a stereotypically narcissistic lesbianism. Like her girlhood friends, Edna has always been "self-contained" (17), but after her "awakening" at Grand

Isle, she turns to the pleasures of her own body and the seductions of interiority; as Patricia Meyer Spacks writes, "the focus of her real interest is entirely within."[32] Alone on the *Chênière Caminada*, Edna stretches, runs her hands through her hair, and strokes her arms, "observing closely, as if it were something she saw for the first time, the fine, firm quality and texture of her flesh" (36). Although Edna's autoeroticism borders on the perverse, the possibility that she, as Harold Bloom puts it, "falls in love with her own body" is finally less problematic than the possibility that she does not fall in love at all, insofar as she refuses to comply with the object-oriented narrative of "love" whose very banality bespeaks its cultural status.[33]

Consider, for example, the passage in which the movement of the ocean evokes the pleasures and the deathliness of female solipsism: "The voice of the sea is seductive; never ceasing, whispering, clamoring, murmuring, inviting the soul to wander for a spell in abysses of solitude; to lose itself in mazes of inward contemplation" (14). Like Whitman, who in "Out of the Cradle Endlessly Rocking" projects a poetic "voice" onto the sea, Chopin conjures a vision of the sea as a speaking subject. But if Whitman's gesture of projection is in some sense solipsistic, it also embraces its reader and the world, attempting to resist mortality by making meaning out of meaninglessness. Chopin's female solipsism, conversely, takes the meaninglessness of the sea's unending movement as the very meaning of a certain "inward" erotics.[34] This image of "solitude" exerts a magnetic, even narcotic, attraction not *despite* but *because*, for all its anthropomorphic "voice," the sea is not properly an object of desire. Providing instead a mirror of the subject's own "mazes of inward contemplation," the "voice of the sea" suggests an eroticism oriented not toward the solidity of the object but toward its obverse, the nothingness of the abyss. As such, Edna's "seduction" figures both the ghastliness misogynistically associated with female sexuality and the vicissitudes of any project of representation: for the "abysses of solitude" in *The Awakening* cannot help but recall the *mise en abyme* that becomes, in the rhetoric of deconstruction, a privileged signifier of the deferral of meaning against which civilization continually struggles.[35] To say more about the abyss of representation, the slippage of referentiality that Western culture takes pains to deny, we must pursue for a moment the abyss of Edna's desire.

If, as Freud memorably suggests, the way to female heterosexuality is a "very circuitous path," Edna's wandering in "mazes" of desire not only bears her away from the logic of object-choice, but also bespeaks a triumph of *circuit* over *destination* in female sexuality.[36] Figures of that endless course recur throughout *The Awakening*, suggesting women's tendency to stray from heterosexuality and from the fixity of object-choice. Later in the text the sea's invitation "to wander for a spell in abysses of solitude" evolves into a parable of women's desire, which Edna relates in response to Doctor Mandelet's therapeutic description of the fall and recuperation of female sexuality:

> He told the old, ever new and curious story of the waning of a woman's love, seeking strange new channels, only to return to its legitimate source after days of fierce unrest. . . . The story did not seem especially to impress Edna. She had one of her own to tell, of a woman who paddled away with her lover one night in a pirogue and never came back. (67)

Edna's story presents a "love" that, like her own, cannot "return to its legitimate source" because it fails to recognize the legitimacy of heterosexual marriage as such a "source." But marriage is not the only sexual relation threatened by female sexuality's "circuitous path." Arobin remarks on Edna's "wandering" thoughts when, during his lovemaking, she insists on discussing Mademoiselle Reisz and seems unwilling to participate in the single-minded enterprise of seduction: "Oh! talk of me if you like" she says, "but let me think of something else while you do" (79).

Shaping the novel both thematically and formally, the infinite "wandering" of female desire in *The Awakening* can end only—and then only in the most literal sense—with the conclusion of the novel, which is itself marked by the stubbornness of transferential energies. The text of *The Awakening* mimics the movement of Edna's erotic displacements in a chain of short chapters not strictly subordinated to the conventions of narrative development and structurally progressing to no logical conclusion. Finally, swimming out into the Gulf, Edna goes "on and on, thinking of the bluegrass meadow that she had traversed as a child, thinking it had no beginning and no end" (109). The final scene stages not only the dead end of the personal "awakening" Edna has sought—inscribing on the female body the putative deathliness of nonoedipal desire—but also the problem of ending as such. The desired end of civilization and the Oedipal family is to postpone their own ending by successfully mobilizing the narrative of reproduction, enshrining the wedding that enables such a reproduction as the conventional narrative conclusion. Chopin's novel, however, pursues contradictory ends: both the perpetuation of Edna's pleasurable movement "on and on" and the closure that, by ending the plot's trajectory, would satisfy the text as to its own meaningfulness.[37] As the antithesis of the marriage plot, the story of erotic displacement allows no ending—no ending, that is, except an arbitrary violence whose very lack of narrative motivation suggests the stereotypical motif of gay suicide. In the end, the movement that for Edna seems to have "no beginning and no end" can take shape only by a return to a beginning, a repetition of the recurring primal scene that places Edna in the bluegrass field that "seemed as big as the ocean" (17).

Creative Writing

Resisting both progress and regression, both the "before" and "after" of preoedipal and Oedipal relations, *The Awakening* brings to light the perversity that inhabits these ideologically constructed distinctions.[38] As Fuss has argued, Freud's account of lesbian sexuality in "Psychogenesis of a Case of Homosexuality in a Woman" focuses on the girl's preoedipal love for her mother, as the site toward which femininity will fall in its gravitational attraction to the "pre-," the moment before culture and language. In Fuss's incisive reading, however, preoedipality is neither pure nor acultural; it depends on socially inscribed notions of sexual difference:

> Preoedipality is firmly entrenched in the social order and cannot be read as before, outside, or even after the Symbolic; the mother-daughter relation, no less than the father-daughter relation, is a Symbolic association completely inscribed in the field of representation, sociality, and culture.[39]

The logic through which the notion of the preoedipal is projected, as Fuss argues, from within the "field of representation" to represent the "outside" of language and culture describes the cultural positing of lesbianism as the outside of female Oedipality (a formulation that also hints at the problem of lesbian visibility in the optic of patriarchal culture). Patriarchal discourse presses lesbianism into service as a name for pleasures that must already have been suppressed or transformed, retroactively reading the preoedipal from the vantage point of Oedipal discourse. Enacting what Eve Kosofsky Sedgwick has called "the killing pretense that a culture does not know what it knows"—in light of which we might recall *The Awakening*'s epistemological axiom "*si tu savais*"—the notion of lesbianism as categorically distinct from female heterosexuality invents lesbian sexuality only the more thoroughly to elide it, rendering unrepresentable the ways in which the deviant inhabits the normative.[40]

Following the same logic, displacement is projected as the outside of a sexual ideology that is itself founded on displacement. The gesture of displacement, I have suggested, represents a certain disavowed perversity *within* female Oedipality that both enables and undermines the "real aim" of heterosexual object-choice. But in psychoanalytic theory, displacement not only forms the precondition of heterosexual femininity—through the erotic transference of a mother- cathexis to the father—but also describes the operations of desire as such. Jane Gallop writes, "what Freud called displacement . . . Lacan calls desire."[41] Both constitute substitutions of one object for another in the pursuit of an object recognized only through misrecognition. The result, as Slavoj Žižek explains, is a "paradox of desire":

> we mistake for postponement of the "thing itself" what is already the "thing itself," we mistake for the searching and indecision proper to desire what is, in fact, the realization of desire. That is to say, the realization of desire does not consist in its being "fulfilled," "fully satisfied," it coincides rather with the reproduction of desire as such, with its circular movement.[42]

Borrowing from Freud's understanding that the object we desire is never truly the object we desire, Žižek suggests that the "thing itself" is available to us only when desire can represent *as* an "object" the objective of its own continuation. The "circular movement" that, in

Žižek's words, constitutes the "reproduction of desire" swerves from the linear course of heterosexual object-choice and returns us to the rhetoric of erotic displacement in *The Awakening*. Addressing the question of female sexuality, Chopin illustrates Žižek's object(less) lessons of desire in, for example, the scene of Edna's first swim, whose "mazes of inward contemplation" pursue what James Justus has called "desire as a thing in itself."[43]

But if, as Freud was acutely aware, we are each condemned to the same inevitable misreading of desire, the same eternal displacement of satisfaction, how does displacement come to represent a distinctly lesbian perversity? Although Freud suggests that a "childhood love" like that of the girl for the mother has "no aim and is incapable of obtaining complete satisfaction," neither can adult genital relations fulfill the Oedipal fantasy of a "satisfaction" that, having attained its proper object, will close desire's circuit and cease its restless movement.[44] Displacement is, in this system, both the mechanism and the object of a certain disavowal. The story of desire that culture would present as "nature" demands the displacement of displacement: it requires that the essential perversity of Oedipal structures be projected onto figures of an abject sexuality in order to deny the fact that desire itself lacks any "real aim" outside the socially imposed imperative of heterosexual reproduction.

Although both are inherent in Oedipal and symbolic structures, displacement and lesbianism are regarded as the negation of meaning as such, relegated to the realm of social unintelligibility figured in *The Awakening* by the abyss. As such, "displacement" names a switchpoint between sexuality and language, between the transference of erotic cathexes and that of signifiers. In Freud's account, the negotiation of the female castration complex operates through the logic of language, establishing the female subject's debt *to* representation through the mechanism *of* representation: "The girl passes over—by way of a symbolic analogy, one may say—from the penis to a child; her Oedipus-complex culminates in the desire, which is long cherished, to be given a child by her father as a present, to bear him a child."[45] That the woman accedes to her place in the Oedipal order of cultural reproduction only through a "symbolic analogy" reveals Oedipality as a paradoxical accomplishment. To borrow from Lee Edelman's account of representation and male homosexuality, the accomplishment of

Oedipality requires the installation of the subject within the realm of "grammar" and socially determinate meaning—thus repudiating the illogical, interminable displacements of "pure rhetoric" that bear traces of a non-Oedipal erotic organization.[46] Edelman argues that heterosexual culture represents gay male sexuality as "the displaced referent within the logic of reference, the figural representation within representational logic, of the Thing that refuses the fixed cathexes from which emerge, as external 'reality,' the referential order of the ego and the symbolic regime of meaning."[47] And as a differently inflected "displaced referent within the logic of reference," lesbianism too is inscribed in the distinction between cultural meaning and non-meaning. Straight culture associates both lesbian and gay male sexuality with the linguistic structure of displacement, although lesbianism never takes on the solidity or distinctness of male homosexuality. While gay male sexuality, even in its association with "pure rhetoric," is produced as a determinate presence that is phobically invested with meaning, lesbian sexuality remains an effect, a figure of negation, a space of incoherence within the Oedipal mythology.

The Oedipal drama thus sets in motion two versions of the same fantasy—the fantasy of the loved object and the fantasy of the signified—which, by positing an ending of the displacements of desire and the slippages of the signifying chain, hold out the promise of futurity. And just as the ideology of the Oedipal family must disavow the "wandering" of female desire, the symbolic order must also banish the traces of its own displacements. To clarify this connection between sexuality and discourse we need only call displacement by its other name, transference. In *The Interpretation of Dreams*, a text published the year after *The Awakening*, Freud uses "transference"—the term that will later, as if transferentially, name a particular erotic substitution that haunts the psychoanalytic narrative—to designate the function of the signifier in the dreamwork.[48] Indeed, transference etymologically refers to metaphor, the very principle of figural language. The *OED* defines "metaphor" as "the figure of speech in which a name or descriptive term is transferred to some object different from, but analogous to, that to which it is properly applicable." Like the circular movement of a desire whose true object is its own perpetuation, and like the process of female Oedipalization whose end is never secure, the transference that we call metaphor can never simply connect one thing to another. Unable to perform the "carrying across" (as the Latin *trans ferre* suggests) of signifier to signified, figural language is, like Edna, condemned to a certain failure as a bridge builder or *pontellier*.[49]

Tracing the evolution of the notion of transference in Freudian discourse, Samuel Weber acknowledges the overdetermined status of transference, *Übertragung*, as a term whose sexual and linguistic functions cannot be separated:

> In *The Interpretation of Dreams*, the German word *Übertragung* is employed to designate the distortions of the dreamwork, which shifts from one representation to another in order to accomplish its goal: that of producing a distorted, self-dissimulating fulfillment of a conflictual wish. *Übertragung*, the German word that literally corresponds to the Greek *metaphorein*, thus describes both the particular dream-device of *displacement* (*Verschiebung*), and the more general instability of psychic energy that is characteristic of the primary process and of the unconscious in general.

Insofar as it corresponds to the metaphoric structuring of symbolic reality, the transferential function of the dreamwork may itself be understood as a kind of dream, the dream of symbolization, from which none of us is destined to awaken. At once general and particular, at once specific to the dreamwork and generally at work in the unconscious, *Übertragung* is also simultaneously static and shifting, as Weber notes: "*Übertragung* presupposes the volatile movement, the 'carrying-over' from one place or thought or image to another; but at the same time, like 'metaphor' itself, it also entails an element of fixity, indeed of fixation."[50] This interplay of movement and fixity within transference mimics the logic of female Oedipalization, in which the mobilization of an erotic displacement is followed by the attempt to lock desire in its normative, heterosexual place. In Edna's erotic movement "on and on," then, we see the abjected mirror image of the movement of civilization toward futurity—a futurity whose limitlessness depends on achieving Oedipal fixity in the register of female desire.

In psychoanalysis, as Gallop notes, displacement means "unfaithful representation," and in American literature, as I have suggested, this equation holds true.[51] The "corruption of language" that seems, for Emerson, to entail the collapse of meaning and with it the foreclosure of national identity corresponds to an anxiety about the transferential properties of figural language. Against this slippage of signifiers Emerson posits a fantasy of coherence, meaning, and futurity, calling for a language both "picturesque" and allegorical, a language founded on the appeal to "visible things" and the faithful correspondence of "thing" to meaning, signifier to signified (20). Yet both Emerson and Chopin rely on the same tropes of displacement that seem to connote the "corruption of language" and a threat to the vitality of meaning. If, for Freud, *displacement* names the exercise of metonymy in the dreamwork, and if, as Roman Jakobson suggests, metonymy is the essence of literary realism, then displacement is fundamental to the generic conventions within which *The Awakening* takes shape.[52] Elaborating Jakobson's argument, Lacan cites Tolstoy's use of synecdoche as an instance of literary realism's debt to metonymy: "[at] the approach of a woman, you see emerging in her place, in a grand-style metonymic process, the shadow of a beauty mark, a spot on the upper lip, etc."[53] In a frequently quoted passage, Chopin introduces the heroine of *The Awakening* through the same rhetorical gesture: "Mr. Pontellier finally lit a cigar and began to smoke, letting the paper drag idly from his hand. He fixed his gaze upon a white sunshade that was advancing at a snail's pace from the beach" (3). Here the substitution of sunshade for woman, replicating the terms of Lacan's reading of Tolstoy, exemplifies the role of metonymic displacement in realism. Its part in regionalism is no less significant, for "local color" writing like Chopin's trades on the fantasy that particulars of regional culture can serve as literary synecdoches of the nation—as the parts that will metonymically evoke the whole of American identity.[54]

These salutary forms of displacement, fundamental to the generic conventions of American literature, ostensibly oppose the morbid, nonreproductive female desire and the "rotten diction," as Emerson puts it, of language detached from referential meaning.[55] In his account of American literature, Emerson links the "corruption of language" to the perversity of a feminine desire that, like Edna's transferential substitution of one love-object for another, resists the imperatives of heterosexual reproduction. Like the symbolic order and the Oedipal family, however, Emerson's American literature can represent itself as natural only through the "unnatural" mechanism of metaphoric displacement, even when representing and repudiating tropes of deviant language and desire. In her published reply to the novel's detractors Chopin herself participates in the cultural displacement of displacement in an effort—ironic or not—to disidentify from the novel whose "morbidity," as we have seen, seems contagiously transferable. Chopin stages a scene of disavowal that trades on the very logic of sexuality and representation that *The Awakening* has laid bare:

> Having a group of people at my disposal, I thought it might be entertaining (to myself) to throw them together and see what would happen. I never dreamed of Mrs. Pontellier making such a mess of things and working out her own damnation as she did. If I had had the slightest intimation of such a thing I would have excluded her from the company. But when I found out what she was up to, the play was half over and it was too late.[56]

Never mind that to disclaim authorial responsibility by protesting that she "never dreamed" of Edna's disorderly conduct requires that Chopin shut down—precisely by reinvoking—the allegory of sleep and "awakening" that would allow us to understand *The Awakening* as a dream-text. At stake here is a rhetorical project of damage control around a transgression whose "slightest intimation" must and will be disavowed. Transferring the onus of "such a thing" to Edna Pontellier, Chopin displaces the text's perversity onto a Mrs. Pontellier who has never seemed so purposeful and casts her lot, instead, with the "company" of characters and readers who embody the proper reproduction of social discourse.

Chopin's comment on *The Awakening* reopens the very question it seeks to dismiss by reanimating the novel's concern with Edna's representativeness, with the trope of synecdoche, and with a distinctly Emersonian individualism. Adding a final chapter to the novel that has shared Emerson's concern with relations between the individual and her "company" or community, Chopin reverses the change that retitling the novel originally effected, making the woman whose "awakening" the text has chronicled once again "a solitary soul." Her remarks on the novel appeal to the rhetoric of the exceptional in order to disavow the possibility that Edna could be, as Olive Chancellor imagines herself in *The Bostonians*, a "representative woman."[57] This relation between the "representative" and the "solitary," of course, also informs Emerson's "Self-Reliance," where it implies the necessity, and the impossibility, of knowing that "what is true for you in your private heart is true for all men."[58] To the extent that Emerson's statement holds true in American culture, however, it is less as a mark of "genius" than as a proof of ideology's coercive power. For it is precisely in the pervasive American myth of individualism that the "private heart" of the individual is made to coincide with the truth of the culture, just as the woman's "subordination to culture" is accomplished through the Oedipal narrative that will both discipline her "private" desires and promise their satisfaction through the reproduction of the heterosexual family.

American literature, then, is inseparable from the figures of lesbian desire that come to *mean*, in dominant ideology, the failure of meaning, even as it claims the status of a discourse designed, in Emerson's words, not for "barren contemplation, but for new creation" (16). If the Oedipal structure seems always to proceed under an Emersonian maxim—"All good is eternally reproductive"— Emerson's vision of American literature in turn mirrors the Oedipal narrative (16). Within structures of symbolization and of female Oedipality, where displacement is both the founding premise and the abject remainder, the transferential properties of both structures, like the supplement as Derrida understands it, come to represent "both humanity's good fortune and the origin of its perversion."[59] Faced with a paradox that is both sexual and linguistic, patriarchal culture must represent, in order to deny, the "morbid" language and desire of which it too partakes, endlessly laboring to shore up heterosexual reproduction on behalf of a social order that only by displacing displacement can deny the *mise en abyme* of its own subjection to desire and language.

chapter three

Modernist Perversity

The Repetition of Desire
in *The Sun Also Rises*

I f *The Awakening*, as a narrative, is structured by a tension between Oedipal teleology and Edna Pontellier's "mazes of inward contemplation," between the fantasy of referential language and the objectless "wandering" of female desire, it
usefully suggests a conflict that is by no means Chopin's alone. In
twentieth-century American literature as well, lesbian sexuality is
construed as a violation of the conventional narrative teleology that
regards a certain closure as the only way to reopen the question of
futurity. Taking up such issues of sexuality and narrative, Hemingway's texts exemplify a distinctly modernist ambivalence: they both
promote narrative experimentation and adhere to the notion of
meaningful language, of what Hemingway calls the "true sentence."[1]
In contrast to that "true" discourse, *The Sun Also Rises* imagines lesbian sexuality as a deformation of language: a kind of compulsive
repetition that threatens both narrative and sexual teleology.

Borrowing a topic and an epigraph from Gertrude Stein's famous
remark, *The Sun Also Rises* represents a group of American expatriates
in Europe after World War I as the "lost generation." That the loss

with which the novel concerns itself is sexual as well as philosophical is demonstrated by the figure of Jake Barnes. Rendered impotent by a war wound, Jake alternately entertains and denies an impossible desire for Brett Ashley, that early and fascinating avatar of the boyish, attractive women who populate Hemingway's texts. The novel follows Jake, Brett, and their circle as they wander from the cafés and nightclubs of Paris to the festival of San Fermin in Pamplona. Throughout their travels Jake is haunted by a sense of repetition that attaches itself to Brett. Near the end of the novel's first section the two visit a club in Montmartre, where after dancing and a conversation about her plans to marry Michael Campbell, Brett's sudden change of mood gives Jake "the feeling as in a nightmare of it all being something repeated."[2] Hemingway declines to name this "something repeated," which marks an intersection of language and sexuality, but surely it belongs to Brett Ashley, the embodiment of the "New Woman" and the representative of a female sexuality that is somehow both alluring and perverse. A recurrent figure in Hemingway's writing, the New Woman combines a masculinized femininity with the suggestion of lesbian desire, reflecting changing gender roles, the link between lesbianism and gay male sexuality in the rhetoric of sexual inversion, and the pressure exerted by masculine sexual anxiety on representations of lesbian figures.

Lesbianism was a subject with which Hemingway considered himself familiar. About "The Sea Change"—a 1931 short story in which a young man and his lover discuss her affair with another woman—he wrote, "I knew the story too too well."[3] But until the posthumous publication in 1986 of *The Garden of Eden*, which describes a male writer's relationship with his bisexual wife and another woman, Hemingway might have seemed an unlikely source of any sustained commentary on lesbian sexuality. Although Hemingway's involvement with the question of lesbianism is now recognized, it still appears visible largely through his biography, as the hint of sexual anxiety adduced to offset or explain his famous *machismo*. We are informed that his mother, Grace Hall Hemingway, enjoyed an intimate friendship with Ruth Arnold; that the sister of his second wife, Pauline, and by some accounts Pauline herself, was a lesbian; and that sapphic love was not uncommon among the members of his Paris literary circle, of whom the most influential, for Hemingway, was Gertrude Stein.[4] More interesting for my purposes, however, is the treatment of lesbian sexuality in Hemingway's writing and in twentieth-century American culture. In addition to Brett Ashley in *The Sun Also Rises* and the nameless woman in "The Sea Change," tropes of lesbian sexuality inform such figures as Pilar in *For Whom the Bell Tolls*, and Catherine in *The Garden of Eden*.[5] Hemingway is most useful to lesbian reading, that is, not as an instance of individual obsession or neurosis, but as an astute recorder of the compulsions and anxieties of masculine literary modernism and modernist culture.

As a cultural and literary phenomenon, of course, modernism responded to a crisis of meaning; in a rapidly changing world, traditional epistemologies seemed inadequate. The writing that took shape under Pound's famous axiom "make it new" celebrated originality, laboring to avoid derivative, imitative prose and the literary repetition-compulsion it implied.[6] Hemingway's own response takes shape, in part, in the anti-style that is his signature style. Like his writer-hero in *The Garden of Eden*, Hemingway attempts to write "simple declarative sentences."[7] His "anti-rhetoric" or "non-syntax," in Leslie Fiedler's words, seems to approach truth only by approaching—or rather, by fantasizing—the eradication of language.[8] In its effort to avoid sentimental indulgence, Hemingway's prose may allude to earlier realist writing; but unlike the writing of James and Chopin, Hemingway's writing is, in its denial of rhetorical embellishment, the stylized reflection of a modernist distrust of style that in turn bespeaks twentieth-century sexual anxieties. *The Sun Also Rises*, which associates perverse and excessive female sexuality with compulsive repetition and the refusal of normative reproduction, reflects modernist culture's distrust of repetition, literary quest for originality, and anxiety about desire and procreation in the face of profound societal changes.

In order to trace the sexual and political stakes of this modernist ideology, my reading of *The Sun Also Rises* calls upon two quite different accounts of repetition: Freud's essay on the uncanny and Judith Butler's discussion of citation as the constitutive gesture of the law. Whereas Freud's notion of the uncanny reads repetition in its most bizarre and unsettling form, Butler's theory of citation presents repetition in its most normative and culturally invisible role. Connecting lesbianism to the logic of repetition and the processes of symbolization, *The Sun Also Rises* and other Hemingway texts position lesbian sexuality at the intersection of Butler's and Freud's theories: at the place where the power of patriarchal law is naturalized through citation, and where lesbianism, pressed into the service of that law, appears as its obverse, a compulsive and unnatural repetition. Yet while *The Sun Also Rises* examines the ways in which American modernist culture seeks to contain lesbianism within regimes of scientific and sexual knowledge, the text also reveals that lesbian sexuality, like repetition itself, is as necessary to that culture as it is intolerable.[9]

A Novel about a Lady

Readers of *The Sun Also Rises* have been quick to identify Brett Ashley as a "New Woman," a figure whose role in fiction had, by 1926, nothing new about it.[10] If Brett Ashley was, as Burton Rascoe wrote in a *New York Sun* review, "the only 'literary' character in the book," she owed her aura of literariness partly to her fictional predecessors—most notably, in early reviewers' opinion, one Iris Marsh in Michael Arlen's 1924 novel *The Green Hat*.[11] Emerging, as a character, from a long line of literary "New Women," Brett Ashley in turn became the prototype of the boyish, athletic, independent woman in Hemingway's writing.

Brett was damned good-looking. She wore a slipover jersey sweater and a tweed skirt, and her hair was brushed back like a boy's. She started all that. (22)

Brett Ashley truly "started all that" as the origin of a feminine type that would return in *The Garden of Eden*'s Catherine Bourne, whose sexual transformation is signaled by a haircut "cropped as short as a boy's," and in "The Sea Change" as the woman to whom no introduction is necessary except a note that she "wore a tweed suit, her skin was a smooth golden brown, her blonde hair was cut short."[12] Like the bisexual woman in "The Sea Change" and the boy-identified, girl-loving Catherine Bourne, Brett Ashley does not fail to attract women's interest—in Pamplona, Jake Barnes recalls, when three women stare at the group from a wine shop, "They were staring at Brett" (137).[13] However, to place her in a lesbian context one need not claim that Brett had or desired to have erotic relations with women, for Hemingway provides Brett with the somatic marks and typical gestures that would signify lesbianism to an American public familiar with the figure of the masculinized New Woman and the myth of the "mannish lesbian."

The New Woman emblematizes the shifts in early-twentieth-century sexual ideology—following on the formulation of lesbian identity in late-nineteenth-century sexology and indebted not a little to the work of Freud—toward modern notions of female sexuality. From the last decades of the nineteenth century through the first decades of the twentieth, the New Woman designated one of several generations of women, usually white and middle-class, who earned higher education, pursued careers, and often postponed or rejected marriage and motherhood. The first generation of New Women participated in the suffrage movement and other social reforms, pursued the educational opportunities men enjoyed, and expanded the "woman's sphere" into the masculine public realm. The second generation went further, claiming their own sexual desire, launching independent careers, and affecting such masculine habits and styles as short hair, smoking, and tailored clothing. From the 1890s through the 1920s, the figure of the New Woman crystallized cultural anxieties about female gender roles and earned widespread criticism in American popular culture and medical discourse; by the 1920s the public imagination had identified the New Woman as a masculinized figure whose manner and dress, if not her erotic cathexes, evoked lesbianism.[14]

Influenced by the work of Krafft-Ebing and Havelock Ellis, early-twentieth-century scientific discourse promulgated a new distinction between normative femininity and lesbianism, even as the rhetoric surrounding the New Woman rendered every woman a potential lesbian. Even while sexology attempted to separate lesbianism from heterosexual femininity, that is, the misogynist reaction to feminism and women's changing roles in the United States strategically conflated the New Woman with the lesbian. From the turn of the century, the notion of lesbianism became in public discourse a weapon against women's education, activism, careers, and sexuality. This equation of New Woman and lesbian owed its rhetorical power to an understanding of lesbianism less as a form of sexual desire or erotic activity than as a perverse enactment of gender, specifically an effect of female masculinization. In Krafft-Ebing's portrait of the "mannish lesbian," lesbian sexuality was legible in masculine social behaviors and morphological signs. The fourth and most extreme category in his schematic account of lesbianism described the woman whose "thought, sentiment, action, even external appearance are those of a man." Indeed, he continued, "Uranism may nearly always be suspected in females wearing their hair short, or who dress in the fashion of men, or pursue the sports and pastimes of their male acquaintances."[15] Elaborating on Krafft-Ebing's understanding of female inversion, Havelock Ellis defined the New Woman as pathologically masculine and linked lesbian sexuality to middle-class women's pursuit of traditionally male privileges.[16] In his own inquiries into lesbian sexuality, Freud departed from his predecessors by attempting to separate sexuality from gender, lesbian object-choice from women's "physical sexual characteristics" and "mental sexual characteristics." Although he located lesbianism in psychic structures and not in external qualities, however, Freud followed Krafft-Ebing and Ellis in positing masculinization as a governing premise of lesbian love. Tracing the lesbian object-choice of one analysand, for example, he proposes that the girl "changed into a man, and took her mother in place of her father as the object of her love."[17]

Hemingway's portrait of Brett Ashley as New Woman suggests some consequences of these notions of female masculinization and the "mannish lesbian." Decked out in the trappings of masculine style, her hair "brushed back like a boy's" (22), Brett wears a "man's felt hat" (28) and boasts a vocabulary of slang and mild profanity. Nor is Brett's masculinization in *The Sun Also Rises* solely a matter of style. As Jake will discover, she lacks maidenly delicacy; watching the bullfight, she finds that she "didn't feel badly at all" (165) about the gore, earning admiration from Jake and the label of "sadist" from Robert Cohn. The opening sentence of Hemingway's original version of the novel seems to underscore Brett Ashley's gender, announcing, "This is a novel about a lady," only to immediately ironize that idea in the following line: "Her name is Lady Ashley."[18] The layering of Brett's femininity with her aristocratic status seems to dismiss both as spurious, no more convincing than the typographical trickery of a capital *L*. Critical responses to the novel have followed suit. Alternately damning Brett Ashley as an excessively sexual woman and excoriating her lack of femininity, they overwhelmingly conclude that Brett Ashley is no lady. For Fiedler Brett is a "bitch-goddess" and for Alan Tate "a nymphomaniac." Yet Theodore Bardake sees her as "a woman devoid of womanhood," and Fiedler himself goes on to remark that "Brett never becomes a woman really," a phrase that echoes Marita's assessment of Catherine in *The Garden of Eden*: "You aren't really a woman at all" (192).[19] It becomes impossible to distinguish between the lesbian "type" and the pathology of femininity *tout court*, for *The Sun Also Rises*, like its readers, both produces and collapses the effect of their difference. Rehearsing an old tenet of patriarchal ideology along with the rhetoric of New Women and lesbians, Hemingway attributes to Brett Ashley both a deviation *from* proper femininity and the deviance proper *to* femininity.

At the same time that their theories distanced lesbianism from an (increasingly evacuated) idea of normative femininity, the sexologists aligned lesbianism with male homosexuality, drawing analogies between these two forms of inversion. As *The Blithedale Romance* demonstrates with its articulation of proto-lesbian and gay male artifice, the metaphorical equation of female perversity with male homosexuality predates the twentieth century. With modernism comes greater emphasis on deceptively simple models of gender dissonance and inversion: male homosexuals are feminine men and lesbians are masculine women. Despite this parallel logic, as Hemingway's texts show, modernist culture also constructs lesbian sexuality and male homosexuality in crucially different ways. Whereas gay male sexuality appears to undermine the coherence of straight male subjectivity and patriarchal discourse, lesbian figures are regarded as simultaneously anxiogenic and attractive. In *The Sun Also Rises*, Brett enters the *bal musette* with a group of young gay men, assuming some of the sexual meaning of their "white hands, wavy hair, white faces" and their "superior, simpering composure" (20). Imagining that sexual inversion is infectiously shared among Brett and the young men, Jake worries that the contagion might extend to himself as well. If his rather histrionic "This whole show makes me sick is all" (21) generalizes the scene as a theatrical "whole show," it also attributes to homosexual pathology the ability to make others "sick" as well. Jake will become preemptively ill with revulsion as if thus to prevent himself from contracting a "sick" desire. But although Hemingway notes that Brett is "very much with" these young men, the novel will exempt her from the onus of gay male identity—as indeed it must, for Jake and the novel itself depend on Brett to prop up their illusions of heterosexual subjectivity and masculine authority (20).

The Sun Also Rises has been the subject of no little critical attention, much of which points out the central place of male sexual anxiety in Hemingway's portraits of Jake Barnes and of modernist culture.[20] But the readers who have usefully identified the roles of misogyny and homophobia in the novel have largely omitted the question of lesbian sexuality, focusing instead on that familiar couple, the (straight) woman and the (male) homosexual. Examining the place of lesbian figures in Hemingway's vision of modernist culture enables a reading not only of Hemingway's anxieties about femininity and male homosexuality, but also of a perversity that *structures* male modernism—its desire, that is, for the lesbian figures it will also condemn as "unnatural," and its effort to conceal the compulsive repetition that underlies its own authority. Consider, for example, a central problem of *The Sun Also Rises*: how to preserve masculine heterosexuality and escape homophobic suspicion while avoiding the feminine in all its forms. The novel opens with a cautionary tale about Robert Cohn, a man who has been "taken in hand by a lady" (5), indicating both how a woman can ruin a man and what sort of man will allow himself to be ruined. In a parable of heterosexual misery that seeks to prove the monstrous and feminizing potential of heterosexual love, Cohn—who is, Hemingway pointedly adds, the author of a "very poor novel" (6)—passively endures Frances's "absolute determination that he should marry her" (5) and her unending mockery when he will not.

It is well known that Hemingway's texts champion masculine camaraderie as an alternative to the feminine, and feminizing, realm of romantic love. Within the terms of the male modernist double bind, with its combination of misogyny and homophobia, men's relationships with one another are no less problematic.[21] If one imperative that shapes Hemingway's text is an aversion to femininity, another is a homophobic repudiation of gay male sexuality. As "the sort of thing that can't be spoken of" (115), Jake's impotence evokes the masculine anxiety about homosexuality, the other unspeakable condition that also signifies, in heterosexual ideology, the loss of phallic authority. Later, in the Pamplona section of *The Sun Also Rises*, Jake's and Montoya's *afición* for bullfighting approaches the Hemingway ideal of male-male relations, but also hints at the homosexual desire that inevitably troubles homosocial bonds. In his passion for the art, Jake recalls, Montoya acted "as though bull-fighting were a very special secret between the two of us; a rather shocking but really very deep secret . . . as though there were something lewd about the secret to outsiders" (131). Projecting the homophobic impulse onto another set of "outsiders" while enacting it himself, Bill acknowledges the possibility of gay male sexuality when, on the fishing trip in Burguete, he tells Jake, "You're a hell of a good guy, and I'm fonder of you than anybody on earth. I couldn't tell you that in New York. It'd mean I was a faggot" (116).

Within the misogyny and homophobia of *The Sun Also Rises*, Brett Ashley may serve as the locus of a displaced gay male desire.[22] Thanks to the same masculine qualities that render her sexually suspect, the figure of the New Woman or the lesbian seems to function as a substitute object that helps fortify straight male subjectivity against the danger of gay male desire.[23] Lesbian sexuality thus constitutes *both* a site of homophobic abjection *and* an essential part of the structure of masculine subjectivity and self-representation. In this, Hemingway and modernist culture demonstrate what we might call a lesbian desire—not the desire *of* the lesbian, but an attraction *to* female figures marked with the signifiers of perverse sexuality and representation, and the desire *to have* such a figure as "the lesbian" that might fantasmatically help to sustain masculine subjectivity, not to say patriarchal culture, against other, more virulent threats. This is surely not to say that lesbianism is exempt from homophobic suspicion and abjection, even when it helps to maintain the illusions of masculine heterosexuality. The problem of homosexuality is not so easily solved in straight culture. Instead, as Hemingway suggests, the substitution of "lesbian desire" for gay male desire is a compromise formation that is only tenuously preserved. Hemingway's later texts "The Sea Change" and *The Garden of Eden* continue his fascination with lesbian figures, but they connect such figures more closely to male homosexuality, each attributing its male protagonist's sexual "change" to his encounter with lesbian sexuality. "The Sea Change" credits the lesbian with transforming her companion into "a different man" (43), a man whom an early draft of the story, leaving nothing of this "difference" to the imagination, calls a "punk" or homosexual.[24] *The Garden of Eden*, alluding to this story, describes Catherine's transformation into something "new and strange" (48) as the force that makes David into "someone else" (84).[25] Catherine's obsessive need to act the role of the "boy" predicts and in some sense explains her eventual lesbian affair, but for Hemingway this role is troubling primarily because it compels her husband to accept a "feminine" position—which is to say, a gay male position—in their relationship. And *The Sun Also Rises* itself shows the instability of the distinction between lesbian and gay male sexuality within the ideology of sexual inversion. Although the novel offers lesbian figures as a site of displaced gay male desire, lesbianism seems endlessly poised to slip back into an identification with gay male sexuality—not least in its association with the uncanny, with a decadent form of literariness, and with the sterile circuit of a compulsive repetition.

Uncanny Returns

Hemingway's early readers were quick to note a certain repetition in the text of *The Sun Also Rises*. To them, Hemingway's text seemed to suffer from the same aimlessness that characterized its "lost generation"—those young people for whom "each day became a replica of the day before."[26] A reviewer for the *Springfield Republican* remarked on the novel's "absence of plot," and Lawrence S. Morris, writing in the *New Republic*, agreed that *The Sun Also Rises* had "no direction whatever." A *Cincinnati Enquirer* review made this complaint brutally plain: "Here is a book which, like its characters, begins nowhere and ends in nothing."[27] Nor was the novel exempt from the charge that, like Brett Ashley and Jake Barnes, it was doomed to repeat what had come before—a damning claim given Hemingway's modernist ambition for originality. Crediting Hemingway with an "extraordinary individuality of style," Conrad Aiken nevertheless asserted that "his literary debts are obvious." Those debts were not, apparently, so obvious that *Time* magazine could resist enumerating them, observing that Hemingway's "title is borrowed from *Ecclesiastes*; his motto about 'a lost generation,' from Gertrude Stein; his widow, Lady Brett Ashley, from Michael Arlen's *Green Hat*."[28]

Hemingway's "literary debts" may reassure those readers who can congratulate themselves on their wide knowledge, but the repetition that Brett signifies remains anxiogenic not only for Hemingway as author, but also for Jake Barnes. If in *The Awakening* Chopin locates Edna's sexuality in the figure of the abyss, in *The Sun Also Rises* Hemingway regards Brett as the site of another circular feminine desire, another endless circuit of displacement. In her first and last scenes with Jake, each set in a taxi that travels toward no particular destination, Brett Ashley comes to emblematize a perpetual, nonproductive return. "Where should I tell him?" Jake asks as they leave the Paris dance hall in the first of these scenes. Brett replies, "Oh, tell him to drive around" (24). That sensation of going "around" in circles, returning again and again to a place one has seen before, is elaborated when, the next night, Brett and Jake visit the club in Montmartre:

> "Oh darling," Brett said, "I'm so miserable."
> I had that feeling of going through something that has all happened before. "You were happy a minute ago." . . .
> I had the feeling as in a nightmare of it all being something repeated, something I had been through and that now I must go through again. (64)

Jake is convinced that to be with Brett Ashley means a kind of compulsion to repeat, although he is unable to locate the original event, the "something" he seems doomed to relive. If the rhetorical repetition in his account of the experience—his emphasis on "feeling" and "something" and his triple use of "through"—literalizes his impression of a "repeated" occurrence, his comparison of the experience to a "nightmare" also hints at the psychic underpinnings of that repetition.

In his essay on the uncanny, Freud predicts Jake's "feeling as in a nightmare" about his own circular relationship with Brett, describing such an experience as an "involuntary repetition" which summons "the sense of helplessness experienced in some dream-states" by reminding us of the "internal 'compulsion to repeat'" in the unconscious.[29] That the repetition-compulsion on which uncanny effects depend is *internal* indicates the role of projection and of the analogous, more "literary" mechanism of displacement in the experience of uncanny repetition. If the uncanny object is a projection, however, it seems drawn to particular objects, objects marked by differences of gender and sexuality. Freud acknowledges that encounters with the uncanny befall men and women alike, but the paradigmatic subject of uncanny effects is the man who feels "there is something uncanny about the female genital organs," taking them as a figure for his mother's womb, the original *unheimlich* home (245). In an autobiographical anecdote, Freud more explicitly identifies repetition-compulsion with the masculine anxiety about a specifically feminine uncanny:

> As I was walking, one hot summer afternoon, through the deserted streets of a provincial town in Italy which was unknown to me, I found myself in a quarter of whose character I could not long remain in doubt. Nothing but painted women were to be seen at the windows of the small houses, and I hastened to leave the narrow street at the next turning. But after having wandered about for a time without enquiring my way, I suddenly found myself back in the same street, where my presence was now beginning to excite attention. I hurried away once more, only to arrive by another *détour* at the same place yet a third time. (237)

Freud's account of his own compulsive repetition, centered on the "painted women" who signify illicit, if not perverse, female sexuality, recalls Jake's aimless wanderings with Brett in *The Sun Also Rises*. Jake's vision of Brett as the emblem of a nightmarish repetition conjures female sexuality as an uncanny power that subjects men to the "helplessness" of involuntary return. The same effect describes David's sense of futility at Catherine's first intimations of her "change" in *The Garden of Eden*: "There aren't many more moves to make," David concludes, except to "go back where we started" (69).

The return of this repetition throughout Hemingway's fiction may, of course, be mere coincidence. One might say that the recurrence of New Women and boyish lesbians in Hemingway's writing and biography means nothing. Yet the idea of meaningless coincidence, as Freud points out, is more troubling than any possible explanation for a figure's recurrence. The very notion of coincidence, Freud suggests, generates uncanny effects in a repetition that seems to be mere "chance," an uninterpretable sequence of events without discernible pattern or motivation (237–38). Noting that the compulsion to repeat is not restricted to neurotics, Freud observes that there are people "all of whose human relationships have the same outcome." A "perpetual recurrence of the same thing," he continues, does not surprise us when it is caused by a person's active behavior, but it becomes more striking when "the subject appears to have a *passive* experience, over which he has no influence, but in which he meets with a repetition of the same fatality."[30]

If lesbian figures in Hemingway's texts evoke the uncanny force of compulsive repetition, however, it is not because there is something essentially lesbian about repetition. In fact, as Judith Butler reminds us, the logic of repetition is fundamental to patriarchal law. The law, Butler argues, is constructed by a series of performative acts, which through "reiteration of a norm or set of norms" enable the law to deny its own contingency by covering over its status *as* repetition.[31] Established metaleptically, the symbolic order does not exist before the citation that rhetorically posits it as an originary law. "The excessive power of the symbolic is itself *produced* by the citational instance by which the law is embodied," Butler writes. As a consequence, the gesture of citation "effectively brings into being the very prior authority to which it then defers" (108–9). How, then, is it possible to distinguish between the repetition that maintains the power of the law and the repetition identified in Hemingway's text with lesbian sexuality? The difference lies in the ability of cultural law to naturalize and elide its own debt to citation, Butler notes. Through this mechanism the law presents itself as an originary force and relegates other forms of citation to the abject space of the bad copy, the debased imitation, the merely or pathologically repetitive. Yet Butler also locates in repetition a subversive potential, albeit one not governed by individual agency: the possibility of "repetitions of hegemonic forms of power which fail to repeat loyally" (124). Her point is well taken: the notion of iterations that "fail to repeat loyally" resists a purely deterministic reading of citation and acknowledges the resignifications of meaning that repetition allows. Indeed, one might ask what repetition, as a representation, ever "repeats loyally." That is, repetition must always be repetition with a difference; and if so, the distinction between the performativity of the law and that of out-law subjects remains an illusion, though a powerful one. It is not the fidelity of its repetition that distinguishes the symbolic order from subversive forces. Rather, it is the ability of symbolic law fantasmatically to remove itself from the realm of repetition and to naturalize the citations through which it is sustained. In contrast, uncanny repetition seems to announce itself as such by resisting the naturalizing, sense-making influence of the symbolic order and appearing as mere contingency or coincidence.

Lesbian sexuality evokes uncanny or compulsive repetition in the rhetoric of the mannish lesbian and sexual inversion, where it is understood as an unnatural, "disloyal" citation of masculine heterosexuality. Krafft-Ebing, for example, views lesbian sexuality as a sort of performance; while he declines to acknowledge masculine subjectivity itself as a role, he diagnoses as lesbian the woman who in erotic fantasies casts herself "in the *rôle* of man."[32] This notion of sexual inversion as performance is shared by Havelock Ellis. Although Ellis stops short of naming feminism as the cause of lesbianism, he sees feminist activity as the "spurious imitation" of a lesbian sexuality that itself, in his view, constitutes a perverse imitation of masculinity.[33] For Freud too, lesbian sexuality implies repetition, although in a somewhat different way. Diana Fuss has observed that the concept of lesbian sexuality returns throughout Freud's writing as the earliest object of psychoanalytic inquiry and the recurrent question it can never fully explain.[34] He describes lesbianism alternately as the subject's return *to* a sexual prehistory and as the return *of* a previously renounced form of desire within adult female sexuality.[35] For Freud as for Krafft-Ebing and Ellis, repetition does not signify exclusively as lesbian; but lesbian sexuality is represented as a kind of repetition: an uncanny, unmotivated, unnatural citation of the law or of male heterosexual privilege and desire. Hemingway's texts similarly represent lesbianism both as a repeated object and as an uncanny form of repetition. Alternately a *thing* and an *effect*, the lesbian figure recalls the oscillation in early-twentieth-century sexual ideology between taxonomic definitions of lesbian identity and more contingent, adjectival understandings of the lesbian potential in femininity as such.[36] Modernist culture, I have suggested, associates lesbian sexuality with repetition not only because it resists the linear teleology of heterosexual culture (which is to say, procreation and the vision of futurity that straight culture reifies in the child), but also because it enacts a spurious citation of straight masculinity. In this sense the lesbian figure in Hemingway's writing bears a structural relation to the citationality of the symbolic order: as the abject form of repetition, lesbianism serves to naturalize, by comparison, the iterations of patriarchal law as well as the fictions of masculine heterosexuality.

I will return in a moment to the status of lesbianism and repetition in *The Sun Also Rises* and in Hemingway's negotiation of literary style, but first it is useful to consider one further aspect of repetition and its uncanny effects. The citations *in* and *of* the symbolic order return us to the ways psychoanalysis links uncanny, compulsive repetition with figural language. In his essay "Freud and the Sandman," Neil Hertz has traced the crucial role of certain "literary" questions—namely, the problem of originality and the function of rhetoric—in mediating relations between the uncanny and the compulsion to repeat. Hertz locates in Freud's discussion of repetition a Hemingwayesque concern with literary priority or originality. Likening repetition to the structure of figural language, Hertz proposes that the repeated thing "colors" the process of repetition, giving it substance and rendering it "visible" or perceptible. Whatever is repeated, Hertz writes, will "feel most compellingly uncanny when it is seen as *merely* coloring, that is, when it comes to seem most gratuitously rhetorical."[37] Jonathan Culler's gloss of Hertz's essay elaborates on this notion of rhetoric: the uncanny, he writes, is a repetition that seems "excessive, the result of no cause but a bizarre manifestation of repetition itself, as if for the sake of literary or rhetorical effect."[38] Uncanny repetition, then, resides in a particular effect of figural language, distinct in degree, if not in kind, from the repetition that constitutes representation. For Freud, Lacan writes, repetition "is fundamentally the insistence of speech which returns in the subject until it has said its final word."[39] And Samuel Weber, explaining Lacan's "return to Freud," characterizes "the ambivalent law of repetition" not as "a return of the same, in any simple sense, but rather as the recurrence of a difference separating what it repeated from its repetition," not as "a faithful rendering of a self-identical original, but as a turn of phrase or a trope."[40]

Surely the notion of repetition as an ambivalent phenomenon has resonance in modernist writing, that famously ambivalent genre, and in view of Hemingway's own ambivalence toward—his attraction to and phobic repudiation of—lesbian figures.[41] As the very concept of ambivalence suggests, however, repetition is fundamentally metaphorical, at home in the province of double meanings. It is impossible, Hertz writes, to "isolate the *question* of repetition from the question of figurative language itself."[42] But figural language, as Hertz observes, can be represented as a form of compulsive repetition only through a figural sleight of hand that disavows the repetitive logic of signification as such. The language Hemingway will designate as corrupt and derivative, analogous to phobic tropes of homosexuality, in fact covers over the perverse repetitions that structure his own text. It is not only in symbolic law that the act of citation, as Butler writes, "brings into being the very prior authority to which it then defers." This metaleptic gesture also characterizes modernist writing, which by citing the authority of literary tradition—even to resist it—establishes the status of that tradition. And it is with this gesture that I want to return to *The Sun Also Rises* to consider Hemingway's relation to his literary predecessors and to male modernist aesthetics.

A Lost Generation

The repetition that psychoanalysis associates with sexual and rhetorical disturbances, but also acknowledges as essential to psychic life, is equally problematic in American literary modernism. As an ambivalent genre, modernism indulges in nostalgia at the same time that it rejects the sentimentality, conventional pieties, and mannered rhetoric of an earlier age. In male modernist texts, the morbidly seductive force of repetition often stands as a token of the effeminacy and sensationalism of Victorian writing.[43] This concern with repetition finds its most salient expression in questions of influence and originality. T. S. Eliot writes in "Tradition and the Individual Talent," "The existing monuments form an ideal order among themselves, which is modified by the introduction of the new (the really new) work of art among them." Despite his disdain for Eliot, Hemingway would also identify good writing with the possibility of the "really new," but the pursuit of the new, as each writer recognized, was not without its own difficulties. When literature seeks "new human emotions to express," Eliot continues, "in this search for novelty in the wrong place it discovers the perverse."[44] The danger of innovation, for Eliot, consists in the "discovery" that deviance is inherent in literature—that the wrong move can show new writing as already infected by the literary corruption it struggles to escape. Rejecting vulgarity and sensationalism yet claiming originality, poised between the "monuments" of the old and the perversion of the new, Eliot's modernism finds itself defined by the desire for and the impossibility of an escape from repetition.

These questions of novelty and perversion, tradition and masculinity become in Hemingway's writing a matter of *style*, or more precisely the repudiation of style. In his essay "End Pleasure," Paul Morrison has suggested that literary stylization—the excessive exercise of an always inherently suspect style—marks the place of perversions both sexual and literary: "Because the novel, like the sexual regime whose interests it serves, understands itself as a 'natural' fact, genres that resist its imperialism are designated as 'stylized.' Or castigated as such." As the obverse of the "natural," stylization has a sexual valence as well. Morrison continues, "the charge of excessive stylization—a variation on the familiar trope of decadence—is broadly legible, from Wilde through Mapplethorpe and beyond, only as a euphemism for perverse."[45] "Stylized" writing, the unnatural antithesis to novelistic propriety, connotes the "decadence" of a corrupt signification and personifies that violation of literary form in the figure of the homosexual. Threatening to expose the literariness or stylization of all language, homosexuality seems to jeopardize "natural" forms of novelistic meaning. It does so through the energies of what de Man, in a reading of Proust, calls "rhetorical seductions"—not only the seductions performed *in* rhetoric but also the seductions *of* rhetoric.[46] One need not go far to find evidence of the long tradition linking both male and female homosexuality with an excess of literary style and with a certain phobic view of literariness as such.

Described by tropes of narcissism, parasitism, and sterility, both homosexuality and "the literary" imply masculine effeminacy and feminine virilization, as well as solipsism, masturbation, and the abdication of productive or reproductive social behavior. And in American literature, lesbian morbidity is frequently figured as a discursive morbidity, as we have seen in Basil Ransom's view of Olive Chancellor, who belongs to the realm of "dead phrases" yet exerts vital influence in James's novel.

Intent on avoiding a stylized presentation, Hemingway exemplifies an emphatically modernist disdain for the mannered, the sentimental, and the derivative. In her discussion of male homosexuality and sentimentality, Eve Kosofsky Sedgwick calls attention to the "modernist aesthetic according to which sentimentality inheres less in the object figured than in a prurient vulgarity associated with figuration itself."[47] Sedgwick sees that abject figurality as located in "a very particular body," the body of the gay man; and the prominence of male homosexual panic in Hemingway, and in modernist literature more generally, can hardly be contested. Yet Hemingway's texts also enable us to see how male sexual anxiety is inseparable from, if never identical to, the lesbian figures that modernist culture no less obsessively conjures. In *The Sun Also Rises*, that same "prurient vulgarity" of figuration is embodied in both perverse female sexuality and the compulsion to repeat, two forces that precipitate the masculine subject's fall into a corrupt world whose very literariness—its empty language and figurative speech—prevents the writing of "true" literature.

It is worth noting that the single explicit reference to lesbian sexuality in *The Sun Also Rises* occurs in the context of literary style and interpretation. During the fishing trip in Burguete, Bill launches a complicated, seemingly interminable monologue about "irony and pity." Along the way he parodies Kipling's poem "The Ladies": "Sex explains it all. The Colonel's Lady and Judy O'Grady are Lesbians under their skin" (116). Whether or not we regard Kipling's "Ladies" as a literary antecedent of Hemingway's own "novel about a lady," the Kipling passage pointedly anticipates the place of the critic—any critic, at least, who is tempted to propose, perhaps in a reading of Hemingway himself, that sex "explains it all."[48] The reader who is more skeptical about such explanatory power might observe Hemingway's use of the lesbian not merely as a figure for sexual deviance but also, perhaps more perversely, as a figure for literary deviance. To define "lesbians," even in jest, as the obscene synonym of Kipling's original "sisters" is to recognize lesbian sexuality, if misogynistically, as the potential fate of any woman. But to assign lesbianism to the place of literary parody, allusion, even "irony," is also to underscore the notion of the lesbian as the bearer of a *rhetorical* repetition-compulsion, manifest in the compulsion to quote literature.

The insistence on quotation in the "irony and pity" passage alludes to Hemingway's earlier story about lesbianism, "The Sea Change," which turns upon an encyclopedic chain of literary references. Refashioning themes from *The Sun Also Rises*, "The Sea Change" presents a young man, Phil, struggling with the problem of how to understand lesbian sexuality—a task that he can address only by quoting a few lines from Pope:

> "Vice is a monster of such fearful mien," the young man said bitterly, "that to be something or other needs but to be seen. Then we something, something, then embrace." He could not remember the words. "I can't quote," he said. (41)[49]

If his young man, by his own account, "can't quote," Hemingway clearly can, and so can Pope, whose account of feminine "vice" itself builds on a reference to Dryden.[50] The sheer excess of quotation in "The Sea Change" (whose title signals in advance an awareness of its literary inheritance) aligns the particular "vice" of lesbianism with the logic of repetition and the endless displacements of the signifying chain. Despite the moralistic and misogynist thrust of the lines from Pope and Dryden, their allusiveness suggests a literary repetition-compulsion of which, for Hemingway, lesbianism is both object and emblem. For even as Hemingway's allusions recall the power of a masculine literary tradition to render lesbian "vice" culturally meaningful, they evoke the circularity, the slippage of meaning, and the sexual deviance associated in modernist culture with a decadent literariness.

For Hemingway, the most influential figure of literary lesbianism and lesbian literature was surely Gertrude Stein. In *A Moveable Feast* Hemingway credits Stein with discovering "many truths about rhythms and the uses of words in repetition" but he objects to the prose of *The Making of Americans*, which, Hemingway complains, "went on endlessly in repetitions that a more conscientious and less lazy writer would have put in the waste basket."[51] Stein's repetition celebrates modes of writing and of sexuality regarded by others, Hemingway included, as waste matter and wasteful expense. Her story "Miss Furr and Miss Skeene," for example, concludes, "she always was living very well and was gay very well and was telling about little ways one could be learning to use in being gay, and later was telling them quite often, telling them again and again."[52] Linking repetition with what "being gay" means for a woman, Stein identifies lesbian sexuality with a kind of repetition peculiar to speech, the act of "telling it again and again."

Unlike Stein, who in "Composition as Explanation" would defend her use of repetition with the remark that "beginning again and again is a natural thing," Hemingway renounced repetition as a kind of figural excess.[53] In *A Moveable Feast* Hemingway describes his goal as writing "true" sentences without "scrollwork or ornament"— without, that is, the rhetorical embellishments that could be construed as useless, circular, or effeminate.[54] In at least one text, *The Garden of Eden*, his writer-hero shares this view. When David asks Catherine why she burned his notebooks, he instantly regrets the question: "the question had been, he realized, a rhetorical one. He disliked rhetoric and distrusted those who used it and he was ashamed to have fallen into it" (224). Should we wonder what exactly is shameful about rhetoric, one early review of *The Sun Also Rises* provides an answer in terms that, though they border on self-parody, are not far from Hemingway's own. According to the *New York Times Book Review*, Hemingway is to be congratulated for "a lean, hard, athletic narrative prose that puts more literary English to shame."[55] If shame is the proper, perhaps the inevitable, response of male modernism to literariness and the linguistic excesses of "scrollwork or ornament," unadorned narrative means, for Hemingway, a masculine language of which he can be proud.

This theory finds expression in the Pamplona section of *The Sun Also Rises*, where Hemingway presents bullfighting as an allegory of literary form. Like the novel as seen by a pessimistic modernism, the bullfight is an institution now in decline, in which inferior bullfighters like Belmonte and Marcial give their work a "fake emotional feeling" while avoiding risk to themselves. Romero, however, has "the old thing" (168). As Hemingway tells us, he shuns the "decadence" and "false aesthetics" (215) that produce only shoddy repetitions of the old style, such as "Belmonte's imitation of himself" and worse, "Marcial's imitation of Belmonte" (218). A true master of the art, Romero strips away his rivals' theatrical gestures, leaving the elegance of pure form: "Romero went on. It was like a course in bullfighting. All the passes he linked up, all completed, all slow, templed and smooth. There were no tricks and no mystifications" (219-20). Indeed, Hemingway suggests, Romero's performance provides "a course in bullfighting" for the edification of the reader as well as Brett Ashley. To appreciate the bullfight, to become a true *aficionado*, one must learn how to read it. By tutoring Brett in the ritual of the *corrido* Jake helps her understand its meaning, "so that she saw what it was all about, so that it became more something with a definite end, and less of a spectacle with unexplained horrors" (167). The bullfight can be recognized as an art form analogous to Hemingway's own novelistic art only through the work of interpretation, the process of deducing meaning—"what it was all about"—in events that might otherwise remain "unexplained" and horrifying. This task of interpretation depends on the transformation of the bullfight from the static tableau of mere "spectacle" into a narrative whose events progress toward "a definite end." Promoting the textual over the visual, Jake insists that the bullfight be "read" as a novelistic text whose "definite end" provides both a conclusion and a sense of purpose.

As with writing, so with sexuality—for the novel and the heterosexual narrative of sexual aims and outcomes allegorize each other in their obsessive drive to conclude. Examining the sexual implications of narrative form and the narrative implications of sexual formations, Morrison argues that the novel constitutes a conservative literary form whose "heterosexual and heterosexualizing conventions are the more insidious for defining themselves against mere literary convention."[56] As one of those narrative forms that, as Morrison suggests, "define themselves against" traditional structures, literary modernism partakes of the same "conventions" as the tradition it would both overturn and revitalize—conventions not lacking in sexual resonance. Indeed, Hemingway's sexual ideology emerges not only in his thematic treatment of such issues as lesbianism, the masculinized

"New Woman," and male homosexuality, but also in the formal structures of his texts. "Like the well-made narrative," Morrison writes, "normative sexuality is end-haunted, all for its end"; in Freud's writing, accordingly, perversion and homosexuality imply "a failure of full narrativization."[57] In both Freudian narratives of sexual processes and Western novelistic traditions, heterosexual normalcy demands teleological progress toward ending or closure, and homosexual deviance appears alternately as the *cause* and the *effect* of a blockage in (or, in *The Awakening*, a wandering from) that trajectory.

Within this narrative landscape, repetition signifies in terms of perversion because it obstructs or diverts both sexual and narrative progress. Judith Roof has argued that Freud's account of the psychosexual economy, which presses both desire and death to the service of narrative conclusion, seeks to "subordinat[e] the potential perversity of repetition to the conservation of the proper (i.e., most resounding, total, and pleasurable) end."[58] Caught amid the perversities of repetition, *The Sun Also Rises* is a text driven less by narrative than by a restless search *for* narrative. As if seeking an image of its own ideal form or a path toward its own proper end, the novel moves from one café to the next, from one tourist destination to another. It pauses only at Pamplona, where it finds in the art of bullfighting a figure for "true" narrative, and in Pedro Romero Hemingway's model of himself as a writer. A new and brilliant rehearsal of an old form, Romero's bullfighting is an apt figure for Hemingway's modernist ambitions, and for Hemingway's desire at once to acknowledge literary tradition and to disavow a decadent, Victorian literary style. If the "imitation" of bullfighters like Belmonte and Marcial signifies only repetitive fakery, Romero's art provides satisfaction in the form of closure. A token of the novel that contains it, Romero's art provides "something with a definite end," and like heterosexuality in Freud's account, offers a productive alternative to the sterile involutions of lesbianism and repetition.

Closing Time

As a text, *The Sun Also Rises* offers little in the way of narrative closure, ending with Jake and Brett, in Madrid, driving around in a taxi just as they did in Paris. But it is not ending as such that the novel pursues. The "definite end" whose importance the bullfight sequence underscores is, after all, an aim as well as a conclusion. *As* an aim, this "end" consists, paradoxically, of a beginning, much as marriage, that conventional narrative conclusion, points toward heterosexual procreation and the reproduction of the family structure. And it is at its beginning that *The Sun Also Rises* most clearly explains its ends, presenting two epigraphs that address issues of narrative and sexuality. The first of these, Gertrude Stein's famous remark "You are all a lost generation," clearly suggests Jake Barnes' impotence and the foreclosure of future generations that the novel will displace onto Brett Ashley. Hemingway explains in *A Moveable Feast* that Miss Stein, as he calls her, overheard the *patrón* of a garage reproaching a young mechanic:

> The *patron* had said to him, "You are all a *génération perdue*."
> "That's what you are. That's what you all are," Miss Stein said. "All of you young people who served in the war. You are a lost generation."[59]

Against this lost generation and against the loss *of* generation it implies, the novel's second epigraph offers a more salutary kind of repetition. Hemingway quotes the passage in Ecclesiastes from which the novel takes its title:

> One generation passeth away, and another generation cometh; but the earth abideth forever . . . The sun also ariseth, and the sun goeth down, and hasteth to the place where he arose . . . The wind goeth toward the south, and turneth about unto the north; it whirleth about continually, and the wind returneth again according to his circuits . . . All the rivers run into the sea; yet the sea is not full; unto the place from whence the rivers come, thither they return again.

With this epigraph, designed, as he noted, "to balance Miss Stein's quotation," Hemingway juxtaposes the morbidity of the "lost generation" with a vision of generations following endlessly upon one another in a natural cycle of return and renewal.[60]

Resisting aimless repetition in favor of narrative progress, Hemingway labors to promote a sense of repetition as reproduction, and to differentiate the perversity of a sterile repetition from the vital repetition of heterosexual procreation. Whereas in "The Sea Change" and *The Garden of Eden* Shakespeare's lines from *The Tempest*—in which nothing "doth fade, But doth suffer a sea-change / Into something rich and strange"—join lesbian sexuality to uncanny transformation, the passage from Ecclesiastes describes a world in which whatever fades returns unchanged, forever adhering to its assigned course. The biblical epigraph champions as its sovereign goal the continuation of natural cycles as figured by the perpetual renewal of the earth. Here the "definite end" of healthy narrative progression is the promise of futurity and of masculine heterosexual generation. Like the law, which elides its own debt to citation, "good" repetition appears as continuity, not redundancy. Hemingway's vision of masculine authorship and originality is similarly framed. In *The Garden of Eden*, for example, after Catherine has burned David's manuscripts, Marita reminds him that he can rewrite the stories. David insists, "When it's once right you never can do it again. You only do it once for each thing" (230). Yet Catherine's destructive act will dispel David's fantasy of an unmediated, "right" relation to writing and force him to confront a world of repetition. David must acknowledge the impossibility of claiming absolute originality and find an image of writing that is not merely derivative; in the end, he will redeem a repetition now recognized as inevitable by finding in it a different form of authority, a model of writing as rewriting in which "there was no sign that any of it would ever cease returning to him intact" (247). But this productive form of repetition can be embraced only when distinguished from the unnatural, uncanny repetition identified *with* and *as* homosexuality. In *The Sun Also Rises*, therefore, Brett is rightly compared to Circe, the mythological daughter of Helios, for she inherits the logic of return first associated with the sun in the passage from Ecclesiastes: the compulsive repetition that straight culture, in order to claim the status of "nature," cannot acknowledge.

However, the epigraphs adduced in *The Sun Also Rises* to mark a boundary between good and bad repetition, between fertility and deathliness, testify instead to the ways productive return always collapses into morbid repetition. Despite its efforts to separate lesbianism and sterility from masculinity and procreation, *The Sun Also Rises* reveals the latter, the sites of Hemingway's identification, to be haunted by their own repetition-compulsion. Like the internal repetition-compulsion that Freud describes, this repetition is merely an external projection of an internal, irresistible gesture of return. The compulsive, perverse repetition of lesbian sexuality is never sufficiently distinct from the compulsory, endless repetition of straight "generations," so that every attempt to combat sterile repetition enacts the very repetition it would escape. Rejecting the effeminacy of a Victorian literariness, Hemingway aspires to male modernist originality, only to find himself enmeshed in the very perversion, the compulsive repetition, he sought to avoid. For although the redundant, excessive elaborations of figural language represent the unmanning of the writer—the possibility of Jake Barnes's impotence, or rather of gay male sexuality—that repetition, in another and equally compulsive form, proves essential to Hemingway's rhetoric of masculine potency. The rehabilitation of repetition requires Hemingway to establish and defend a distinction between two forms of repetition: on the one hand, the fruitful reproduction of future generations through heterosexual coupling, and on the other, the sterile circuit of imitation culturally ascribed to lesbian sexuality. But surely it is not far from Jake Barnes's nightmarish experience of "going through something that has all happened before" to this vision of "nature" in all of its *un*naturalness, a "nature" whose elements, predicting Jake and Brett's taxi rides, circle about and "return again" with a blind, compulsive force.

If patriarchal culture, then, equates lesbianism with a refusal of language—if it is, as the woman in "The Sea Change" puts it, a desire to which "You don't have to put any name" (42)—lesbian sexuality at the same time represents figural language in all its uncanny excess. In language as well as sexuality, Hemingway seeks to preserve the distinction between morbid repetition and "natural" cycles. Like the symbolic law, which as Butler suggests establishes its authority by differentiating itself from debased, compulsive repetition and concealing its own citationality, Hemingway's writing works to differentiate two kinds of repetition. The "natural" reproduction of meaning must be distinguished from the sterile rhetoric that can only appear, to borrow Culler's term for the uncanny, as "a bizarre manifestation of repetition itself." Invoking, by way of Pope and Dryden, its own relation to canonical literature, "The Sea Change" cannot separate the redundancy of lesbian sexuality from the allusive logic of the masculine literary tradition and of clinical accounts of feminine "vice." And although Hemingway's refusal of "literariness" profoundly shapes the American literary tradition, in *The Sun Also Rises* the prose dedicated to the renunciation of style becomes stylized, in the name of the "true sentence" returning to the discourse it deems most untrue. Summoning quotation and allusion, the accoutrements of style, to contain the recurring figure of lesbian sexuality, Hemingway compulsively repeats the logic he would repudiate, finding the only anodyne for repetition in repetition itself.

c h a p t e r   f o u r

Oral Narratives

"Race" and Sexuality
in *Their Eyes Were Watching God*

Although as Hawthorne, James, and Hemingway suggest, patriarchal ideology construes lesbianism as "impossible"—both unthinkable and intolerable, both alluring and anxiogenic—the fate of impossibility is not lesbian figures' alone. American hegemony also designates other figures as discursively "impossible," abjecting from its symbolic order that which seems unassimilable to white, bourgeois, and patriarchal values. Others who share the status of the unrepresentable, each framed by different tropes of resistance to symbolization, include gay men, colonial subjects, and "racial" others. In her essay "Unspeakable Things Unspoken," Toni Morrison argues that the notion of "race"—which is to say, inevitably, "racial" difference—remains "a virtually unspeakable thing" within the discourse of white America:

> We can agree, I think, that invisible things are not necessarily "not-there"; that a void may be empty, but is not a vacuum. In addition, certain absences are so stressed, so ornate, so planned, they call attention to themselves; arrest us with inten-

tionality and purpose, like neighborhoods that are defined by the population held away from them.[1]

In the regime of "racial" discipline, Morrison writes, the African American subject is the site not of nonexistence, the "not-there," but of a glaring erasure, a "void" that marks the presence of "race" as a conspicuous "absence." That cultural order of visibility is also a structure of discourse, which, if it regards "race" as "unspeakable," consigns African American women to a particularly overdetermined place. In *Their Eyes Were Watching God*, Zora Neale Hurston suggests that black women's subjectivity occupies a peculiar, insistent blind spot in white American culture. Relegated by gender and "race" to the space of the other, and as I will argue, to the realm of pure materiality, African American women come to seem "impossible" within an ideology that fails to recognize their subjectivity, their desire—and their voice.

Henry Louis Gates Jr. has argued that *Their Eyes Were Watching God* is a "speakerly text"—a text, that is, "whose rhetorical strategy is designed to represent an oral literary tradition."[2] Published two years after Hurston's study of black folklore, *Of Mules and Men*, the novel explores African American oral traditions through Janie's progress toward the narrative voice that enables her to tell the story of her life. *Their Eyes Were Watching God* is in this sense a novel *about* speaking—about Janie's accession to the status of speaking subject, about the power of speech itself to constitute communities and their relations to the world, and about cultural articulations of "race" and gender. Early in the novel Nanny tells Janie, "Ah wanted to preach a sermon about colored women sittin' on high, but they wasn't no pulpit for me."[3] When her status as a black woman born into slavery prevents Nanny from preaching her sermon, her dream is passed on to Janie, whom Nanny reminds, "Ah said Ah'd save de text for you" (32). In Hurston's novel, Janie realizes Nanny's ambition when she returns home and, taking "self revelation" (18) as the "text" of her "sermon," relates her story to her friend Phoeby, who will pass on that narrative to the community.

"Designed to represent an oral literary tradition," as Gates suggests, *Their Eyes Were Watching God* consists largely of oral narrative, in the tale Janie tells Phoeby while "the kissing, young darkness became a monstropolous old thing" (19). But the novel is also about orality in another, more literal sense. In the central trope of Hurston's first chapter, Janie takes the mouth as a figure for (and figure of) speech, metaphorically equating embodied "orality" with oral narrative. The porch-sitting gossips she names "Mouth-Almighty" (16), for example, are people who "wastes up too much time puttin' they mouf on things they don't know nothin' about" (17). This trope extends to oral activities such as eating, as when Janie enjoys the dinner Phoeby brings her before beginning her tale, then finds encouragement in Phoeby's "hungry listening" (23). If, for Hurston, the act of eating complements that of speech, the act of kissing seems to stand for speech itself. "If they wants to see and know," Janie says of the town gossips, "why they don't come kiss and be kissed?" (18). To Phoeby, who does come to hear her story, Janie says "We been kissin'-friends for twenty years, so Ah depend on you for a good thought" (19). And again, when Phoeby urges Janie to "make haste and tell 'em" how she decided to marry Tea Cake and why she has returned alone, Janie responds: "You can tell 'em what Ah say if you wants to. Dat's just de same as me 'cause mah tongue is in mah friend's mouf" (17).

Equating eating, kissing, and speaking, *Their Eyes Were Watching God* proliferates the meanings of orality. Surely the "oral literary tradition" that Gates locates in Hurston's text is meant to signify certain culturally specific African American modes of discourse; but Hurston's own "oral tradition" goes further, associating these discursive formations with questions of gender and lesbian desire. In the novel's frame story, the naming of Janie and Phoeby as "kissin'-friends" represents talk as embodied and eroticized, just as the phrase "mah tongue is in mah friend's mouf" imagines the women's exchange of words as a shared kiss.[4] Yet Hurston's narrative appears to focus on Janie's heterosexual relationships; if it metaphorically embodies speech in the figure of the kiss, it hesitates to grant that kiss between female friends more than figurative status. In order to decipher the role of lesbian eroticism both in mediating Janie's relationship with Phoeby and in elaborating Hurston's heterosexual narrative, we must consider Hurston's figures of speech. To examine the multivalent forms of orality with which, as its first chapter suggests, *Their Eyes Were Watching God* is fundamentally concerned requires that we trace the connections among oral eroticism, the question of speech, and African American narrative traditions. Although a number of valuable readings of the novel, including Gates's own, have focused on its discursive strategies and tropological structures, I choose, for the moment, to be rather more literal. I want to examine the "obvious" bodily referents of orality and the oral tradition precisely in order to address the differences between the literal and the figural, the material and the ideal. For these are the differences that inform the status of the phallus and the notion of whiteness; hegemonic constructions of gender and "race"; the distinction between speech and writing in the Western philosophical tradition; and the psychoanalytic notion of lesbian sexuality as preoedipal or "prehistoric."

Speech and "orality" are not, of course, synonymous. In Western philosophy, as Derrida has argued, the valuation of speech over writing depends on an understanding of speech as internal and unencumbered by materiality, and of writing as "sensible matter and artificial exteriority."[5] Orality cannot represent ideal speech insofar as it refers back to the body—and, in the "racial" logic of Euro-American culture, to the notion of the "racialized" body. If, as Morrison suggests, "race" constitutes an "unspeakable" subject in white American literature, it is a subject whose very interdiction returns us to the issue of speech. In Hurston's novel, I want to consider how black and female speech—forms of the spoken word that appear materialized, "already a writing" in Western dominant culture—reveal speech, the phallus, and whiteness as cultural ideals constituted by a disavowed "idolatry." One task of this reading, then, is to apply the deconstructive analysis of speech and writing to social formations of racism and patriarchy. Another goal is to use Freud's theory of the oral stage in sexual development to investigate the ways in which orality, as a discursive and a sexual mode, resists such dominant formations. For Freud, orality marks a "primitive" organization of desire that must yield to genitality; for women in this narrative, the oral phase characterizes the preoedipal mother-love to which lesbianism seems to be a regression. *Their Eyes Were Watching God* links lesbian sexuality to orality in a number of resonant ways, not only in Hurston's metaphors for the conversation of female friends, but also in a figure of the mother's voice, which betokens the preoedipal, the "prehistoric," and the pregenital. These different senses of orality offer critical purchase on Hurston's novel, which anatomizes and resists the fundamental logic of racist and masculinist ideology by acknowledging the interrelations of "pure sign" and materiality, speech and writing, women's speech and a "lesbian" orality.

At the beginning, however, it is necessary to say a few words about the shape of the argument that follows, specifically its relation to psychoanalytic theories of sexuality, difference, and representation. The preceding chapters have been grounded in the premise that psychoanalysis and post-structuralist theory offer valuable tools for the study of sexuality and representation in American culture and literature. But the relation of psychoanalysis, in particular, to matters of "race" remains an open question, even at a time when psychoanalytic concepts increasingly inform readings of African American texts and "racial" discourses in Western culture. In a 1989 essay Hortense Spillers asked, "is the Freudian landscape an applicable text (to say nothing of appropriate) to social and historic situations that do not replicate moments of its own historic origins and involvements?"[6] Feminist criticism has long enjoined us to recall the genesis of psychoanalysis in turn-of-the-century white bourgeois European culture and to interrogate the tendency of Freud and his followers to replicate in varying degrees the dominant ideologies of their cultural surround. Such cautions are no less crucial in readings of "race," which must attend to the historical specificity of American racism and the wrenching effects of the institution of slavery, for example, on gender, desire, and family structures.

With such caveats in mind, the question becomes *how* Freudian concepts might be appropriate or applicable to the question of "race"—and how "race," in turn, might apply to psychoanalysis. While it is true, as Jean Walton has suggested, that the field of psychoanalysis has systematically overlooked the "racial" concepts upon which its insights frequently rely, this failure itself reveals the interpenetration of the two discourses.[7] Barbara Johnson observes that the so-called "Jewish science" of psychoanalysis from its beginning engaged questions of race, albeit in underexamined or resistant ways: "Race, then, is at the heart of Freud's discovery. It is not outside but inside psychoanalysis."[8] Johnson alludes to Spillers's recent work on the question of "race" and psychoanalysis, in which Spillers proposes that "the 'race' matrix was the fundamental interdiction within the enabling discourse of founding psychoanalytic theory and practice itself." Although this statement would not be true in the reverse (we cannot say that psychoanalytic theory is fundamental to "race"), the "private," subjective psychic formations that Freud made it his business to interrogate are in fact, Spillers argues, at the heart of "race" questions in the form of "fantasy, desire, and the 'unconscious,' of conflict, envy, aggression, and ambivalence."[9] Psychoanalysis promises a way to read the psychic causes and consequences of "racial" structures and a ground from which to intervene in such structures, as Spillers's theory of "internal intersubjectivity" endeavors to do. Considering the articulation of orality, subjectivity, and phallic authority, then, both in *Their Eyes Were Watching God* and in psychoanalytic theory, I mean to suggest not only that psychoanalytic texts can speak to formations of "race" and gender in America, but also that American literature has something to say to psychoanalysis. Indeed, Hurston's novel, with its own complex theory of desire, illuminates the ways in which the intersection of "race," gender, and sexuality has long been a site of absence or blockage, both in psychoanalytic knowledge and in the optic of American culture.

Idolatry and Inscription

In a frequently quoted passage of *Their Eyes Were Watching God*, Nanny describes the cultural location of African American women at the intersection of racist and patriarchal economies:

> de white man throw down de load and tell de nigger man tuh pick it up. He pick it up because he have to, but he don't tote it. He hand it to his womenfolks. De nigger woman is de mule uh de world so fur as Ah can see. (29)

Hurston has defined the oppressive weight of the "load" imposed on black women somewhat earlier, in Nanny's account of her own experience as a woman born into slavery. "Ah done been on mah knees to mah Maker many's de time askin *please*—for Him not to make de burden too heavy for me to bear" she says; "Ah done bore de burden in de heat uh de day" (27). The "mule uh de world" parable explains how a form of oppression is displaced across lines of "race" and gender from the white man to the black man to the black woman. If the heavy "load" that white men and black men seek to displace onto another is also the "burden" Nanny herself must bear, what does that burden mean? Of what does it consist? The word "burden" designates a load that is carried as well as the main idea of a text, the refrain of a song, and a child carried in the womb. Within the context of African American history, the notion of burden as child seems to allude to the rape of black women, epitomized in their compulsory reproduction within the slave economy. In *Their Eyes Were Watching God* this burden is manifest in the stories of Nanny and her daughter, each of whom bears a child conceived by rape. Yet while such a reading recognizes the intersection of racism and patriarchal law in slavery—under the rule of the white man who, as Frederick Douglass writes, "in cases not a few, sustains to his slaves the double relation of master and father"—it does not fully account for the theory of racism and misogyny presented in Hurston's parable of "de mule uh de world."[10]

If the notion of burden as child bodies forth the horror of slavery as a specific form of white male violence, the rhetorical sense of "burden" as a principal theme of a text—or the burden, as they say, of a speech—suggests the discursive construction of this oppression within American culture. One could say that the load transferred from the white man to the black man and finally to the black woman in Hurston's parable is a culturally significant theme or idea. This load suggests the cultural weight of representation itself: not the burden *of* a speech but the burden that *is* speech, the burden of discourse as such. One burden that makes the African American woman "de mule uh de world" is meaning itself, as distinguished from the signifiers whose chainlike structure of displacement Hurston's metaphor describes. In *Their Eyes Were Watching God* and in American culture, Hurston suggests, the "white man's burden" is all too real. *Contra* Kipling, however, it consists not in a sentimentalized fiction of responsibility that thinly masks colonial violence, but in the insupportable weight of the "racial" and sexual differences that create and sustain the authority of the "white man" and of the culture that operates in his name.

In Nanny's account of black women's cultural status, the imposition of this burden effects a striking reversal, attaching weightiness and material density not to the load that is borne but to the body on which it is imposed. Naming "racial difference" in Western culture as an effect of overembodiment and reification, Frantz Fanon explains the reduction of the "racialized" subject to the status of material object: "the occasion arose when I had to meet the white man's eyes. An unfamiliar weight burdened me."[11] In this "racial" interpellation, the "weight" of white ideology imposes itself on a body that is thus, Fanon writes, "overdetermined from without."[12] When it produces the "racialized" subject as *all* body, white discourse mirrors the logic of patriarchy, in which women, "becoming" the phallus so that men may have it, will come to emblematize not meaning but sheer matter.[13] As Hurston recognizes, African American women are "de mule uh de world" because they must fantasmatically assume the weight of materiality so that the phallus and whiteness, as cultural ideals, can float free of material embodiment and appear in the invisible place of the transcendent—a process allegorized in Joe Starks's favorite trope of authority, the "big voice," or more properly, in Janie's words, by "the making of a voice out of a man" (134).

Thirteen years after the publication of *Their Eyes Were Watching God*, Hurston would return to the question of "racial" embodiment in an essay titled "What White Publishers Won't Print." Her essay argues that the racist ideology of the United States excludes African Americans as subjects of writing and inquiry, constructing them instead as already known, self-evident exhibits in what Hurston terms "THE AMERICAN MUSEUM OF UNNATURAL HISTORY":

> It is assumed that all non–Anglo-Saxons are uncomplicated stereotypes. Everybody knows all about them. They are lay figures mounted in the museum where all may take them in at a glance. They are made of bent wires without insides at all. So how could anybody write a book about the non-existent?[14]

Produced as pure surface, "without insides at all," people of color seem to lack the interiority that signals subjectivity. Predicting Fanon's argument, Hurston proposes that racist logic operates through the reduction of persons to the status of *things*. This overembodiment renders them culturally "non-existent," read and written by regimes of white knowledge but barred from the status of speaking subjects. The conspicuous place of nationality in Hurston's

"American museum" of "racial" ideology is not incidental. As Lauren Berlant has argued, the paradigmatic American citizen is an abstract subject whose whiteness and maleness are both presupposed and obscured: "if in practice the liberal political public sphere protects and privileges the 'person's' racial and gendered embodiment, one effect of these privileges is to appear to be disembodied or abstract while retaining cultural authority."[15] In his discussion of "the invisibility of whiteness" Richard Dyer summarizes the "racial" aspect of this logic: "white power secures its dominance by seeming not to be anything in particular" within dominant representations of "race"; it seems, like the phallus in the logic of patriarchy, "to be everything and nothing."[16] In contrast to white culture's fetishistic investment in the bodies of "racial" others, whiteness, like the phallus, becomes a locus of meaning and value only by maintaining its invisibility—by remaining, like the Word, divinely disembodied.

The phallus and whiteness are each identified, as if interchangeably, with the "transcendental signifier" whose authority depends on its claim to invisibility and immateriality. Although Lacan designates the phallus as the signifier that "stands out as most easily seized upon in the real of sexual copulation," he also insists that the phallus is not an object and "even less the organ, penis or clitoris, which it symbolises."[17] As Jacqueline Rose notes, "anatomical difference comes to *figure* sexual difference" in a metaphorical substitution of material sign for transcendent ideal. For Lacan, she continues, "The phallus symbolises the effects of the signifier in that having no value in itself, it can represent that to which value *accrues*."[18] This paradoxical account of the signification of the phallus can also help us understand the cultural stakes of whiteness in racist ideology, as Samuel Weber's gloss of Lacan suggests:

The phallus thus operates as the pure representation of absence, a representation that is pure because it represents nothing, and hence, coincides, qua representation, with what it represents, without leaving the slightest trace or residue. . . . The phallus then would be pure sign, were it not for the fact that it does not completely disappear or dissolve into diaphany; instead, it reappears inscribed as the distinctive trait of the male body, and above all, of the paternal body.[19]

The disembodiment of the phallus and whiteness as "pure signs"—to the extent that they are incommensurate with the penis and what is taken as a visibly Caucasian morphology—allows them cultural authority. Conversely, the overembodiment of black and female persons in the rhetoric of racist culture renders them meaningless as subjects and significant, instead, as bodies inscribed by "scientific" taxonomy and social discipline.

Seeking to forestall the collapse of the "pure sign" into bodily form, Western philosophy demands a fantasmatic distinction between the world of things, of sheer materiality, and the realm of the transcendent and the ideal—a distinction that, in turn, structures the production and naturalization of "race" and "gender." But the transcendental signifier of cultural value, be it phallus or whiteness, is in double jeopardy. Its authority is threatened both by the *collapse* of the relation between penis and phallus, between whiteness and "racial" morphology, into an excessive closeness, and by the *dissociation* of that relation, which would undermine the hegemonic power of white and male subjects. The logic of patriarchal and racist culture, that is, requires *both* that the phallus and whiteness remain transcendently immaterial, *and* that they be identified with the penis and skin color, conferring on white male subjects the authority of the ideal signs. It insists on having it both ways, preserving the phallus and whiteness as "pure" signs while identifying certain persons, and certain bodies, as their material corollaries.

Just as the reign of whiteness requires the overembodiment of "racial" others, the authority of the phallus requires that women be made to bear the burden of materiality, as Janie does when she accedes to Joe's ambition to "be," as he puts it, "a big voice." Joe's body is imposing, "kind of portly like rich white folks" (56), but his corpulence says less about his authority than does his voice—not the largely unremarkable voice that he *has* but the voice that he *is*. Joe's exercise of speech and authority depends on the separation of transcendent word from material form. In the exchange that seals Janie's claim to her own "voice" and precipitates Joe's downfall, Janie points out that Joe habitually criticizes her looks but will not allow his own body to be scrutinized. "Ah'm nearly forty and you'se already fifty. How come you can't talk about dat sometimes instead of always pointin' at me?" (122). Janie continues, "Humph! Talkin' 'bout *me* lookin' old! When you pull down yo' britches, you look lak de change uh life" (123). Although comparing Joe's sexual potency to the state of menopause is surely less than flattering, the metaphor itself is less significant than the way it exposes and names the penis, dissociating it from phallic authority. Janie takes from Joe "his illusion of irresistible maleness that all men cherish" (123) by robbing the penis of the mystification that allows it to stand for the phallus, as cynosure of the logocentric thought in which, like whiteness, it appears to be "everything and nothing."[20]

In *Their Eyes Were Watching God*, Hurston describes both the overvaluation and the debasement of the phallus and whiteness through the notion of *idolatry*. An episode toward the end of the text introduces Janie's "color-struck" (220) Everglades neighbor, Mrs. Turner, who, as if enacting the meaning of her name, has turned against African American people and culture. Having internalized the racist ideal of whiteness, she urges Janie, whose physical characteristics seem more "white" than her own, to leave the darker-skinned Tea Cake. Hurston represents this disavowal of blackness and aspiration to the ideal of "whiteness" not only as a pathological condition but also as a form of religious devotion. "Mrs. Turner," Hurston writes, "like all other believers had built an altar to the unattainable—Caucasian characteristics for all" (216). Yet in her "fanaticism to defend the altars of her god" (216), Mrs. Turner betrays the imposture through which whiteness appears as divine or transcendent. If, that is, Mrs. Turner takes as the object of her worship the material, visible property of whiteness—fetishizing "Caucasian characteristics" like Janie's light skin and long hair—she exposes that "god" as a mere image. The conflation of the transcendental signifier with the bodily site where it is culturally enshrined is the prohibited gesture into which social representation incessantly falls and whose exercise it must endlessly disavow. Compelled by her identification with and pursuit of whiteness, Hurston tells us, Mrs. Turner subscribes to a sort of profane faith: "Once having set up her idols and built altars to them it was inevitable that she would worship there" (215). In *The Blithedale Romance*, Hawthorne's description of love between women as "idolatry" charges lesbian desire with the crime of mistaking a crude image for the true deity; here Hurston accuses Mrs. Turner, and with her white culture, of a similar offense. Echoing the Mosaic prohibition of graven images, white patriarchal law ostensibly rejects visible "idols" or images lest that construction repeat the sin of the Israelites, as Hurston writes in *Moses, Man of the Mountain*, "howling in idolatry" before the golden calf.[21] Yet racism and patriarchy cannot survive without idolatry; they are *founded on* idolatry. Even while they insist on the "worship" of whiteness and the phallus as immaterial and invisible, such structures demand and enjoy the cultural privileges enabled by the location of authority in white and male bodies.

Hurston's Alphabet

White patriarchal ideology does not, of course, operate purely in the realm of the social and the public; in *Their Eyes Were Watching God* it also shapes the processes of individual subjectification through which Janie "recognizes" herself as black and as female. When Janie, "full of that oldest human longing—self revelation" (18), begins telling her story to Phoeby, she starts by relating two incidents that, while not structurally implicated in the narrative's other events, constitute its very foundation. These moments of identity formation mimic the retrospective structure of Hurston's narrative by presenting "race" and femininity as belated formations. Janie first explains her entrance into "racial" awareness through the recognition of her image in a photograph, and then describes her accession to heterosexual femininity through an identification with a blossoming pear tree. Of "race" Janie says, "Ah was wid dem white chillun so much till Ah didn't know Ah wuzn't white till Ah was round six years old." She "found it out," Janie continues, only when she saw a photograph of herself:

> So when we looked at de picture and everybody got pointed out there wasn't nobody left except a real dark little girl with long hair standing by Eleanor. Dat's where Ah wuz s'posed to be, but Ah couldn't recognize dat dark chile as me. So Ah ast, 'where is me? Ah don't see me.'
>
> Everybody laughed, even Mr. Washburn. Miss Nellie, de Mama of de chillun who come back home after her husband

dead, she pointed to de dark one and said, 'Dat's you, Alphabet, don't you know yo' ownself?' (21)

As Priscilla Wald has explained, this "lesson in cultural subjectivity," like other such scenes in African American novels from the late nineteenth and early twentieth centuries, stages the alienation of identity in specifically "racial" terms.[22] The lesson not lost on Hurston is the contingency of the "racial" identity whose "discovery" masks its social production. In Janie's photographic memory, Hurston suggests, "racial" identity is written on the body through the technology of a social discourse, which, like the medium of photography, retroactively "invents" the subject it claims merely to represent.[23]

Hurston offers a similar account of her own entrance into "racial" subjectivity in her essay "How It Feels to Be Colored Me." "I remember the very day that I became colored," Hurston writes, "I was not Zora of Orange County any more, I was now a little colored girl."[24] As in *Their Eyes Were Watching God*, the imposition of a cultural fantasy of "race" as visible difference seems to require a certain renaming. "Zora" will be replaced by "a little colored girl," just as Janie, or "Alphabet" as she is called, will become a "dark little girl." Remembering Miss Nellie's question, "Alphabet, don't you know yo' ownself?" Janie explains, "Dey all useter call me Alphabet 'cause so many people had done named me different names" (21). For both Zora and Janie, the renaming that marks one's entrance into the social order of "race" entails the suppression of proper names and a reconstitution of identity around a description, an external form. Although, as Gates has noted, "race" is a trope and "racial" identity constitutes a social inscription, for Hurston the trope of "race" also works against inscription, replacing writing with image, "Alphabet" with a "dark little girl."[25] As Barbara Johnson points out in her reading of *Their Eyes Were Watching God*, "the acquisition of color is a *loss* of identity"; no longer a person signified by a name, Janie becomes merely a body marked by "racial" difference.[26]

In the photograph passage the name "Alphabet," *as* a name, evokes Derrida's notion of speech as a form of writing and predicts Hurston's use of free indirect discourse.[27] Derrida has suggested that the distinction between speech and writing in the Western tradition depends upon the distinction between ideality and materiality:

writing, the letter, the sensible inscription, has always been considered by Western tradition as the body and matter external to the spirit, to breath, to speech, and to the logos. And the problem of soul and body is no doubt derived from the problem of writing from which it seems—conversely—to borrow its metaphors.[28]

If, as Hurston's notion of "idolatry" suggests, hegemonic systems of "race" and gender both demand and mystify the perverse substitution, or overvaluation, of the material sign in place of its abstract, ideal referent, writing constitutes a form of "idolatry" in Western philosophy because it offers the material sign in place of the transcendent word. Within this ideology, Derrida writes, the subversion of the proper reign of speech by writing seems to produce "the perverse cult of the letter-image," analogous to the "sin of idolatry" and to what Saussure names the "superstition of the letter."[29]

Although the authority of writing is generally predicated on that of speech, Gates argues that the "racial" logic of nineteenth-century European and American culture claimed writing as the discourse of white reason. "While several superb scholars give priority to the *spoken* as the privileged of the pair," Gates writes, "most Europeans privileged *writing*—in their writings about Africans, at least—as the principal measure of the Africans' humanity, their capacity for progress, their very place in the great chain of being."[30] As a result, Gates explains, writing became a crucial arena in which African Americans, addressing a white readership, sought to demonstrate their humanity and claim their social rights; indeed, he writes, "Anglo-African writing arose as a response to allegations of its absence."[31] According to the speech / writing relation Derrida describes—a relation structured by the internal and the external, the ideal and the material—racist ideology could not construe African American speech *as* speech. The African American voice could not be understood as essential "to the spirit, to breath, to speech, and to the logos" because it could only appear as overembodied. Instead, African American speech seems *like a writing*, material and secondary, in white and patriarchal Western cultures. As such, it recalls the place of dialect writing, including Hurston's text, in American literature. When conventional dialect literature employs a nonstandard orthography to reflect the intonations of speech, this "disfigurement" of the word highlights the materiality not only of the written word, but also of the voice it represents.[32] As the written form of a spoken word, that is, dialect writing alludes to speech, but this allusion, rather than securing its authority, instead marks it as a marginal, "racial" discourse.

In its negotiation of speech and writing, the transcendent and the material, the ideology of patriarchy mirrors that of racism. Patriarchal discourse, as Kaja Silverman notes, promotes "the close identification of the female voice with spectacle and the body, and a certain aspiration of the male voice to invisibility and anonymity."[33] The female voice must signify externality and embodiment in order to preserve for masculine speech the exalted status of presence and authority. This is the binary logic that in *The Blithedale Romance* renders the Veiled Lady an object of uncanny fascination and in *The Bostonians* enables Basil Ransom to dismiss Verena Tarrant's speech as pretty noise. Heard within an ideology that associates female speech with embodiedness, Verena's feminist arguments are reduced to the "charming notes" of her voice; violating the logic of this system, the Veiled Lady appears as a "disembodied spirit" who seems to usurp the "invisibility and anonymity" proper to masculine discourse. But if the burden of materiality falls on feminine speech—as the repository of what masculine discourse, in its claim to transcendence, cannot acknowledge—African American women's speech bears the double burden of "race" and gender. Hazel Carby notes the reception that white audiences gave the nineteenth-century African American lecturer and writer Frances E. W. Harper: "because she was so articulate and engaging as a public speaker, audiences concluded that she couldn't possibly be a black woman. Some even speculated that she must be a man, while others reasoned that she was painted to look black."[34] The audience's obsessive interrogation of the black female body, which eclipses Harper's voice and message, is symptomatic of African American women's struggle to be heard in the American public arena. Taking up the matter of black women's speech in *Their Eyes Were Watching God*, Hurston connects Nanny's frustrated desire to "preach a sermon about colored women sittin' on high" with Janie's difficult attempts at public speech. Perhaps most vivid among these is her testimony in the Florida courtroom, when a white audience, intrigued but not entirely sympathetic, "all leaned over to listen while she talked" (278).[35] The white audience's somatic reaction, its physical movement toward the object of fascination, attributes an almost contagious embodiment to blackness and femininity, reducing Janie's testimony to the status of spectacle. Caught in the double bind of this racial and sexual ideology, Janie's voice, like writing, appears as the material trace and inferior copy of the speech celebrated by Western philosophy.

"The Inaudible Voice"

While the notion of an overembodied speech, a speech *as* a form of writing, structures Janie's "racial" identity, a different but equally problematic form of speech marks her place within cultural orders of gender and sexuality. Having described the photograph episode and her social interpellation as a "dark little girl," Janie proceeds to the moment in which, under a blossoming pear tree, she "recognizes" herself not only as female but also as heterosexual. If at the opening of Janie's narrative Hurston underscores a crucial metaphor—"Janie saw her life like a great tree in leaf with things suffered, things enjoyed, things done and undone"—a tree, a pear tree in particular, will become an emblem of Janie's sexual life. As the governing trope of her heterosexual desire, the pear tree presides over Janie's union with Logan Killicks, her remarriage to Jody Starks, and finally her love for Tea Cake Woods. Comparing each of her relationships to this central figure, Janie recalls that she had wanted "things sweet wid mah marriage lak when you sit under a pear tree and think" (43). After she learns that Logan's crude pragmatism cannot realize her dream, she will see Jody's ambition and pretension take "the bloom off of things" (70) before she can welcome Tea Cake as the man who will be "a bee to a blossom—a pear tree blossom in the spring" (161).

Robert Hemenway's widely cited biography of Zora Neale Hurston introduces Hurston's best-known novel with the statement "*Their Eyes Were Watching God* is a love story."[36] Hemenway is not alone in identifying eros as the novel's principal theme. While Richard Wright criticizes *Their Eyes Were Watching God* for a lack of political engagement, manifest in its "romantic" heroine and in

Hurston's language, whose "facile sensuality," in Wright's view, seems to mirror the novel's own "romantic" failing, other critics have approvingly cited Hurston's representation of Janie's search for heterosexual love.[37] As many readers note, that "romantic" plot both issues from, and labors to re-create, Janie's encounter with the blossoming pear tree—a moment that Cheryl Wall and others have called an "organic union."[38] But according to other readers, including some of Hurston's most astute recent critics, the pursuit of heterosexual love is a secondary theme or, as Houston A. Baker Jr. writes, "a deceptively prominent construct" in a novel more pointedly interested in Janie's search for her own identity, her acquisition of the power of speech, and as Baker argues, the economic structures of black middle-class culture.[39] Although I take sexuality to be a fundamental concern of *Their Eyes Were Watching God*, I would want my reading of the text to resonate with the skepticism of those other readings that do not simply accept the marriage plot as its preeminent structure. I want, that is, to examine how the heterosexual love story assumes in Hurston's novel, as in American culture, the seeming inevitability of an "organic" process and the exalted status of nature itself.

Perhaps the most surprising thing about the heterosexual plot in *Their Eyes Were Watching God*, after all, is the tremendous effort required to set it in motion. Staging for Janie the erotic union of bee and blossom, the pear tree is so extravagant a trope, so breathlessly prolonged, and so endlessly repeated throughout the novel that its claims for heterosexual enjoyment may seem, to say the least, overstated. After days of watching the "mystery" of the pear tree's blossoms, whose gradual unfolding suggests her own movement toward adult femininity, Janie is aroused by a vision:

> She was stretched on her back beneath the pear tree soaking in the alto chant of the visiting bees, the gold of the sun and the panting breath of the breeze when the inaudible voice of it all came to her. She saw a dust-bearing bee sink into the sanctum of a bloom; the thousand sister-calyxes arch to meet the love embrace and the ecstatic shiver of the tree from root to tiniest branch creaming in every blossom and frothing with delight. So this was a marriage! (24)

While it dazzles Janie with the "revelation" (24), as Hurston calls it, of her sexuality, this vision also ushers her into "conscious life" (23), marking her accession to subjectivity within the symbolic order of patriarchal culture. Announcing the imperative *to* pair, the pear tree metaphor promotes a sexual union that can only be imagined within the heterosexual register of bees and blossoms—or, as some would say, of birds and bees. The desire inaugurated in this moment and sustained by recurring allusions to the pear tree image is structured by penetration—the bee "sink[ing]" into the blossom—and explicitly named as "marriage."

Presenting desire in heterosexual form, the pear tree figure insists that to be a woman is to be a subject of heterosexual desire. So although Janie protests, "Naw, Nanny, naw Ah ain't no real 'oman yet" at Nanny's insistence that she is just that, she is launched on the seemingly irreversible course toward her marriage to Logan Killicks (26). By prompting Janie to take its fecund "delight" as an image of her own desire, the pear tree passage masks the discursive production of sexual identity as a recognition or "revelation." Janie's enjoyment is rooted not in the "organic"—which could in any case be meaningful only through the discourse of culture—but in social discipline, whose articulation of sexual pleasure creates the experience it comes to describe. The pear tree metaphor constructs female heterosexuality through catachresis, by imposing grammar on enjoyment and giving name to what would otherwise be nameless. Through this figure, Janie *becomes* the blossom, not the bee, and assumes the bodily form required by the heterosexual metaphor: "she had glossy leaves and bursting buds" (25). The assumption of gender proceeds through what Judith Butler has called a "fantasy of literalization or a *literalizing fantasy*," which by inventing bodily sites as the figurative marks of gender vivifies certain pleasures and forecloses others.[40] This fantasy subordinates Janie's inchoate sensations to the decisive figure of bee and blossom, straightening the "circuitous path" of female sexual development into a beeline toward heterosexuality.[41]

Like her realization of her "racial" identity, then, Janie's acceptance of gender proceeds through a form of literalization that is, in a sense, a literalization of form: the social inscription of gender and sexuality on the body. Yet in conjuring Janie's heterosexual desire, the pear tree vision evokes another figure, and with it a somewhat different story of female sexual development. As the pear tree's foliage unfolds, Hurston writes, barrenness yields to budding new growth, and finally to a mature, sexually poised "virginity":

> From barren brown stems to glistening leaf-buds; from the leaf-buds to snowy virginity of bloom. It stirred her tremendously. How? Why? It was like a flute song forgotten in another existence and remembered again. (23)

While its movement from "barren brown stems" to "snowy" blossoms suggests an inverse image of Janie's "racialization" in the photograph passage, its "flute song" evokes another kind of backward movement: the resurrection, however fleeting, of "forgotten" pleasures and cathexes associated with the "other existence" of preoedipality and the mother. In the psychoanalytic account of female sexual development, heterosexuality is a secondary formation, following upon the girl's acceptance of castration, her entrance into the Oedipal stage, and her repudiation of a mother-cathexis. Psychoanalysis often describes lesbianism as a displaced form of mother-love; in "The Psychogenesis of a Case of Homosexuality in a Woman," Freud confirms "beyond all shadow of doubt that the lady-love was a substitute for—her mother."[42] Although the girl's desire for the mother must therefore be erased in her progress toward female heterosexuality and toward the reproduction of culture itself, the mother remains a marker, for Freud, of the alternative, pregenital organization of desire out of and against which female heterosexuality develops and to which it perpetually threatens to return.

A trace of that maternal presence appears in the pear tree's "glistening leaf-buds," a figure for an early stage of female sexual development that also recalls the unusual name of Janie's mother, "Leafy." Having no proper place in *Their Eyes Were Watching God*, Leafy marks the site of something unassimilable but essential to Hurston's heterosexual narrative. Janie's mother is never physically present in the text; as Janie tells Phoeby, "Mah mama . . . was gone from round dere before Ah wuz big enough tuh know" (20). Indeed, Hurston writes, Janie "had no interest in that seldom-seen mother at all" (137). Yet Janie observes that the image of the pear tree "connected itself with other vaguely felt matters that had struck her outside observation and buried themselves in her flesh" (24)—matters that had been "forgotten in another existence and remembered again." There is perhaps no better description of the unconscious than that "buried" site of "vaguely felt matters" whose affective energies remain "outside observation" and unavailable to conscious scrutiny. Interestingly, in her autobiography *Dust Tracks on a Road*, Hurston describes the composition of *Their Eyes Were Watching God* as a kind of burial. Writing after the failure of a love affair with a man, Hurston says, she "tried to embalm all the tenderness of my passion" in the novel itself.[43] However, the delights and disappointments of heterosexuality first require that another kind of love be embalmed. The "buried" figure of the mother in Janie's vision wavers between familiarity and alienation, evoking Freud's notion of the uncanny as an effect reminiscent of "infantile complexes" and the maternal body. The phantom "song" or "inaudible voice of it all" represents for Janie the uncanny effect Freud attributes to "something which is familiar and old-established in the mind and which has become alienated from it only through the process of repression."[44] In *Their Eyes Were Watching God*, this return of the repressed is short-lived: the forgotten "matter" is conjured up only to be cast aside, and the "buried" *mater* is remembered only to be forgotten, summoned only to be transformed into the female heterosexuality that, blossoming from the structure of an earlier love, requires the repudiation of the mother.

Janie hears the "flute song" of the mother's voice as it assumes its own burden, the refrain of patriarchal culture that intones the eternal reproduction of heterosexuality. But the figuration of that maternal presence as voice is significant in a novel so fundamentally concerned with women's speech. The "voice" or "song" that accompanies Janie's "revelation" under the pear tree functions as a switchpoint, an implicit pun, marking the crossing of discursive and sexual senses of orality. While Hurston's discussion of idolatry and signification enables us to see orality as a "racialized" understanding of speech in white Western culture, the "other existence" recalled in the pear tree passage points toward a rather different, though no less "racialized," understanding of orality. In a recurring analogy, Freud compares the teleology of individual development with that of cultural evolution, describing the early, pregenital stages of sexual life as a "primitive" organization of desire, a kind of ancient history. "The

Question of Lay Analysis," for example, famously compares female sexuality to the "dark continent" of Africa: "We know less about the sexual life of little girls than of boys. But we need not feel ashamed of this distinction; after all, the sexual life of adult women is a 'dark continent' for psychology."[45] The construction of adult femininity as "racialized" in Freud's figure of the "dark continent" has been frequently acknowledged; but it is worth noting that in the argument that precedes this passage Freud also equates "darkness" with infantile sexuality. Rehearsing a favorite idea, Freud argues that children's imaginations create "the same product as the imaginative activities of primitive man." Indeed, he continues, "in the mental life of children to-day we can still detect the same archaic factors which were once dominant generally in the primaeval days of human civilization."

Within this historical / sexual metaphor, as Diana Fuss has explained, orality dwells in a "primitive" or "primordial" realm.[46] In *Introductory Lectures on Psycho-Analysis*, Freud names the oral phase as the first, "most primitive" stage of sexuality. As he explains in *Three Essays on the Theory of Sexuality*, it is the "prototype" whose pleasures must be relinquished in the normal course of sexual development.[47] As such, orality becomes associated with the sexual perversions, including both male and female homosexuality, that Freud locates in a "primitive" era of individual and cultural development.[48] Not only did early psychoanalysis and sexology see "primitive" cultures as inclined to homosexual practices, as Fuss has noted, but Freud also places homosexuality or "inversion" in a "prehistoric" epoch of sexual life. Arguing in *Three Essays* that homosexuality is not limited to a clearly bounded group, Freud proposes that both homosexuality and heterosexuality have as their origin the "choice of an object independently of its sex," which exists "in childhood, in primitive states of society and early periods of history." Heterosexuality requires that this object-choice be restricted; but in "inverted types," Freud continues, "a predominance of archaic constitutions and primitive psychical mechanisms is regularly to be found."[49]

Although Freud's account of homosexuality, orality, and the "primitive" remains focused on gay male sexuality, notions of orality and of sexual, if not cultural, prehistory play important roles in his analyses of lesbianism. If, as the figures of repetition and return in

The Sun Also Rises suggest, twentieth-century American sexual ideology deems lesbian desire a disruption of narrative teleology, psychoanalysis too sees lesbianism as a failure of sexual progress—a kind of freak of history. In "A Case of Homosexuality in a Woman," Fuss argues, Freud construes lesbianism as "foundational, as primeval, as primitive" as well as preoedipal and even presexual.[50] In Freud's view, lesbian sexuality's retrograde tendency takes shape notably, though by no means exclusively, in its susceptibility to oral fixations. The Dora case is perhaps the best-known and most evocative instance. Although it connects lesbianism with orality through the nexus of hysteria, the case study stresses the significance of an oral overinvestment manifest in Dora's aphasia and coughing. This oral fixation was predicted, Freud claims, by a history of infantile thumb sucking, which recalls the "prehistoric impression of sucking at the mother's or nurse's breast."[51] In designating Dora's oral pleasures as "prehistoric," Freud links her sexual pathology, only later recognized as lesbian desire, to the "primitive" and the preoedipal. While sexual prehistory and preoedipality *as such* are by no means "lesbian," Freud understands lesbianism as a particular form of displaced preoedipality, an adult female sexuality that seems to reproduce or resuscitate an older form of desire and thus to allude to the imaginary.

Recalling the speech of the Veiled Lady in *The Blithedale Romance*, the disembodied maternal "song" in *Their Eyes Were Watching God* remains an *imaginary* voice, an artifact of preoedipality. The imaginary marks the symbolic order's own "prehistoric" past—the site of a relation to the mother that will be broken by castration, subjectification, and entrance into the symbolic order. Yet the imaginary, like the real, exists only within sociality and language; these notions of what precede symbolization are metaleptic *effects* of the symbolic order that ostensibly follows them. Janie's pear tree vision suggests that female sexuality may itself be structured by this retroactive logic, in which the primordial state of preoedipal mother-love will be "remembered" as an "inaudible voice" or forgotten "song" only from the vantage point of an emergent heterosexuality. If preoedipality and mother-love belong to the imaginary, and if the preoedipal organization of desire is a precondition of adult female heterosexuality, as both Hurston and Freud suggest, then it is only when signs associated with the preoedipal stage appear in the wrong place, within

Oedipality and the symbolic order, that they evoke the traumatic effect of the real. Whereas in *The Blithedale Romance* the eruption of an acousmatic female voice within the symbolic order comes to signify the "morbid" resistance to heterosexual femininity that would, later in the century, be named as lesbian, in *Their Eyes Were Watching God* the disembodied maternal voice is subordinated to the heterosexual narrative. In Hurston's image of the blossoming pear tree, this "forgotten" prehistory forms the necessary precondition of Janie's subjectifying vision and her path toward marriage. But although the image of the blossoming pear tree recurs throughout Janie's tale as a reminder of her heterosexual desire, the "inaudible" voice has its own pervasive effects as a "prehistoric" form of Janie's own oral narrative.

Orality and Lesbianism

Their Eyes Were Watching God presents at least three forms of female speech: the buried trace of a maternal "song," the courtroom speech Janie delivers under the shadow of white law and racist ideology, and Janie's own story, framed by Janie and Phoeby's eroticized speech. Tracing the relations among these oral narratives, Hurston seeks to resist dominant sexual and "racial" discourses and to recuperate orality, in several senses, from the logic that would posit it as "primitive" or abject. To counter racist and misogynist constructions of African American women's speech, the text attempts to move beyond both disembodied and overembodied discourse, incorporating the imaginary, ephemeral voice of the mother into a symbolic and authoritative form of narrative. It does so in the frame story of *Their Eyes Were Watching God*, where Janie's own oral narrative translates the "inaudible voice" under the pear tree into the audible, even tangible, form of speech figured by the phrase "mah tongue is in mah friend's mouf."

In the frame story the dimly recalled "song" that Janie remembers, and as quickly forgets, at the moment of her entrance into heterosexual femininity is transformed into the conversation that makes Janie and Phoeby "kissin'-friends" through reversals of before and after, inside and outside. And in this sense the text's interrogation of "race" is inextricable from its investigation of female sexuality. Revising the relation of "race," gender, and sexuality to representation, Hurston offers her own oral narrative in place of the "unnatural history" of American hegemony, whose worship of whiteness and the phallus depends on the manichean division of ideality and materiality. Resisting this hierarchical organization of ideal and material, speech and writing, interiority and externality, *Their Eyes Were Watching God* acknowledges the incoherence of white, phallic ideology while also documenting the brutal effects of that ideology on communities and individual subjects. One emblem of this effort, analogous to Hurston's treatment of sexuality and narrative form, is the use of free indirect discourse to bring together the divergent modes of speech and writing. As Gates and Johnson have both noted, free indirect discourse unites speech (imagined as pure interiority) and writing (materiality and exteriority) so that their difference is, in Johnson's words, "both transgressed and preserved."[52] If oral traditions are, within the terms of white Western philosophy, forms of speech that resemble writing, free indirect discourse is, conversely, a writing akin to speech. Janie's remark "mah tongue is in mah friend's mouf" thus allegorizes the novel's own language. Not only does it name Phoeby's role as interlocutor between Janie and the community—or, as Janie calls it, "Mouth-Almighty"—but it also suggests the sharing of narrative voice between Janie and other speakers, and between Janie and Hurston herself, the writer who alternately puts words in Janie's mouth and presents herself as amanuensis, recording Janie's oral narrative in the writing that is the novel.[53]

Much as Hurston's use of free indirect discourse joins speech with writing, the narrative structure of *Their Eyes Were Watching God* turns upon a reversal of outside and inside. In Hurston's novel the convention of the frame story and the "interior" narrative it encloses exemplify the textual effect Derrida calls "invagination." As Jonathan Culler explains, "An external frame may function as the most intrinsic element of a work, folding itself in; conversely, what seems the most inner or central aspect of a work will acquire this role through qualities that fold it back outside of and against the work."[54] This folding together of the text's outside and inside describes the infinitely reversible relation of Hurston's frame story and embedded narrative. Acknowledging the obstacles to black female speech while simultaneously calling that speech into being, the novel attempts to fulfill both Nanny's ambition to "preach a sermon" and the promise of Leafy's "inaudible voice." It moves toward the place from which Janie can finally speak, where the "burden" of racism and misogyny is transformed into the fullness of Janie's own narrative—an aim accomplished in Janie's story to Phoeby, and when that story is done, in Hurston's final image of Janie gathering up a "great fish-net" with "so much of life in its meshes" (286). Prior to this the text has taken shape as a kind of search—not only Janie's quest for love or self-expression, but also the story's attempt to create the conditions of its own existence—which, seeking the point of its own beginning, produces a metaleptic reversal of cause and effect.

Mirroring the lesbian sexuality psychoanalytically understood as a history that refuses to remain in the past, Hurston's frame story is no mere container for a more significant narrative, but instead a site where the novel turns inside out. In patriarchal ideology, the preoedipal stage functions as the frame story that precedes and introduces the more central narrative of Oedipal, heterosexual desire and reproduction, a story our culture never tires of retelling. Unlike Hurston's novel, the patriarchal narrative of female sexuality intends never to return to the frame that launched it; instead, it promotes heterosexual relations and motherhood as ends in themselves, perpetually displacing (through the pursuit of substitute objects such as the phallus and the child) the closure of female sexuality's lesbian frame. This distinction between the central and the marginal narrative of femininity, however, can only be fantasmatic. The primary and the secondary story are always invaginated, so to speak, susceptible to exchange and interpenetration, and like feminine preoedipality and Oedipal heterosexuality, impossible to disentangle. In *Their Eyes Were Watching God* the coherence of Janie's heterosexual narrative, moving from Logan Killicks to Joe Starks to Tea Cake, relies on the discursive relation between Janie and Phoeby; and the outer frame story, with its suggestion of a lesbian orality shared by Janie and Phoeby, imbues the embedded heterosexual narrative with less orthodox forms of discourse and enjoyment.

We might say that when orality returns in the frame story, with it returns the lesbian sexuality elsewhere figured by the "forgotten" voice of preoedipal mother-love. But to do so is not fully to acknowledge the imbrication of lesbian eros and heterosexual femininity throughout the text. Readings of *Their Eyes Were Watching God* differ significantly in their assessment of the text's lesbian possibilities. Lorraine Bethel, for example, asserts that the novel is lesbian because "it acknowledges and asserts the validity of primary love relationships between women," while Molly Hite suggests that through "highly sexual" images the heterosexual couple in *Their Eyes Were Watching God* is "replaced by interchangeable versions of the same-sex couple."[55] Carla Kaplan also identifies Janie and Phoeby's relationship as sexual, hinting at the ways in which, for Hurston, discourse is erotic and eros discursive. "Telling her story to Phoeby supplies the erotic fulfillment Janie misunderstands as 'marriage' " and makes Phoeby "the 'bee' to Janie's 'blossom,' " although the meaning of that "revelation," Kaplan argues, is "talk itself, the experience of conversation, the act of storytelling and self-narration."[56] The problem of locating lesbianism in *Their Eyes Were Watching God* does not stem from a lack of lesbian signifiers, either in Janie and Phoeby's conversation or in the pear tree passage. Instead it lies in the text's rejection of an either / or logic. Rather than attempting to adjudicate the relationship between Janie and Phoeby, Hurston describes this love of "kissin'-friends" as a site where femininity and lesbianism fold together, a site that can be neither named simply as lesbian nor purified of lesbian signs. Staging the intersection of orality as speech and orality as a name for certain bodily pleasures, Hurston's novel insists on the interrelations between discourse and sexuality, the figural and the literal, the ideal and the material, the prehistoric and the present, female heterosexuality and lesbian desire. Taking orality as a doubled, recurring theme, Hurston's novel translates an "inaudible voice" into an oral narrative that aspires neither to the status of speech in the white Western tradition nor to the sexual "development" that would abrogate lesbian sexuality. Finally, if *The Bostonians*, noting Verena Tarrant's ability to articulate a "magical voice" by taking "words from her friend's less persuasive lips," imagines lesbian sexuality as a kind of erotic ventriloquism, *Their Eyes Were Watching God* goes far toward explaining, on behalf of a quite different voice, how a word between women can become a kiss.

chapter five

Love's Substitutions
Elizabeth Bishop and the Lie of Language

In *Their Eyes Were Watching God*, Hurston suggests that Janie's entrance into adult femininity, and into a heterosexual erotic economy, requires not only the resonant image of the pear tree but also the stirring of "other vaguely felt matters that had struck her outside observation and buried themselves in her flesh." Such "matters" are, I have argued, the province of the mother, the first love whose loss, for women, constitutes a precondition of femininity. In psychoanalytic terms, the loss of the mother prompts the production of feminine gender identity through the transformation of the girl's desire *for* the mother into identification *with* her.[1] Hurston's text represents this process as a kind of melancholic incorporation that sustains the lost object within the psyche as an encrypted object of identification. "Buried" within Janie, "in her flesh," the absent mother is banished from consciousness to a "forgotten" realm "outside observation," where she is enshrined as the fantasy that motivates Janie's recognition of her femininity and her heterosexual desire. Whereas Janie once longed to *have* her mother, she will now aspire to *be* her. Through identification she will come to resemble that lost object of love by emulating the feminine attributes displaced onto the anthropomorphized pear tree.

While Hurston's pear tree figure thus describes femininity as a melancholic formation, the negotiation of gender and sexuality elsewhere in *Their Eyes Were Watching God* raises further questions. For Janie, after all, the pleasures associated with the mother are neither wholly abolished nor fully converted into identification. That desire persists in Janie's friendship with Phoeby in the form of an oral eroticism that unites symbolic meaning and material body, calling upon both figurative and literal meanings of orality. As an emblem of orality and of a certain same-sex love, the presence of the absent mother pervades the text, a cynosure of both feminine identification and lesbian desire.[2] Imagining in this way a double relation to the mother, Hurston's text asks that we consider the relation of mother-love and loss not only to gender formation but also to lesbian sexuality. It thus returns us to the problem of differentiating between lesbianism and femininity, and by locating this vexed distinction amid the figural operations of the pear tree passage, suggests the structuring role of signification in mediating the relation between "lesbian" and "woman." To pursue these questions of femininity and lesbianism, identification and desire, I want to consider two somewhat later texts that refract issues of lesbianism, femininity, and mourning through the lens of figural language. Elizabeth Bishop's short stories about her early childhood, "The Country Mouse" and "Gwendolyn," examine the meaning of normative femininity by mapping the child Elizabeth's growing awareness of what it means to be a "little girl" within a linguistic system of sexual discipline.[3] Linking the ambiguities of sexuality with questions of language that will by now, no doubt, seem familiar, these texts also represent the love of little girls as something more complex than straight culture likes to acknowledge.

Two versions of the same story, "The Country Mouse" and "Gwendolyn" offer two accounts of the relations among desire, loss, and the substitutive logic of figural language. Taking their place among the many texts in the American literary tradition that define lesbian sexuality in relation to abjected modes of discourse, each elaborates lesbianism *in* and *as* metaphor, transference, and displacement—rhetorical gestures that "The Country Mouse" will name as the "lie" of language. Each is haunted by the loss of the mother and concerned with the diversion of the energy of maternal attachment into other channels of identification and desire. Connecting lesbian love to Elizabeth's multiple and often contradictory ways of addressing the loss of her mother, "The Country Mouse" and "Gwendolyn" invite us to reevaluate the system of psychic processes that the mother serves to anchor. That inquiry, I will argue, has significant consequences for lesbian theory in at least two ways. "The Country Mouse" and "Gwendolyn" ask that we consider lesbian sexuality as inextricable from femininity as such; and insist that we recognize lesbian desire as operating, like all desire, *within* language and linguistic displacements. In this sense Bishop's texts elaborate two of this study's major concerns: first, the problem of defining lesbian particularity with respect to femininity, and second, the notion of lesbianism, both in heterosexual literary and cultural discourses and in recent lesbian criticism, as beyond symbolization, in the place of the unrepresentable real.

In the context of the hegemonic representations of lesbian sexuality examined elsewhere in this book, Bishop's texts may seem somewhat anomalous. Although Bishop herself chose not to identify publicly as lesbian, the knowledge of her lifelong relationships with women inevitably colors readings of her texts, certainly in the context of figures—Hawthorne, James, Chopin, Hemingway, Hurston—who are, to say the least, not commonly regarded as lesbian writers. Bearing the burden of lesbian authorship within the present study, Bishop asks us to consider what that category might mean and what it might *not* mean. If it is all too easy, reading Hawthorne, Hemingway, or Hurston, not to see the traces of lesbian sexuality, it is all too easy, reading Bishop in this context, not to see anything else—not to see, that is, those aspects of Bishop's texts that trouble and exceed notions of "subversive" lesbian authorship. Bishop's texts are, therefore, presented here not as representative of lesbian discourse as such, but instead as accounts of lesbian sexuality, written *both* within and against the sexual mythologies of American culture, that can assist the project of reading those cultural fantasies.

Written around 1961 but published posthumously in 1984, "The Country Mouse" recounts Elizabeth's removal at the age of six from her maternal grandparents' home in Nova Scotia to her paternal grandparents' house in Worcester, Massachusetts. Some time after her mother suffered a "nervous breakdown" and was institutionalized, Bishop writes, her American grandparents arrived in Canada to escort her to the United States. The long trip southward by train marks the beginning of a new life for the child in a household whose every custom seems foreign. But the strangeness of that dislocation also works in the opposite direction, bringing to light the strangeness of everything Elizabeth has taken as normal, including the meaning of her identity as a "little girl." At the beginning of the journey Elizabeth's grandmother, who is herself "very pretty, in a doll-like way," offers Elizabeth a new doll, whose "bright blue eyes" and "pink cheeks" both epitomize feminine charm and, perhaps as a result, render the doll "totally uninteresting" to young Elizabeth. "That seemed to be one of Grandmother's ideas," Bishop writes; "a 'little girl' should carry a doll when she went travelling."[4] As Elizabeth is soon to learn, that "idea" is only one of the rules governing the behavior of the "little girl." The equation of grandmother with doll, and doll with "little girl," is the first intimation that gender consists of an array of signs within a cultural grammar whose interpretation becomes the child's primary task. In her incipient awareness of her gendered place in the world, it is the designation of the "little girl" *as a sign* that most impresses Elizabeth. Her grandmother, Bishop writes, has "such a confusing way of talking":

> She would speak of "grandma" and "little girls" and "fathers" and "being good"—things I had never before considered in the abstract, or rarely in the third person. In particular, there seemed to be much, much more to being a "little girl" than I had realized: the prospect was beginning to depress me. (16)

With the alternately trivial and ominous phrase "being good," the "little girl" is installed in Elizabeth's vocabulary not simply as an idea but as an entry in a kind of foreign phrasebook of gender. Like Hurston, who recounts in "How It Feels to Be Colored Me" her interpellation as a racialized subject—"I was now a little colored girl"—Bishop sees identity, in this case gender identity, as constituted through the retroactive work of naming. But if Bishop's notion of the "little girl" presents gender in quotation marks, it also renders subjectivity, like femininity—or, shall we say, *little-girlness*—"in the third person." Her own little-girlness exists in both the past and the future, as both a disheartening "prospect" and a depressing fait accompli, as a fact Elizabeth "had realized" but whose reality she had not, it seems, fully grasped.[5]

Thrust into a foreign household and into new codes of feminine decorum, Elizabeth must take up the task of interpretation and assume her place within a new world of signs. She regards the bewildering signifier "little girl" much as she does the American national anthem, whose verses her patriotic grandmother makes her learn even though "most of the words made no sense at all" (27). Unable to embody such standards of propriety, Elizabeth identifies instead with her grandparents' nervous, self-punishing Boston terrier—who seems, she notes, "on the same terms in the house" as herself (21). If to be a "little girl" means acceding to a place within language, Elizabeth imagines herself, like the dog Beppo, living outside language. Listening to her grandmother's conversations with neighbors, Bishop writes, she "understood, like Beppo, by tone of voice rather than by words" (23). Elizabeth substitutes the sound of the grandmother's speech for its sense, much as Basil Ransom in *The Bostonians* dwells on Verena's "tone of voice." She acts out her painful bafflement at the linguistic code of "little-girlness" by renouncing "words," with their (unrealized) potential for sense making, and puts acting itself in place of language as a way to signify her inexpressible unhappiness. Shortly after her arrival in Worcester, Elizabeth begins to suffer from eczema and asthma, illnesses that promote her identification with the "hysterical" (21) Beppo during those uncomfortable nights when the two, Bishop writes, "scratched together" (29). Attributing her illnesses to the environmental, if not the psychic, irritants of the new surroundings, Bishop presents Elizabeth herself as a kind of hysteric. Her symptoms literalize on Elizabeth's body her resistance to the role of "little girl" and to the language that would secure her in that role. As Jane Gallop suggests in her reading of the Dora case, hysterical "symptoms are ways of speaking": Elizabeth replaces her words with symptoms.[6]

Although Elizabeth's hysterical illness thus mimics her mother's "hysteria," her undiagnosed mental illness, this identification with the mother serves to undermine gender propriety rather than to secure it. To her grandparents, Bishop tells us, Elizabeth's maternal connection has always implied an improper relation to language and to gender. Removing her from Nova Scotia, her grandparents are determined to rescue her from "a life of poverty and provincialism, bare feet, suet puddings, unsanitary school slates, perhaps even from the inverted *r*'s of [her] mother's family" (17). Among this catalog of class-specific offenses, the "inverted *r*'s" stand out as remarkable, as if the graphological crime were a hereditary trait to which Elizabeth, through her maternal lineage, might be susceptible.[7] The "inverted *r*'s" of her mother's family cannot help but also evoke another kind of backward character. The notion of inversion as a form of desire is pointedly mentioned in Bishop's early poem "Insomnia," where the image of "that world inverted" in a mirror offers a glimpse of a place "where the heavens are shallow as the sea / is now deep, and you love me."[8] "The Country Mouse" takes inversion further, figuring linguistic deviance as a kind of sexual deviance manifest in visible signs of regression. Fulfilling their role as guardians not only of the child but also of the law, the grandparents would prevent Elizabeth from following the maternal line. In a reversal of the psychoanalytic model, to successfully become a "little girl" she must break off her identification with the mother—a bond that, too tightly held, promises an "inverted" relation not merely to the word but also to desire.

School slates and backward letters need not have concerned Elizabeth's grandparents, for in her resistance to little-girlness, Elizabeth has turned against language itself, shunning words in favor of other forms of symbolization. Alone in her bed in Worcester, Bishop writes, "I lay blinking my flashlight off and on, and crying" (31). In that odd gesture of switching the flashlight "off and on," Elizabeth replicates the fort-da game wherein, as Freud writes in *Beyond the Pleasure Principle*, an infant came to terms with his mother's absence by reenacting her departure with a wooden reel on a string. "This, then, was the complete game—disappearance and return," Freud writes.[9] In her own drama of "disappearance and return," Elizabeth attempts to establish some measure of control over her mother's loss by representing her absence and presence in the flickering of the flashlight. As Samuel Weber has noted, Freud's account of the fort-da game is a kind of origin myth of symbolization that explains how the experience of loss, specifically the loss of the mother as primal love-object, prompts the subject's entrance into the order of metaphoric substitution. Bishop's anecdote describes part but not all of this narrative. Elizabeth participates in a kind of symbolization, using what Weber calls the "language of things," but she refuses verbal language, the language of signifiers.[10] The child in Freud's account accompanies his manipulation of the wooden reel with sounds, the "o-o-o-o" and "da" that Freud interprets as meaning *fort* and *da*, "gone" and "there." Elizabeth signifies her abandonment through such bodily signs as her tears, and through such symbolic objects as the flashlight and its flickering beam. If part of the text's project, then, is hermeneutic, chronicling Elizabeth's gradual mastery of interpretation in her new surroundings, its other impetus is linguistic, tracing Elizabeth's attempts to represent the loss of her mother in the language of words as well as things. But in order to explain how both projects reach fruition at the conclusion of "The Country Mouse"—in what Bishop adduces as the story of her "first lie" and the intimation of a "great truth"—we must first briefly consider what is at stake for Bishop and her readers in the rhetoric of truth and falsehood.

True Lies

Writing to Robert Lowell in 1962, Elizabeth Bishop described her fidelity to truth as "my George-Washington-handicap": "I can't tell a lie even for art, apparently; it takes an awful effort or a sudden jolt to make me alter facts."[11] In public remarks throughout her writing life Bishop insisted on the veracity and accuracy of her poems, appealing to the certainties of "truth."[12] The discourse of truth telling recurs in critical readings of Bishop's life and work, which at the risk of making a fetish of truthfulness seek to evaluate Bishop's relation to empirical and experiential "facts." While recent readings of Bishop's work have largely abandoned the prevailing themes of earlier criticism, praise of the poet's keen eye and genius for minute detail, notions of mimetic accuracy remain a central concern. In a survey of Bishop's years in Brazil, for example, Lorrie Goldensohn terms Bishop "the ultimate realist" but deplores her reluctance to represent the autobiographical.[13] Reversing these terms, Joanne Feit

Diehl compares Moore's somewhat prudish evasions with Bishop's more active engagement.[14] And after suggesting that Bishop's poems disavow "camera-like mastery," Bonnie Costello goes on to assert that the poet "invents a rhetoric of exact recall."[15] It comes as no surprise that such assessments of Bishop's engagement with—or as they more often conclude, her evasion of—the "realities" of her experience are most intricately knotted around questions of sexuality.

"Experience," the "personal," and "the real," to borrow Goldensohn's terms, have assumed a prominent role in discussions of Bishop as a lesbian author. For Goldensohn, the fact of the matter lies in the "particular experience" of the poet, which, she argues, Bishop's poems simultaneously represent and occlude. Her reading of the poem "Crusoe in England," for example, enjoins us to recognize the "subterranean desire of the 'real' shadow speaker" and in so doing, to imagine a subject and a sexuality grounded in "real," lived experience.[16] Locating Bishop's sexuality not *within* language but *beneath* the surface of discourse, this approach not only names lesbianism as essential, "subterranean," reality but also, like *The Blithedale Romance* and *The Bostonians*, locates lesbian reality outside symbolic structures. The relation of lesbianism to truth and falsehood, of course, has a history of its own. When Havelock Ellis describes the problem of distinguishing the "true invert" from other women's "spurious imitation" of lesbianism, his effort to establish a diagnostic rubric for the condition of inversion not only posits lesbianism as a copy or repetition but also locates lesbian desire in the epistemological realm of truth and falsehood ("imitation").[17] Ellis adopts the goal of classification that characterized nineteenth-century medical taxonomy, but his notion of truth is ultimately as murky as the desire toward which his diagnostic efforts are bent. Even if, as Goldensohn argues, lesbian desire were to constitute the truth of Bishop's "particular experience," it is by no means clear what constitutes the truth of lesbian sexuality. Bishop offers a useful caution in her letter to Lowell, where, having asserted that she "can't tell a lie even for art," she continues, "sometimes I think I'm telling the truth when I'm not." Even the truth, Bishop suggests, can be a lie; as Diehl observes, " 'fidelity' or 'truthfulness' may itself, of course, contain an element of self-deception"—certainly, as Freud has shown, where sexuality is concerned.[18]

This much, however, is certain: the rhetoric of truth and lying in Bishop's writing provides a fundamental way of understanding desire. For Bishop the question of sexuality is always a question of language, located in the same metaphoric register as Bishop's self-description under the unlikely name of "George Washington." Desire, for Bishop, depends on a representational logic that inexorably returns the speaker to a slippage of meaning—what Bishop calls a "lie"—even, or perhaps especially, in those moments when, as Bishop puts it, she thinks she is telling the truth. In "The Country Mouse," Bishop's meditation on her status as a "little girl" concludes with three anecdotes that summarize the child's efforts of interpretation, among them the story of her "first lie." "Three great truths came home to me during this stretch of my life," Bishop writes. One "truth" reveals social and economic class differences in and around the Worcester household, another visits the scene of terrifying self-consciousness also described in the poem "In the Waiting Room," and another, placed first among the anecdotes, concerns loss, lesbian desire, and a form of language named as "lying."

This "great truth" emerges from a conversation in which Elizabeth's young friend Emma asks her about her parents. Elizabeth explains that her father is dead, but has difficulty accounting for her mother, who is, Bishop notes, "in a sanatorium, in another prolonged 'nervous breakdown.' "[19]

> What about my mother? I thought for a moment and then I said in a *sentimental* voice: "She went away and left me . . . She died, too." Emma was impressed and sympathetic, and I loathed myself. It was the first time I had lied deliberately and consciously, and the first time I was aware of falsity and the great power of sentimentality—although I didn't know the word. (31–32)

Meditating on her lie, Bishop adds,

> I didn't know then, and still don't, whether it was from shame I lied, or from a hideous craving for sympathy, playing up my sad romantic plight. But the feeling of self-distaste, whatever it came from, was only too real. I jumped up, to get away from my monstrous self that I could not keep from lying.

While candor is no doubt an admirable virtue, there is more at stake here than moral lessons.[20] The lie appears as another fort-da game, like Elizabeth's gesture of switching the flashlight "off and on." This attempt to address the problem of her mother's absence, however, replaces the language of objects with verbalization. Laboring to understand how the mother can be dead *to her* and still living in the world, Elizabeth puts her mother's death and life in place of the infant's *fort* and *da*, "gone" and "there": "She went away and left me . . . She died, too."

More striking than the fact of the lie, however, is the enormous rhetorical energy this text directs toward its repudiation and toward the creation of a "monstrous" self as an object of disavowal. Elizabeth's somatic response to her lie and its consequences—"I jumped up"—echoes the "awful effort" and "sudden jolt" that in the letter to Lowell Bishop associates with choosing to "alter facts." Like that letter, "The Country Mouse" locates the source of the lie simultaneously inside and outside the subject, who exerts an "awful effort" but also suffers, as if passively, a "sudden jolt." The lie divides the subject, making Elizabeth wish she could "get away from my monstrous self that I could not keep from lying." The lie carries so phobic a charge that Elizabeth, we are asked to believe, finds herself loathsome, distasteful, "hideous," and "monstrous"—a rhetoric of abjection sufficiently overwrought to merit the charge of lying, if not melodrama. Surely Elizabeth's "self-distaste" responds in part to the moral injunction against lying and in part to the superstitious energy attached to the child's fantasy of her mother's death; but this self-loathing also echoes the language of a specifically homophobic abjection. It is not necessary to argue that the scene between the six-year-old Elizabeth and her friend Emma is "erotic" in order to hear in these lines the intimation of lesbian sexuality, though it is also not impossible to recognize, in Elizabeth's attempt to disavow her "hideous craving," the reverberations of an erotic excitement turned against itself. It is enough that this passage describes the young girl's transference of a libidinal energy originally devoted to the mother onto another female object. Describing the failure of the normative Oedipal transference onto the father (or his substitute), Freud suggests that lesbianism is a displacement of a primal love for the mother. And if the persistence of an elusive mother-love, "shadowy and almost impossible to revivify," obstructs the girl's Oedipal transference from mother to father, Elizabeth's lie enacts a *lesbian* transference, a displacement of the maternal attachment onto her female friend.[21]

Bishop locates lesbian love at the very moment when loss enters language, presenting the child's lie as a return to symbolization amid a violent struggle to transform melancholic identification into transferential desire. The scene of Elizabeth's "first lie," that is, evokes both the metaphoric structures of mourning and the inward-turning aggression of melancholia. Elizabeth's intense self-loathing and split subjectivity recall Freud's account of melancholia as a formation in which "one part of the ego sets itself over against the other, judges it critically, and, as it were, takes it as its object." The melancholic's "reproaches against a loved object which have been shifted away from it onto the patient's own ego" are replicated in Elizabeth's "self-distaste." Bearing the hallmarks of melancholic "feelings of shame," Bishop's account of the lie produces a recriminatory rhetoric of its own, tracing the shame of her dissimulation to the shame of her mother's illness.[22] Indeed, Elizabeth's self-loathing about her lie replicates the lie's aggressive impulse, which by "killing" the mother exacts a kind of revenge for her abandonment. The fantasy of the mother's death frees the child to pursue other objects of desire even as it more firmly enshrines the mother as the primal lost object that every other love will only impersonate. Yet in this sense the lie also functions within the register of mourning. While melancholia is anti-metaphorical or literalizing, mourning is essentially metaphorical, adhering to the substitutive logic of desire and of language. Elizabeth strives to overcome the mother's loss by naming it as absolute, by weaving a fantasmatic narrative in which "she died, too." Having turned away from words toward the language of things, Elizabeth now seeks to express her grief in language. The lie works to acknowledge Elizabeth's loss through a misrepresentation; and it sacrifices the mother on the altar of another object of desire, the all too easily "impressed" Emma. Designating the mother as lost, Elizabeth's lie not only opens up the possibility of metaphoric substitution (of Emma for the mother) along the axis of desire, but also *enacts* metaphor by simultaneously naming and misnaming the mother's fate.

The movement of the story is thus toward the reassertion of figural language over more recalcitrant, compromised modes of symbolization such as hysterical symptoms and symbolic objects.[23] If in *Their Eyes Were Watching God* the lost mother enables a melancholic assumption of femininity, in Bishop's scene of the "first lie" mourning seems to challenge, then supersede, melancholia as a strategy for the mediation of loss. Lesbian desire emerges in a liminal moment; the transference of maternal attachment to another female object is located in the conflict between mourning and melancholia. By showing mourning and melancholia as overlapping, if separate, mechanisms, Bishop invites us to reconsider the psychoanalytic framing of their relation, and the relation, as well, between lesbianism and femininity. Although he notes the many ways their paths converge, Freud presents mourning and melancholia as alternative responses to loss. This distinction is stressed in the either / or formulation of Abraham and Torok's title: "Mourning *or* Melancholia: Introjection *versus* Incorporation." If femininity requires a melancholic identification with the mother and lesbianism describes the displacement of mother-love onto other female objects, the notion of melancholia and mourning as separate and antithetical alternatives would seem to divide lesbianism from femininity.[24] It would then be true, to invoke Monique Wittig's famous phrase, that "lesbians are not women."[25] For Bishop, however, mourning and melancholia seem not to be mutually exclusive. Instead, Elizabeth's double relation to her mother's loss locates lesbianism *at the site of* their meeting. Horrified into self-loathing by her lie, but accomplishing through that lie the transference of her desire from the mother to Emma, Elizabeth exemplifies a subject who is at once "woman" and "lesbian"—or, more precisely, a "little girl" for whom the "little girl," no less than the mother, becomes in this moment an object of both identification and desire.

The Lie of Language

There is another psychoanalytic sense in which Elizabeth's "first lie" connects the problem of lesbian specificity with that of metaphoric language. In "The Psychogenesis of a Case of Homosexuality in a Woman" Freud takes up questions of lesbian desire and lying language in remarkably similar ways. Reframing Ellis's ontological inquiry into "true" lesbianism in psychoanalytic terms, Freud turns his attention to a young "girl" who is in love with an older "lady." Although the girl cooperates in allowing Freud mastery of the first stage of analysis, her stubborn attachment to homosexual objects of desire causes Freud to break off both the treatment and his own study of lesbianism before their completion. Despite Ernest Jones's claim that in this case "both Freud and the patient obtained a clear insight into the essential nature and genesis of her condition," Freud's conclusions are less than clear.[26] The case study conceived under the aegis of psychoanalytic research is in fact a story of its failure—the failure both of the interpretive strategies of psychoanalysis and of interpretation itself. In its struggle with the problem of lesbian specificity, Freud's own account displays the "gaps" and slippage of meaning he will associate with lesbian desire, whose constitutive qualities can be defined only through negation and fields of ontological uncertainty. The case study posits female homosexuality as utterly perverse and absolutely normal: the girl, who is "not in any way ill," nonetheless can be classed among those who "fall a victim to homosexuality" (150, 168). Her deviance is located neither in interiorized psychic formations nor on the surface of the sexed body, explained neither by inheritance nor by experience.

Lesbian sexuality is thus defined as a resistance to definition that obstructs efforts to produce it *as* meaningful. Such a resistance is explained, for Freud, by the relationship of homosexuality to dissimulation: the "secret plan" of the homosexual, he writes, is "the striking failure of [the psychoanalytic] attempt" (151). During her analysis, the girl produces a series of dreams that prove "false or hypocritical" although they can be "easily translated with certainty" (165). These dreams express a desire for heterosexual normalcy but ultimately reveal only the stubbornness of the girl's homosexual investments. Their meaning too eagerly anticipated and too easily grasped, the false dreams testify at once to her deviance and to her normalcy. The lie both characterizes the utterance of the lesbian and signals the imbrication of lesbianism with the lying nature of femininity, for in patriarchal ideology duplicity not only *belongs to* women but also *constitutes* "woman" as such. Joan Riviere's well-known discussion of femininity as masquerade posits "womanliness as a mask, behind which man suspects some hidden danger."[27] Citing Nietzsche's remark on feminine duplicity—"her great art is the lie"—Stephen

Heath suggests that if, for Riviere, the woman's "lie," her representation of "woman," is her gender then "femininity is representation."[28] As in "The Country Mouse," in Heath's reading the notion of the lie stands for the troubling, figural aspect of signification that is aligned with feminine duplicity.[29] At stake in the production of the lesbian as distinct from the woman, therefore, is an effect of difference that reifies lesbian figures as the abject, duplicitous, "lying" side of femininity. Within a patriarchal ideology that defines "normal" femininity as perverse, lesbianism becomes an *emblem* of femininity—that is, of an ostensibly feminine corruption—without being identical to it. And like Ellis's notion of femininity as prone to the "spurious imitation" of lesbianism, or Dr. Mandelet's struggle, in *The Awakening*, to distinguish between the exemplary woman and the exceptional one, Freud's diagnosis in this case fails to distinguish between the "very peculiar" creature that is woman and the peculiar circumstances of homosexual desire.

To complicate this definitional impasse between "woman" and "lesbian," it is the very banality of the lesbian analysand's "lying dreams" that makes them remarkable. The lie that typifies a specifically lesbian pathology in the case study also exemplifies the workings of the unconscious as such. Though Freud points out that his analysand's lying dreams are not actually the unconscious, but rather representations of it (165), Lacan suggests that the unconscious can also lie. Indeed, insofar as it is structured like a language, the unconscious may *only* lie.[30] Returning to "A Case of Homosexuality in a Woman" in "Of the Subject of Certainty," Lacan addresses Freud's notion that "the unconscious may operate in the direction of deception." He asks, "how could there not be truth about lying—that truth which makes it perfectly possible, contrary to the supposed paradox, to declare, *I am lying*?"[31] For Lacan, the very effect of subjectivity, the ability to say "I am," rests on a kind of lie, a denial of the fact that subjectivity is compromised by the very language that constitutes it. To put this in somewhat different terms, the lesbian's "lying dreams" in Freud's case study enact what Paul de Man calls "the exemplary 'lie' of language." Only through a "false literalism," de Man suggests, can we forget "the rhetorical, symbolic quality of all language"—as we do at our own peril when we deny the metaphorical status of the subject.[32] Even the assertion that the subject is a lie, a mere figure, as de Man points out, can only replicate a doomed attempt to posit a truth of subjectivity. Confronting lesbian duplicity and metaphoric displacement, then, "A Case of Homosexuality in a Woman" construes lesbian desire as the abject face of representation, as the aspect of discourse that resists the certainties of scientific meaning. The psychoanalytic attempt to represent lesbian desire finally installs the lesbian in the place of representation, or more accurately, of figural language, where figural language becomes a token of the endless displacements of signification.

If for Bishop the child's "first lie" unveils a "great truth," it is perhaps because, as Lacan writes, there is always a certain "truth about lying." And there is always a certain lying about truth. Bishop's categorical insistence on truth telling—her claim that "I can't tell a lie"—hints at the interchangeability of truth and deception. Lacan's pronouncement that "a letter always arrives at its destination," that is, can be summarized in Bishop's only slightly more cautious words from an earlier letter to Lowell, which meditates on "that desire to get things straight and tell the truth."[33] Foregrounding the desire for truth, if not the truth of desire, this remark seems dedicated to an effort to "get things straight" that can only have a straightening effect. Bishop, however, concludes, "it's almost impossible not to tell the truth in poetry, I think." As a common instance of figural language, poetry exemplifies the circular movement of a chain of signifiers that, like the circuitous "maze" of transferential desire in *The Awakening*, never comes to rest in the truth of referentiality, making the "lying" substitution of sign for sign the only truth we can know.

It is thus appropriate that "The Country Mouse" links lying with a specifically literary form of "monstrous" figural language. Her lie about her mother, Bishop writes, was "the first time I was aware of falsity and the great power of sentimentality." Sentimentality is not, strictly speaking, synonymous with "falsity," but in both modernism and twentieth-century American popular culture that definition frequently passes as common knowledge. According to Wallace Stevens, sentimentality is "a failure of feeling."[34] If nineteenth-century rhetoric sees sentimentality as a kind of *excess* of feeling, twentieth-century readers regard sentimentality as a "failure" to precisely the extent that it can be construed as *false* feeling. In the absence of any authentic response, sentimentality fills up the space of "feeling" with unearned or vicarious emotion. This understanding of sentimentality as a kind of figural substitution or imposture becomes a hallmark of a male modernist aesthetic, which, as in Hemingway's writing, associates sentimentality with the vicariousness of figural language as such.[35] For twentieth-century readers like Hemingway, Stevens, and Bishop herself, sentimentality also alludes to the feminine tradition of the Victorian sentimental novel. As Jane Tompkins notes, the dominant twentieth-century views of sentimental fiction "equate popularity with debasement, emotionality with ineffectiveness, religiosity with fakery, domesticity with triviality, and all of these, implicitly, with womanly inferiority."[36] Hemingway's writing is exemplary in decrying those literary styles that, like inferior bullfighters, produce a "fake emotional feeling" without actual risk. In the context of this tradition, Bishop's disavowal of sentimentality goes hand in hand with her insistence on truthfulness—for, while her style could hardly be called Hemingwayesque, it relies on the masculine craft of the "true sentence," not the feminine exercise of sentimentality, for its claims to literary authority.[37] Equating sentimentality with "falsity" in "The Country Mouse," Bishop relegates a part of her maternal literary heritage, nineteenth-century American women's writing, to *the place of* the mother. Like Elizabeth's own mother, that is, sentimentality will be declared "dead," but that repudiation merely repositions sentimentality—which, as Tompkins notes, finds its deepest pathos in tales of "salvation through motherly love"—as a discourse that haunts the writer as the lost mother haunts the child.[38]

What Are Little Girls Made Of?

To go further we must go back in Bishop's prose to another short story, "Gwendolyn," which prefigures the questions of desire, identification, and language raised in "The Country Mouse."[39] Published in 1953, this tale of little girls offers scenes from an earlier moment in Bishop's Nova Scotia childhood and fixes Elizabeth's prior ideas of little-girlness in the vocabulary of cultural meaning. Engaged with issues of mourning, desire, and the circulation of figural language, "Gwendolyn" connects gender to sexuality and charts the affiliations between sexual and metaphoric displacement.[40] Like "The Country Mouse," "Gwendolyn" is a story of little girls and their dolls, although "Gwendolyn" goes further in exploring the consequences of the identifications—and the dizzying series of analogies—among them. As the story begins, an ailing Elizabeth delightedly discovers her aunt's fragile, drooping "girl doll," whose loose joints and costume, we are told, "went very well with the doll's personality, which in turn was well suited to the role of companion to an invalid" (214). "When you held her up," Bishop recalls, "her head fell gently to one side, and her outstretched hand would rest on yours for a moment and then slip wearily off" (214). The doll thus becomes a tiny version of Elizabeth herself, but Elizabeth is not the invalid with whom the narrative is most concerned. That honor belongs to the lovely, spoiled Gwendolyn, who seems the true living embodiment of the mesmerizing doll.

Taking up that iconic theme in American literature, the death of a little girl, Bishop presents her eponymous "beautiful heroine" as a pale and "delicate" diabetic who survives only long enough to befriend Elizabeth and earn her adoration. If in "The Country Mouse" Elizabeth will feel that there is "much, much more to being a 'little girl' than I had realized," here Gwendolyn Appletree provides her with an exquisite model of feminine perfection:

> to me she stood for everything that the slightly repellent but fascinating words "little girl" should mean. In the first place, her beautiful name. Its dactyl trisyllables could have gone on forever as far as I was concerned. (216)

How appropriate that the question of little-girlness, which Bishop pointedly identifies in "The Country Mouse" as a *linguistic* problem, should here be embodied by a little girl who is herself, above all, a gorgeous *name*—as if her material form, though not without its own magnetism for Elizabeth, were the conduit, the grammatical conjunction, between the abstraction of "little girl" and the mathematical elegance of prosody. For Elizabeth, Gwendolyn "played the role of beautiful heroine" like a theatrical part that "grew and grew until finally it had grown far beyond the slight but convincing talents she had for acting it" (217–18). Still, Gwendolyn's resemblance to the heroines of fiction can hardly be accidental. "Delicate," blonde, dressed in white, she was, Bishop writes, "pink and white, exactly like a blossoming apple tree" (216)—and exactly, in more literary terms, like Stowe's Little Eva, who in her "perfection of childish beauty" reminds Tom of "one of the angels stepped out of his New Testament."[41]

Such perfection has its uses. For Elizabeth both the intriguing "girl doll" and the doll-like Gwendolyn open up identificatory possibilities, becoming not only external models of successful little-girlness, but also internalized objects imbued with meaning. In the world of little girls, of course, the doll is a paradigmatic example of identification and its cultural consequences. As a token of what is to come, a baby doll encourages the little girl to identify with the maternal role, which she will eventually assume, so the conventional wisdom goes, all the more effortlessly for having practiced it so long.[42] Bishop is concerned with another sort of doll, however, which invites the child to perfect her role *as* little girl by modeling herself on its feminine example. As such, the identifications anchored by both the doll and Gwendolyn herself might seem to have a wholly conservative function. But as Diana Fuss has explained, identifications are by no means purely benign; instead, founded on ambivalence, identification implies a kind of violence, not least when it approaches its supposed opposite, desire.[43]

Elizabeth's relationship with Gwendolyn is no exception. Believing that her friend's illness is caused by "too much sugar," Elizabeth envisions Gwendolyn's sweetness in newly concrete terms:

> that in itself made Gwendolyn more attractive, as if she would prove to be solid candy if you bit her, and her pure-tinted complexion would taste exactly like the icing-sugar Easter eggs or birthday candle holders, held to be inedible, except that I knew better. (216)

Smitten as she is with the charms of this terribly conventional little girl, Elizabeth is quick to disregard conventional wisdom when it stands in the way of an enjoyment deemed impossible or unhealthy. She recognizes her attraction to Gwendolyn as somehow like other proscribed behaviors, although neither the prohibition of cannibalism nor the milder injunction against "inedible" Easter eggs and birthday candle holders seems to trouble her excessively. Combining a shy admiration of her friend's virtues with a more aggressive fantasy of incorporation, Elizabeth's question of what would happen "if you bit her" literalizes Freud's notion of melancholic identification as the interiorization of the loved object.[44] Her relation to Gwendolyn in this orally organized fantasy seems to conjure a shade of the lost mother, even if, since Gwendolyn is not yet lost to her, that relation cannot be properly melancholic. Indeed, this persistent vestige of melancholia appears through the substitutive logic characteristic of mourning: Elizabeth takes her friend in place of the mother. That paradoxical relation of mourning and melancholia is not incidental to the structure of Bishop's text, for "Gwendolyn" is a story *about* mourning—about the substitution of one object for another—which *as* a story is melancholic, unable to name or acknowledge the mother's loss.

Although her candy-colored beauty appeals to Elizabeth's hungry imagination, Gwendolyn's sweetness is not, as it turns out, for all tastes. Her angelic femininity is wedded to images of filth and waste, Bishop explains; when Elizabeth and Gwendolyn spend a day together,

> Our play was not without a touch of rustic corruption . . . I can't remember what happened, if anything, but I do remember being ordered out of the whitewashed privy in the barn after we had locked ourselves in and climbed on the seats and hung out the little window. (220)

The notion of the privy as an indecorous site is no novelty to Bishop, whom Marianne Moore once chastised for the vulgar language in her poem "Roosters." In a 1940 letter Moore repeated her objection to the poem's distasteful terms, then added, "I think it is to your credit, Elizabeth, that when I say you are not to say 'water-closet,' you go on saying it a little."[45] If, reading "Gwendolyn," we recall the "dropping-splattered floor" of the outhouse in "Roosters," the scatological crudeness of the privy gives the lie to Gwendolyn's radiant sweetness, showing, as if we did not know already, the angelic little girl as somewhat less than divine. Unlike Stowe's Little Eva— the vision "always dressed in white" who "seemed to move like a shadow through all sorts of places, without contracting spot or stain"—Gwendolyn retains the stain of her outhouse adventure.[46] Like the "whitewashed" privy, she is a thing of contradictions, a combination of dazzling whiteness with the suggestion of filth and "corruption."

One might ask what exactly the girls *did* in the privy—a question that Bishop's claim "I can't remember what happened, if anything" both invites and renders inordinately intriguing. That effect of amnesia recurs throughout "Gwendolyn," always associated with some nameless "corruption," some offense against the codes of proper little-girlness. Gwendolyn seems to produce in Elizabeth an epistemological panic, a lapse of memory regarding what she has heard and seen.[47] This crisis erupts again when, after the outhouse incident, Gwendolyn has been invited to spend the night: "Gwendolyn was going to sleep in my bed with me. I was so overwrought with the novelty of this that it took me a long time to get ready for bed" (220). And when she is preparing for bed, Elizabeth hears her friend remark that she is going to die. "At least," Bishop continues, "that was what I thought she said. I couldn't quite believe I had really heard her say it and I certainly couldn't ask her if she had said it." Her "heart pounding," Elizabeth says her prayers, but "the pounding went on and on" (220) until the surprise of Gwendolyn's remark is followed by another. Picking up her friend's clothes from the floor, Elizabeth notices that "her drawers had lace around the legs, but they were very dirty. This fact shocked me so deeply that I recovered my voice and started asking her more questions" (220).

No doubt the bedroom incident owes its "shock" in large part to Elizabeth's recognition of death as more than a romantic possibility. But the pressure of materiality also bears on Elizabeth's fantasy of Gwendolyn in the knowledge gained in the privy and the bedroom— the knowledge of a sweetness now inextricably connected to "dirt." In a sense the privy and the dirty drawers enact a return of the repressed, asserting what must be excluded and denied in the fantasy of Gwendolyn's edible sweetness. Yet for Elizabeth that "corruption" seems no less compelling than Gwendolyn's feminine charms, producing an adrenaline "shock" of both terror and excitement. After Freud, of course, we know better than to imagine children as outside the forces of sexuality. In psychoanalytic writing (and in grade-school girls' culture, where traces of romantic friendship still linger), an immature same-sex love may be tolerated, if not wholly approved, provided that these attachments will later yield to heterosexual cathexes. As Freud notes in "A Case of Homosexuality in a Woman," the notion of lesbianism as the prehistory of femininity also hints at the potential failure of this developmental narrative and the disintegration of the fragile boundary between lesbianism and feminine heterosexuality. So if Gwendolyn represents, for Elizabeth, all that the proper " 'little girl' should mean" (216), she seems at the same time to stand for something else. Like Gwendolyn herself, the girls' relationship is poised on the boundary between the normal and the perverse, between delicacy and filth, between identification and desire, between the cloying sweetness of childish devotion and Elizabeth's *frisson* of horror and curiosity.

The Missed Encounter

While Elizabeth's intimacy with Gwendolyn may seem a "novelty," therefore, it is a novelty with a certain history. Like "The Country Mouse," "Gwendolyn" raises the question of lesbian attachment in the failure of Elizabeth's Oedipal transference onto a father figure and the displacement of a mother-love onto feminine objects instead. Reading "The Country Mouse" underscores the importance of the mother, in "Gwendolyn," as the original object of both desire and mourning. If in "Gwendolyn," the girl who takes the place of the mother for Elizabeth must, like the mother, be lost, Bishop's story of her death can be understood as another lie about her mother's death, another fiction that appeals to the displacements of language to accomplish the work of mourning.

In that substitutive process, Gwendolyn is above all a *signifier*, and her death produces for Elizabeth a crisis in signification, manifest in a vision that seems, even in its utter clarity, to be excessive, unreal, and "impossible." After Gwendolyn's death, Elizabeth observes the preparations for her funeral, as the church bell tolls across the village green: "I wasn't even supposed to know what was taking place, but . . . I knew quite well, and my heart began to pound again, apparently as loudly as the bell was ringing" (221). Creeping into the front parlor, Elizabeth stares across the field at the church through the curtains: "I had a perfectly clear, although lace-patterned, view of everything" (222). Veiled by curtains, that vantage point presents

Elizabeth Bishop and the Lie of Language 137

Elizabeth with a "perfectly clear" but absolutely mysterious vision of another kind of veiling or occlusion. This "impossibility," as Bishop calls it, is a bizarre image of Gwendolyn's coffin:

> Two men in black appeared again, carrying Gwendolyn's small white coffin between them. Then—this was the impossibility—they put it down just outside the church door, one end on the grass and the other lifted up a little, to lean at a slight angle against the wall. Then they disappeared inside again. For a minute, I stared straight through my lace curtain at Gwendolyn's coffin, with Gwendolyn shut invisibly inside it forever, there, completely alone on the grass by the church door. (22–4)

The abandoned coffin or unburied corpse recalls not only the phobic tropes of lesbian morbidity, but also, as something "left over" and out of place, the site of lesbian sexuality in the narrative of straight culture. The identification that forms a precondition of Oedipal heterosexuality itself requires the girl to bury her desire for the mother, then represses the "morbidity" of its own development.

In "Gwendolyn," Elizabeth's loss of Gwendolyn mimics her loss of her mother in "The Country Mouse," as the girl suffers, then overcomes, a traumatic blockage of symbolization to reenter the world of language. In the funeral scene, Elizabeth's appalling vision seems to defy interpretation and momentarily to arrest the movement of signification. Bishop's image of Gwendolyn "shut invisibly inside" her coffin literalizes the logic of melancholic identification and renders Gwendolyn, like the mother, a ghostly presence "shut invisibly inside" Elizabeth herself. Installing the lost object in an "imaginary crypt" or "secret tomb," Abraham and Torok explain, incorporation implies the *annulment of figurative language*."[48] Yet the "impossible," inexplicable sight in the churchyard also prompts Elizabeth to efforts of interpretation. As Bishop writes, it is "Something that could not possibly have happened, so that I must, in reality, have seen something like it and imagined the rest; or my concentration on the one thing was so intense that I could see nothing else" (223). The three alternatives designate three ways of reading: the scene may be simply untrue, a lie outright ("something that could not possibly have happened"); or it may be a lie of language, either a displacement ("I must . . . have seen something like it") or condensation ("my concentration on the one thing was so intense") of what actually occurred in the churchyard. If its apparent power to disable signification brings Elizabeth's vision into alignment with melancholic incorporation, however, its simultaneous ability to *inspire* interpretation recalls another figure for the failure of representation. Both an uncanny object and the space of a terrible absence, the "impossible" vision of Gwendolyn's coffin produces the effect that Žižek calls the *"answer of the real,"* holding out the promise of a yet-to-be-deciphered meaning.[49]

As a figure for the real, Elizabeth's vision leads us back to questions of lesbian representation. If, as I have argued, Western patriarchal ideology phobically presents lesbianism as a figure for the real, as *like* the real in its apparent resistance to interpretation and meaning, it is curious that this same notion should have gained the aura of "subversive" insight in recent lesbian criticism. A number of arguments have explicitly or implicitly claimed lesbianism as the real—understood as that which rejects or escapes the symbolic order of patriarchal culture. In an essay that brings Lacanian and Žižekian insights to bear on Bishop's work, David R. Jarraway suggests that "Bishop's implicitly lesbian subjectivity becomes possible only as a function of a real that eludes symbolic articulation within reality's dark holes."[50] This articulation of lesbian sexuality via the inarticulate real, Jarraway argues, carries political force in the form of a "transgressive and empowered subjectivity—a spectral lesbian identity."[51] Borrowing the trope of ghostly, "spectral" lesbian sexuality from Terry Castle's *The Apparitional Lesbian*, Jarraway also revivifies—albeit in quite different theoretical terms—the central premise of that text's "Polemical Introduction." Castle's introduction, finding its polemical impetus under the banner of lesbian "presence," seeks to vindicate "real," "embodied" lesbians against the discursive regimes that relegate lesbian sexuality to apparitional status. Lesbian sexuality, Castle writes, is not only "vaporized by the force of heterosexual propriety" but also threatened by the "murderous allegorizing" of patriarchal discourse—and implicitly by the possibility that allegory may itself be nothing other than murderous.[52] Like those readings that seek to discover the unrepresented truth of Bishop's sexuality, this lesbian variation on the repressive hypothesis imagines desire as confined within representation, "shut invisibly inside . . .

forever" like the unfortunate Gwendolyn in her coffin, awaiting the critic whose task it is to uncover lesbian "reality."[53]

But before we commit ourselves, like Hawthorne's Coverdale, to uncovering the "realities" hidden behind the surface of things, it is worth reconsidering Bishop's texts. Although Castle regards lesbian sexuality as victimized and Jarraway celebrates it as subversive, both Castle's notion of lesbian "reality" and Jarraway's notion of the Žižekian real locate a "real," essential lesbian desire outside the symbolic order. Two sides of the same coin, these readings trade in the currency of heterosexual ideology: the idea of lesbianism as unassimilable to meaning and to language. If for no other reason, the privileged status of this idea in the homophobic discourse of American dominant culture should make us wary of acceding to its terms. Bishop's writing further problematizes the appeal to a space outside the symbolic by suggesting that lesbian sexuality is inextricable not merely from the sexual rhetoric of phallocentric culture but also from the logic of figural language. For Bishop there is no subjectivity not indebted to the cultural vocabulary of, among other things, "little girls," and no desire outside the linguistic structures of displacement and transference.

"Gwendolyn" is above all a story of love's substitutions. As an account of the ways in which loss enables metaphorical processes of identification and desire, the text locates the threat to lesbian attachments not in the activity of representation but conversely, in the possibility of an end to it. If Elizabeth's "impossible" vision of Gwendolyn's funeral appears as a fragment of the real, that trauma marks a loss so profound that it seems momentarily to strip the world of meaning. Gwendolyn's fascination will survive her death, but in this moment, seemingly cast out of the world of signs, Gwendolyn herself—for Elizabeth, the "beautiful heroine," the lovely trisyllabic name, the very meaning of "little girl"—becomes unrecognizable. It is not Elizabeth's desire for Gwendolyn that produces the effect of the real; rather, it is her loss, her absence, that seems to take shape as a material thing, obtruding into the space of reality and arresting the linguistic play in which that desire had found form.[54] Whatever the love between little girls might mean, it is propped up by a system of signs that Elizabeth must try at all costs to sustain. Like any human attachment, Bishop suggests, lesbian sexuality exists only within the symbolic, only through endless displacement, only, like metaphor, as a lie of language. In simplest terms, the truth of love is a lie, but this imposture, this misnaming, is the most poignant and most powerful lie we know, taking its place alongside the fiction of subjectivity as the inescapable fate of each subject within the symbolic.

Restaging and Representation

Finally, the task of Bishop's narrative is to overcome its "missed encounter" with the real by returning Gwendolyn to the economy of signs. Joining her cousin Billy in a symbolic game, Elizabeth re-creates the churchyard scene on her own terms, staging a mock funeral in which the doll takes the place of Gwendolyn. One day, Bishop writes, when all other entertainments have been exhausted, "finally I did something really bad: I went in the house and upstairs to my Aunt Mary's bedroom and brought down the tissue-paper-wrapped, retired doll." The children play at decorating "the nameless doll" with flowers until the meaning of their game occurs to them:

> We laid her out in the garden path and outlined her body with Johnny-jump-ups and babies'-breath and put a pink cosmos in one limp hand. She looked perfectly beautiful. The game was more exciting than "operation." I don't know which one of us said it first, but one of us did, with wild joy—that it was Gwendolyn's funeral, and that the doll's real name, all this time, was Gwendolyn. (226)

Appropriately, the doll that Elizabeth first finds embalmed in a "bottom bureau drawer," "well wrapped in soft pink tissue paper" (213), exits the story in a funeral scene. In the mock-funeral the doll that enters the story conspicuously lacking a name—"It was a girl doll, but my grandmother had forgotten her name" (213)—also gains an identity. And what better name for this privileged emblem of substitution and feminine identification than that of Gwendolyn, the figure who has throughout the text embodied the allure of the "beautiful name" and the seductions of language itself?

The children's reenactment of the funeral thus returns Gwendolyn and the experience of her loss to the register of language and reengages the chain of displacement of which Gwendolyn has been the linchpin. Adding another identificatory link, Elizabeth takes the doll in the place of the lost girl who had taken the primal place of the mother. The second funeral, an act that articulates loss within the symbolic, recalls Elizabeth's lie in "The Country Mouse," but with one signal difference: it stages the scene of mourning in classically Oedipal terms. Following Freud's story of sexual development to its (only seemingly inevitable) conclusion, Elizabeth assumes the mother's place in the family tableau, whose triangular structure Billy conveniently completes. Within the narrative conventions of Western literature, as we know, such a heterosexual coupling is not only *a* satisfying conclusion, but *the* satisfying conclusion. Granted, "Gwendolyn" celebrates that traditional closure with a funeral rather than a wedding, but the difference is not as great as it might seem. Indeed, as the title of one recent film would suggest, a certain sort of funeral can handily enable the heterosexual wedding. As if the garden path where these rites are observed were the royal road to heterosexual maturity, Elizabeth seems to bury the juvenile attachments that, in Freud's account, must die so that the "exciting" business of marriage and procreation can go forth. Forsaking the "circuitous path" of lesbian attachments in this normative story of feminine development, Elizabeth must, as in "The Country Mouse," fantasmatically bury earlier loves—for the mother and for Gwendolyn—in order to take her place in the Oedipal triangle.

However satisfying this conclusion may be, if not for the sake of Elizabeth's sexual development then for the admirable symmetry it lends Bishop's narrative, it reveals Oedipality as another lie. The mock-funeral scene creates Oedipal order only *through* a certain perversity, only through substitution and imposture, only through the sentimentality that "The Country Mouse," observing modernist conventions, repudiates as false. An ersatz Little Eva, Gwendolyn might be expected in dying to enact the scene that Tompkins names "the epitome of Victorian sentimentalism."[55] If the text's occlusion of Gwendolyn's death and its hallucinatory account of the funeral scene are stoically, if surreally, antisentimental, Gwendolyn does get her moment of high drama. Reveling in the spectacle of the doll-Gwendolyn entombed in flowers, the children's funeral "play" renders pathos as pleasure, finding a sentimental excess in theatricality, vicariousness, and sheer morbid enjoyment. Stagey and melodramatic, this reenactment functions to ironize "reality." The two funerals come to mirror each other in a kind of chiasmus, the "real" one experienced only vicariously, from behind the parlor curtain across the green, and the "false" one acted out closer to home.[56] Both are revealed as representations, the first hallucinatory and the second theatrical, of a loss that can be neither understood nor even experienced except through displacement. Having lingered on the Oedipal scene, Bishop's text cannot rest there. The garden path game ends with the arrival of Elizabeth's grandparents, who, as if recognizing this role playing as Oedipal imposture, save the doll from its undignified fate and apparently punish Elizabeth for her transgression although, Bishop writes, "I don't remember now what awful thing happened to me" (226). Ending with this gap in memory, the text reverts again to its previous logic, to the forgetfulness that partially erased each fascinating encounter with Gwendolyn and to the restless movement of a desire that remains always elsewhere.

If Bishop's thematic concern with mourning, her acute awareness of how loss inaugurates both desire and discourse, seems to recall other images of lesbian morbidity in American literature—the Veiled Lady's communion with the "refuse-stuff" of "past mortality" in *The Blithedale Romance*, perhaps, or Basil Ransom's banishment of Olive Chancellor to the realm of "dead phrases" in *The Bostonians*—Bishop's texts also help us see the relation of lesbian sexuality to language in somewhat different terms. In "Gwendolyn" lesbian attachment must function as metaphor, rendering one loved object in place of another through an allegorical chain of primal loss and elusive enjoyment. If metaphor is nothing but a lie, it is also, in its own way, enormously productive, resisting meaning only insofar as it forever proliferates meanings, much as the displacement of same-sex desire and identification in "Gwendolyn" yields an unending, vertiginous series of substitutions. And perhaps this is the real pathos in Bishop's story: for having "stood for" femininity as the "beautiful heroine" of Elizabeth's fantasy, Gwendolyn will come to stand for a world of lost objects, living on as a signifier of the impossibility of language and the impossibility of desire, from which lesbian figures are not exempt.

conclusion

There is some irony in presenting conclusions about the lesbian figures that in many texts signify a resistance to closure. Imagined as derailing teleological progress, such figures seem to obstruct or deviate from narrative, epistemological, and socio-sexual goals. If *The Sun Also Rises* aligns lesbianism with the insistence of circular logic and the failure of narrative conclusion, *The Blithedale Romance* and *The Bostonians* construe the lesbian "type" as an epistemological problem. For their own part, *The Awakening* and Bishop's stories present same-sex love as an interminable, anti-Oedipal displacement of desire and meaning. When Bishop's "Gwendolyn" finally produces an Oedipal tableau that promises conclusive progress in sexual development, it does so only to set the stage for another fall, with Bishop's final "I don't remember," into the metaphorical substitutions that the text has associated with lesbian love. In each case the possibility of lesbian sexuality signals the impossibility of narrative closure and interpretive certainty. It seems that lesbianism is an always unfinished business.

But reading lesbian sexuality in American literature also underscores the political stakes of the demand for closure. In the illogic of patriarchal culture, the most salient tropes of lesbian sexuality are tropes of despecification—figures, that is, of the failure of boundaries and the collapse of form—which feed the homophobic myth of lesbianism as contagious, colonizing, and vampiric. While describing this tropology, the preceding chapters have also sought to identify some of the other signs by which lesbian sexuality is known. Although the cultural composite sketch of lesbian sexuality concludes, in its inconclusive way, by linking the radical instability of figural language to the elusive quality of female sexual perversity, no single trope defines lesbianism across historical shifts in American sexual ideology. In the broadest terms, American literature from the 1830s to the 1960s reflects a redefinition of sexual ideology that shifted the focus of female perversity from a violation of reproduction to a deviation in object-choice. Within that historical trajectory, the lesbian potential of female sexuality takes shape as female "morbidity" in *The Blithedale Romance* and *The Bostonians*; as the repudiation of proper reproduction, both familial and social, in *The Awakening*; as the masculinization of the "New Woman" in *The Sun Also Rises*; as a "wandering" in and from object-choice in *The Awakening*; as the persistence of mother-love in *Their Eyes Were Watching God* and Bishop's stories; and as an uncanny, eroticized female speech in *The Bostonians*, *The Blithedale Romance*, and *Their Eyes Were Watching God*.

Throughout these texts, the question that *The Awakening* frames as the difference between the exemplary woman and the exceptional one remains central. James asks that we consider how Olive Chancellor might be "typical," and of what, in a novel that itself aspires to the "very national, very typical," while Hemingway calls on notions of the "New Woman" to conflate sexual deviance with changing gender roles. The negotiation of the difference between lesbians and women, and between perverse and normative femininity, in American literature suggests that in American culture, at least, that distinction is by no means absolute. In patriarchal ideology, of course, femininity itself occupies an ambiguous place, as Lacan's famous axiom indicates: "There is no such thing as *The* woman."[1] If "woman," defined by lack and negativity, marks the limit of masculine epistemology, what is the difference between lesbianism and femininity? Represented as formless, engulfing, and without essence, lesbian sexuality functions metaphorically as a condensation of troubling qualities that patriarchal discourse attributes to femininity. If women appear in masculine ideology, as Michèle Montrelay has suggested, as "the ruin of representation," lesbian sexuality becomes the paradigmatic instance of that resistance to symbolization.[2] But patriarchal culture does not simply imagine "women" and "lesbians" as synonymous, nor does it posit lesbian sexuality as merely a metaphor for femininity. The tropes of lesbian sexuality are never wholly reducible to the signs of normative femininity. Instead, retaining as a rhetorical possibility (and strategy of antifeminist intimidation) the collapse of "lesbian" and "woman," patriarchal ideology attempts to separate lesbianism from a female heterosexuality that only then can appear as normative.

At a time when much lesbian criticism dedicates itself to the task of theorizing lesbian specificity—a project that inevitably describes the scope and ambitions of lesbian theory itself—it may seem politically retrograde to question the possibility of such definition. To choose uncertainty over certainty as a critical strategy, however, is not to minimize the oppression of women identified as lesbians in patriarchal culture, nor is it to deny the phobic energies at work in many American literary representations of lesbian sexuality. Rather, it is an effort to gain critical purchase on the mechanisms of sexual knowledge that both posit lesbianism as the limit of epistemology and continue to insist, paradoxically enough, that they know a lesbian when they see one. In particular, this book has attempted to consider lesbian sexuality in less literal terms by expanding the meaning of "lesbianism" beyond familiar public (and private) identities, sexual acts, and even object-choices; by willfully asking what "lesbian" desire might mean *avant la lettre* in mid-nineteenth-century American literature; and by recognizing lesbian thematics in texts that do not announce themselves as concerned with perverse sexuality. Acknowledging the problem of lesbian specificity is, in this sense, essential to understanding the complex and contradictory articulations of lesbian sexuality in American literature. Moreover, resisting the impulse to define lesbian specificity may help lesbian theory avoid the boundary policing that defines disciplinary mechanisms of heterosexual culture—or at least, to consider with open eyes the risks of adopting, in the name of lesbian identity, an exclusionary logic that also structures the homophobic repudiation of lesbian sexuality. While the question of what constitutes lesbian sexuality is not an empty one, that is, any serious answer must include consideration of the question's own cultural construction. As an historical antecedent of contemporary lesbian-feminist struggles to theorize lesbian specificity, the hegemonic fantasy of defining lesbianism—visible in Freud and James, Ellis and Hemingway—provides a useful caution. What motivates straight culture's "lesbian desire"? What fantasy informs its interest in knowing and representing such a figure as the lesbian? What are the epistemological fantasies of lesbian theory? How do the political goals of lesbian criticism imply or demand new ways of knowing?

While some lesbian readings of American literature have addressed "representation" in a different light, emphasizing the politics of inclusion and identity, this book has foregrounded the rhetorical sense of lesbian representation in an effort to think beyond essentialist notions of lesbian identity. To take lesbian desire as a figure, indeed as a figure for the instability of figural language, may seem to prioritize the rhetorical over what passes, perhaps too innocently, for material reality or "lived experience." This methodology, however, does not presuppose that lesbian sexuality is exclusively produced by patriarchal discourse, nor does it deny that oppositional lesbian politics and the actions of lesbian individuals can and do influence American culture. Rather, it suggests that sexual codes and ideologies exist in language, from whence they extend their effects even to those identities and desires we experience as most intimately "real." While this study appreciates the importance of other approaches within the repertoire of lesbian criticism—including readings of lesbian authors, lesbian history, and the subversive potential in literary and cultural texts—it has attempted to develop a rhetorical and psychoanalytic approach to the lesbian figures constructed by hegemonic discourses. It has investigated how discourses of power are productive of, and inextricable from, those persons and practices they will regard as sexual "others," in order to examine the various roles played by lesbian sexuality in American writing and in the cultural machinery of sexual knowledge and sexual discipline within and against which lesbian theory has taken shape.

I have argued that lesbian sexuality occupies the site of a structuring incoherence in the nationalist ideology of the United States and in the thematic and generic concerns of American literature. In Hawthorne, James, and Emerson, the articulation of lesbian figures helps to establish and secure the meaning of an "American literature" by distinguishing between proper and perverse forms of representation and reproduction. Imagining the birth of American literature out of a marriage of masculine thought and feminine nature, Emerson yokes meaningful symbolization to the teleological project of reproduction and the Oedipal development of female sexuality toward marriage and motherhood. Attributing "corrupted" language to a "barren" and deathly female desire, this notion of proper "generation," as Hemingway names it, construes lesbianism as a danger to both reproduction and representation. Within an American ideology driven by anticipation and dedicated to self-invention, lesbian sexuality thus plays a signal role as token of a threat to futurity, although, like castration, this is a threat that paradoxically also empowers. Recognizing lesbianism as a structuring trope in canonical as well as noncanonical American literature thus illuminates the role of sexuality in defining the relations of American genres and traditions—romance, realism, modernism, sentimentality, the African American oral tradition—to one another and to fantasies of "American literature." While James and Hawthorne describe romance and realism in generic crises at the site of lesbian desire, *The Sun Also Rises* presents a modernist renunciation of perverse repetition, circular logic, and stylistic indirection. *Their Eyes Were Watching God* gestures toward its own literary inheritance by comparing oral eroticism with African American oral traditions; and Bishop's antisentimental rhetoric, as a response to male modernism like Hemingway's, suggests the dilemma of the American woman writer and the lesbian writer in the twentieth century.

One larger goal of this project is to complicate the dialogue between American literary criticism and lesbian theory. For its part, lesbian theory has sometimes shown a distinctly American sensibility. Surely its profound awareness of its own struggle for self-invention has rivaled that of nineteenth-century American writing: in the title of a groundbreaking 1981 essay, Bonnie Zimmerman identified the project of lesbian theory as the articulation of a new discourse, the writing of "What Has Never Been."[3] At once anticipatory and retrospective, this continuing work of self-production has required lesbian criticism to sustain a vision of its future even as it undertakes the unending work of self-revision. But if their shared search for meaning and identity makes the project of reading American literature along with lesbian theory especially provocative, their relation to rhetoric makes it especially difficult. A certain strand of American literature and literary criticism has, in its long love affair with the concrete, the specific, and the material, nurtured a lasting distrust of language. Turning pointedly away from rhetorical structures, such writing aligns itself with David in *The Garden of Eden*, who "disliked rhetoric and distrusted those who used it and . . . was ashamed to have fallen into it."[4] Following Hemingway's lead, it seeks to divorce American literature from a "literariness" that seems only to signify the antiquated, the elitist, the morbid, and the effete.

In this respect the concerns of American literature and criticism speak trenchantly, if unexpectedly, to those of lesbian theory. Despite its grounding in oppositional politics and its productive engagement with psychoanalytic theory, lesbian criticism at times seems to mimic the ideology of American literature, performing the same gestures of abjection and mobilizing similar efforts to police "corrupted" rhetoric, dangerous metaphors, and language as such.[5] It seems that our own perversity may be slighter, or that of the dominant culture greater, than we would like to think. But this distrust of discourse and the concomitant resistance to "theory," when they appear in lesbian criticism, are also cause for concern. The preceding chapters have worked to demonstrate how, in American literature, the project of distinguishing "good" language from "bad" is part and parcel of a sexual ideology that phobically represents lesbian sexuality alternately as the unrepresentable real and as the circuitous wandering of figural language. Within this system, lesbian sexuality must occupy the place of linguistic failure or that of linguistic perversity: the site of the real or the site of a language emptied of meaning. As I have suggested in the context of Bishop's stories, the resistance to rhetoric in contemporary lesbian theory repeats at its own peril the disciplinary gestures of the patriarchal order, for when it subscribes to the same ideology lesbian theory cannot effectively address the ways in which hierarchies of "race," gender, and sexuality in American culture are sustained by notions of proper and perverse language.

Taking as a point of reference psychoanalytic and deconstructive understandings of language and desire as structured around a certain impossibility, this study has sought to explain how American literature not only betrays the sexual preoccupations of national ideology, but also makes visible the logic of the symbolic order with regard to lesbianism. Reading hegemonic inscriptions of lesbian "impossibility" and locating desire amid the displacements of language does not therefore place lesbian theory under the sign of failure or fatalism. Rather, it enlarges the possibilities for a criticism that, setting aside the metaphysics of truth, might perceive the multiple and shifting forms of lesbian figures in patriarchal culture and shed light on the cultural work performed by such figures. What would it mean to build a theory—which is always to say, a politics—on "impossibility"? While this question may inevitably be no more than rhetorical (and as such, a truly queer question), it asks that we recognize as the task of oppositional criticism the interrogation not only of meanings handed down by cultural authority but also the socially contructed category of meaning itself. It implies an effort to conceptualize, within gay and lesbian studies, a methodology based not on the truth of language and desire but on their uncertainty. And it offers an alternative to the critical gesture Eve Kosofsky Sedgwick has called "We Know What That Means"—for as Sedgwick notes, both straight culture's and queer critics' readings of homosexuality are susceptible to a strategic pose of knowingness whose homophobia consists in its refusal of difference, of uncertainty, of surprise.[6] Resisting this logic, recent lesbian critics have begun to map the imbrications of sexuality and representation in ways that both locate sexual discourses in social and historical contexts and acknowledge the contingency of subjectivity and "lived experience." To read against the grain of homophobic culture is always, in a sense, to attempt the impossible. In that effort, lesbian theory can bring a new attention to the stubborn contradictions and endless proliferations of language and desire—an attention whose cost and whose reward will be to render both more radically strange.

n o t e s

Introduction

1. Carroll Smith-Rosenberg, *Disorderly Conduct: Visions of Gender in Victorian America* (New York: Oxford University Press, 1986), 287.

2. Terry Castle, *The Apparitional Lesbian: Female Homosexuality and Modern Culture* (New York: Columbia University Press, 1993), 30–31. On lesbianism as impossibility, see also Judith Roof, who persuasively argues that lesbian sexuality, construed as "excess, immaturity, impossibility," marks a "point of failure" and also recuperation in patriarchal symbolic structures; *A Lure of Knowledge: Lesbian Sexuality and Theory* (New York: Columbia University Press, 1991), 242.

3. Castle's own reading, however, seems to turn away from this linguistic sense of lesbian impossibility. Rather than regarding lesbian sexuality in Foucauldian terms, as *produced by* the disciplinary mechanisms of heterosexual discourse, her notion of lesbianism as "apparition" suggests that lesbianism lies outside patriarchal ideology, as a "real" presence that is repressed, erased, and "ghosted" by patriarchal representation. For further discussion of Castle's approach, see chapter 5.

4. In psychoanalytic terms, language and sexuality are both substitutive mechanisms, endlessly displacing an elusive referent or object of desire. Governed by lack and haunted by difference, each is fundamentally a story about absence. Although each is pressed to the service of social hegemony, language and desire also bear with them the potential for disruption, whether in the slippage of figural language, the operations of transference and displacement,

or the anarchic impulses of the unconscious. As Lacan and Foucault remind us, language and sexuality are not only parallel but also intersecting; hegemonic discourses produce the desires and identities they claim only to regulate or suppress, while symbolization plays a constitutive role in formations of individual subjectivity and desire. See Jacques Lacan, *Écrits: A Selection*, trans. Alan Sheridan (New York: W. W. Norton, 1977), 284; and Michel Foucault, *The History of Sexuality: An Introduction* (New York: Vintage, 1990), 10, 34–35.

5. See, for example, Judith Butler, *Bodies That Matter: On the Discursive Limits of "Sex"* (New York: Routledge, 1993) and *Gender Trouble: Feminism and the Subversion of Identity* (New York: Routledge, 1990); Teresa de Lauretis, *The Practice of Love: Lesbian Sexuality and Perverse Desire* (Bloomington: Indiana University Press, 1994); Diana Fuss, *Identification Papers* (New York: Routledge, 1995); Judith Roof, *A Lure of Knowledge*, and *Come As You Are: Sexuality and Narrative* (New York: Columbia University Press, 1996).

6. Butler, *Gender Trouble*, 17.

7. Ibid., 77. Butler writes, "for heterosexuality to remain intact as a distinct social form, it *requires* an intelligible conception of homosexuality and also requires the prohibition of that conception in rendering it culturally unintelligible."

8. Judith Roof, "The Match in the Crocus: Representations of Lesbian Sexuality," in *Discontented Discourses: Feminism, Textual Intervention, and Psychoanalysis*, ed. Marleen S. Barr and Richard Feldstein (Chicago: University of Illinois Press, 1989), 103. Lynda Hart echoes Roof's formulation when she suggests that, within feminism, lesbianism is "charged with a divine mission—an impossible one—to represent the unrepresentable." *Between the Body and the Flesh: Performing Sadomasochism* (New York: Columbia University Press, 1998), 54.

9. Julia Kristeva, "Women Can Never Be Defined," trans. Marilyn A. August, in *New French Feminisms*, ed. Elaine Marks and Isabelle de Courtivron (Amherst: University of Massachusetts Press, 1980), 137. Hélène Cixous offers a more ambivalent discussion of femininity as "impossible" and "unrepresentable" in "The Laugh of Medusa," in *New French Feminisms*, 245–64 passim.

10. Paul de Man, *Allegories of Reading: Figural Language in Rousseau, Nietzsche, Rilke, and Proust* (New Haven: Yale University Press, 1979), 18; *The Resistance to Theory* (Minneapolis: University of Minnesota Press, 1986), 19.

11. Slavoj Žižek, *Looking Awry: An Introduction to Jacques Lacan through Popular Culture* (Cambridge: MIT Press, 1991), 47.

12. Lauren Berlant, *The Anatomy of National Fantasy: Hawthorne, Utopia, and Everyday Life* (Chicago: University of Chicago Press, 1991), 5.

13. On the revolutionary-era and early-nineteenth-century American rhetoric that presented the family as a figure for the nation, see Shirley Samuels, *Romances of the Republic: Women, the Family, and Violence in the Liter-*

ature of the Early American Nation (New York: Oxford University Press, 1996), 15–18, and "The Family, the State, and the Novel in the Early Republic," *American Quarterly* 38, no. 3 (1986): 381–95.

14. Ralph Waldo Emerson, "Nature," in *The Collected Works of Ralph Waldo Emerson*, vol. 1, ed. Robert E. Spiller and Alfred R. Ferguson (Cambridge: Harvard University Press, 1971), 19–20.

15. There is, of course, no single, monolithic American culture. The dominant ideology I examine here includes an endlessly multiplying constellation of ideological formations, economic relations, and political forces within American culture. Despite this fragmentation, however, it would be naive to suppose that some ideas, beliefs, and values are not commonly celebrated above others, or that certain ideologies—among them the family, patriotism, individualism, and (hetero)sexual propriety—are not imbued with an all too recognizable disciplinary power.

16. Nancy Cott, *The Bonds of Womanhood: "Woman's Sphere" in New England, 1780–1835* (New Haven: Yale University Press, 1977), 185.

17. Smith-Rosenberg, *Disorderly Conduct*, 60.

18. On the role of sexology and changing gender roles in the shift from the ideology of romantic friendship to that of lesbianism between 1895 and 1915, see John D'Emilio and Estelle B. Freedman, *Intimate Matters: A History of Sexuality in America* (New York: Harper and Row, 1988), 222–29; Smith-Rosenberg, *Disorderly Conduct*, esp. 273–75; Lillian Faderman, *Surpassing the Love of Men: Romantic Friendship and Love between Women from the Renaissance to the Present* (New York: William Morrow, 1981), 235–53, and *Odd Girls and Twilight Lovers: A History of Lesbian Life in Twentieth-Century America* (New York: Penguin, 1991), 34–61.

19. On the first published appearance of the term "lesbian" in America, see Smith-Rosenberg, *Disorderly Conduct*, 272.

20. Martha Vicinus, " 'They Wonder to Which Sex I Belong': The Historical Roots of Modern Lesbian Identity," *Feminist Studies* 18, no. 3 (1992): 467–93. See also Martha Vicinus, "Distance and Desire: English Boarding School Friendships, 1870–1920," in *Hidden from History: Reclaiming the Gay and Lesbian Past*, ed. Martin Duberman, Martha Vicinus, and George Chauncey Jr. (New York: New American Library, 1989), 212–32. Although Vicinus focuses on England rather than America, such anxieties around female intimacy are visible throughout nineteenth-century American literature. Other discussions of sexual love between women before the formulation of lesbian identity include Marylynne Diggs, "Romantic Friends or a 'Different Race of Creatures'? The Representation of Lesbian Pathology in Nineteenth-Century America," *Feminist Studies* 21, no. 2 (1995): 317–40; Castle, *The Apparitional Lesbian*, 8–10; and Mary E. Wood, " 'With Ready Eye': Margaret Fuller and Lesbianism in Nineteenth-Century American Literature," *American Literature* 65, no. 1 (1993): 1–18.

21. Diggs, "Romantic Friends," 321.

22. Smith-Rosenberg, *Disorderly Conduct*, 260.

23. On changes in birthrate and motherhood, see D'Emilio and Freedman, *Intimate Matters*, 173–74. Smith-Rosenberg discusses the conflation of "lesbianism" with resistance to traditionally feminine roles, dress, and behavior (*Disorderly Conduct*, 271, 278–79).

24. The notion of the "lesbian continuum" is Adrienne Rich's; see "Compulsory Heterosexuality and Lesbian Existence," in *Blood, Bread and Poetry: Selected Prose, 1979–1985* (New York: W. W. Norton, 1986), 23–75.

25. Further discussion of the relation between lesbianism and femininity can be found in chapters 2, 4, and 5 and the conclusion.

26. Annamarie Jagose, *Lesbian Utopics* (New York: Routledge, 1994), 9. The repressive hypothesis, as Foucault explains, proposes that "sex is outside of discourse and that only the removing of an obstacle, the breaking of a secret, can clear the way leading to it" (*The History of Sexuality: An Introduction*, 34).

27. Valerie Traub, "The Psychomorphology of the Clitoris," *GLQ* 2, nos. 1–2 (1995): 102. Jagose offers a similar Foucauldian argument, noting that "the lesbian body is not forbidden by the supreme law of some sovereign power but actually produced by those power relations with which it is thoroughly saturated" (*Lesbian Utopics*, 4).

28. Slavoj Žižek, *The Sublime Object of Ideology* (New York: Verso, 1989), 164, and *Looking Awry*, 43.

1. The Romance of the Real: *The Blithedale Romance* and *The Bostonians*

1. Henry James, *Hawthorne* (New York: AMS Press, 1968). J. Hillis Miller's discussion of "The Minister's Black Veil" provides a valuable account of allegory and realism in James's reading of Hawthorne. See *Hawthorne and History* (Cambridge, Mass.: Blackwell, 1991). On *The Bostonians* and *The Blithedale Romance*, see Millicent Bell, *Meaning in Henry James* (Cambridge: Harvard University Press, 1991), 129–51; Elissa Greenwald, *Realism and the Romance: Nathaniel Hawthorne, Henry James, and American Fiction* (Ann Arbor: UMI, 1989), 79–104; Alison Rieke, "Two Women: The Transformations," in *Faith of a (Woman) Writer*, ed. Alice Kessler-Harris and William McBrien (Westport, Conn.: Greenwood, 1988), 71–81; Richard Brodhead, *The School of Hawthorne* (New York: Oxford University Press, 1986), 147–65; and Robert Emmet Long, *The Great Succession: Henry James and the Legacy of Hawthorne* (Pittsburgh: University of Pittsburgh Press, 1979), 117–57.

2. James, *Hawthorne*, 62–63.

3. Ibid., 114, 124.

4. For one formulation of the type as the "central category" of realism, see Georg Lukács, *Studies in European Realism* (New York: Grosset and Dunlap, 1964), 6.

5. Henry James, *The Complete Notebooks of Henry James*, ed. Leon Edel and Lyall H. Powers (New York: Oxford University Press, 1987), 20.

6. The notion of the "typical invert" can be found in Havelock Ellis, *Studies in the Psychology of Sex: Sexual Inversion* (1897), cited in Lillian Faderman, *Surpassing the Love of Men: Romantic Friendship and Love between Women from the Renaissance to the Present* (New York: William Morrow, 1981), 241.

7. Henry James, *The Bostonians* (New York: Bantam, 1984), 13, 207. All further references will be cited in the text.

8. Slavoj Žižek, " 'In His Bold Gaze My Ruin Is Writ Large,' " in *Everything You Ever Wanted to Know about Lacan (But Were Afraid to Ask Hitchcock)*, ed. Slavoj Žižek (New York: Verso, 1992), 239.

9. On the real as internal resistance, see Slavoj Žižek, *Enjoy Your Symptom!* (New York: Routledge, 1992), 49. On the real and homosexuality, see also Lynda Hart, *Between the Body and the Flesh: Performing Sadomasochism* (New York: Columbia University Press, 1998), 54–55, 91–92.

10. Jacques Lacan, *The Seminar of Jacques Lacan: Book 1*, ed. Jacques-Alain Miller, trans. John Forrester (New York: W. W. Norton, 1991), 66–67.

11. Henry F. Chorley, review of *The Blithedale Romance*, *Athenaeum*, July 10, 1852, 741–43; James, *Complete Notebooks*, 19.

12. The term "arguing with the real" comes from Judith Butler in *Bodies That Matter: On the Discursive Limits of "Sex"* (New York: Routledge, 1993), 187–222. Butler's response centers on Žižek's *Sublime Object of Ideology* (New York: Verso, 1989); see also Žižek's *Looking Awry: An Introduction to Jacques Lacan through Popular Culture* (Cambridge: MIT Press, 1991).

13. James, *Hawthorne*, 132. The *OED* defines "morbid" in the sense "of mental conditions, ideas, etc." as "unwholesome, sickly," bringing morbidity into alignment with nineteenth-century notions of those sexual impulses, including what we now call gay and lesbian desire, that were construed as sterile or pathological.

14. Review of *The Blithedale Romance* in *Graham's Magazine*, cited in James K. Mellow, *Nathaniel Hawthorne in His Times* (Boston: Houghton Mifflin, 1980), 402; "Modern Novelists—Great and Small," unsigned review of *The Blithedale Romance*, *Blackwood's Magazine* 77 (May 1855): 562–66; unsigned review of *The Blithedale Romance*, *American Whig Review* 16 (November 1852): 417–24.

15. *Southern Quarterly Review*, cited in Mellow, *Nathaniel Hawthorne in His Times*, 402.

16. Barbara F. Lefcowitz and Allan B. Lefcowitz, "Some Rents in the Veil: New Light on Priscilla and Zenobia," *Nineteenth-Century Fiction* 21 (1966): 263–75; and Frederick Crews, *The Sins of the Fathers: Hawthorne's Psychological Themes* (New York: Oxford University Press, 1966), 194–212.

17. *The Blithedale Romance*, Norton Critical Edition, ed. Seymour Gross and Rosalie Murphy (New York: W. W. Norton, 1978), 67. All further references will be cited in the text.

18. On the psychoanalytic notion of lesbianism as a kind of regression, see Diana Fuss, *Identification Papers* (New York: Routledge, 1995), 57–82; and Judith Roof, *A Lure of Knowledge: Lesbian Sexuality and Theory* (New York: Columbia University Press, 1991), 210.

19. Charles Swann discusses Fauntleroy as a forger in *Nathaniel Hawthorne: Tradition and Revolution* (New York: Cambridge University Press, 1991), 118, 124.

20. While the text asks us to understand that Priscilla "is" the Veiled Lady, the two figures never coalesce, making the relationship between Zenobia and Priscilla, in a certain sense, a *ménage à trois*.

21. "Modern Novelists—Great and Small," 562–66.

22. James, *Hawthorne*, 137, 132.

23. Brodhead, *The School of Hawthorne*, 155; Lefcowitz and Lefcowitz, "Some Rents in the Veil," 348. Elizabeth Bronfen offers a valuable reading of Zenobia as a figure for allegory in *Over Her Dead Body: Death, Femininity, and the Aesthetic* (New York: Routledge, 1992), 242–49.

24. On connections between Coverdale's subjectivity and voyeurism, see, for example, Richard H. Millington, *Practicing Romance: Narrative Forms and Cultural Engagement in Hawthorne's Fiction* (Princeton: Princeton University Press, 1992), 155.

25. Lauren Berlant notes that in *The House of the Seven Gables* Hawthorne praises the "private and domestic view," which reveals "the vast discrepancy between portraits intended for engraving, and the pencil-sketches passed from hand to hand, behind the original's back." See *The Anatomy of National Fantasy: Hawthorne, Utopia, and Everyday Life* (Chicago: University of Chicago Press, 1991), 232 n. 55.

26. Nathaniel Hawthorne, *Selected Tales and Sketches* (New York: Penguin, 1987), 193. On the veil as a figure for allegory, see Greenwald, *Realism and the Romance*, 84.

27. Lacan, *The Seminar of Jacques Lacan: Book 1*, 229.

28. Žižek, *Sublime Object*, 161–170 passim. One might say, borrowing from de Man's account of the resistance to theory, that the resistance to symbolization is in symbolization itself—or rather, that the resistance to symbolization represented by the real is in fact a product of the symbolic order; *The Resistance to Theory* (Minneapolis: University of Minnesota Press, 1986), 19.

29. Lacan, *The Four Fundamental Concepts of Psycho-Analysis*, ed. Jacques-Alain Miller, trans. Alan Sheridan (New York: W. W. Norton, 1981), 55, 53.

30. Butler, "Arguing with the Real," 192. For Butler's critique of Žižek, see 195–207. In *The Metastases of Enjoyment* Žižek responds briefly to Butler, acknowledging the need to historicize the real (New York: Verso, 1994), 199–200.

31. Butler, "Arguing with the Real," 206.

32. Žižek, *Looking Awry*, 32. Lee Edelman has argued that male homosexuality functions within heterosexual culture as the "arbitrary sign" whose exclusion from symbolization enables the signifying practices of the dominant culture, even as the foreclosure of that desire from representation and the domain of knowledge renders it endlessly subject to disciplinary scrutiny. Lee Edelman, *Homographesis: Essays in Gay Literary and Cultural Theory* (New York: Routledge, 1994), xv–xvi. At the same time, Edelman argues, cultural representations of certain unassimilable scenes stage "the occlusion of the real by the symbolic" by veiling over the homosexual desire that threatens to obtrude into cultural visibility (140).

33. On the real as enjoyment and *jouissance*, see Žižek, *Sublime Object*, 164. Leo Bersani discusses the displacement of a cultural aversion to sexuality onto the figure of the gay man; see "Is the Rectum a Grave?" in *AIDS: Cultural Analysis, Cultural Activism*, ed. Douglas Crimp (Cambridge: MIT Press, 1988), 197–222. Edelman traces the production of male homosexuality as figure for "the unknowability of sexuality as such" in the preface to *Homographesis* (xv).

34. Žižek, *Sublime Object*, 164; and Lacan, *Four Fundamental Concepts*, 59. The prohibition of the impossible is also discussed in Žižek, *Looking Awry*, 43.

35. Terry Castle, *The Apparitional Lesbian: Female Homosexuality and Modern Culture* (New York: Columbia University Press, 1993), 6, 240 n. 5.

36. Judith Roof, "The Match in the Crocus: Representations of Lesbian Sexuality," in *Discontented Discourses: Feminism, Textual Intervention, and Psychoanalysis*, ed. Marleen S. Barr and Richard Feldstein (Chicago: University of Illinois Press, 1989), 102.

37. Hart, *Between the Body and the Flesh*, 91. Although her primary emphases are performance and the body, not textuality and rhetoric, Hart's provocative discussion of the connection between the unsymbolizable real and lesbian sexuality enables and supports my argument here.

38. Žižek, *Enjoy Your Symptom*, 49.

39. Hart, *Between the Body and the Flesh*, 193.

40. Ibid., 102.

41. Roof, *A Lure of Knowledge*, 242. In a similar formulation, Roof writes, "Operating as points of systemic failure, configurations of lesbian sexuality

often reflect the complex incongruities that occur when the logic or philosophy of a system becomes self-contradictory, visibly fails to account for something, or cannot complete itself" (5).

42. Žižek, *Sublime Object*, 163; see also Lacan, *Four Fundamental Concepts*, 55.

43. Žižek, *Looking Awry*, 31.

44. On the relation of the voice to questions of sexuality in Hawthorne's novel, see Brodhead, *The School of Hawthorne*, 149; and Lauren Berlant, "Fantasies of Utopia in *The Blithedale Romance*," *American Literary History* 1 (1989): 43–44.

45. Sigmund Freud, *Three Essays on the Theory of Sexuality* (1905), *Standard Edition* 7:224.

46. Kaja Silverman notes the "profoundly ambivalent nature" of this fantasy, in which the maternal voice is resonant with preoedipal wholeness yet tinged with a claustrophobic horror. See *The Acoustic Mirror: The Female Voice in Psychoanalysis and Cinema* (Bloomington: Indiana University Press, 1988), 72–140. Claire Kahane addresses Chion's, Winnicott's, and Kristeva's notions of the maternal voice in *Passions of the Voice: Hysteria, Narrative, and the Figure of the Speaking Woman, 1850–1915* (Baltimore: Johns Hopkins University Press, 1995), 16.

47. Michel Chion, *La voix au cinéma* (Paris: éditions de L'étoile, 1982), 32–33, cited in Silverman, *The Acoustic Mirror*, 50. Silverman offers a useful discussion of Chion on 49–50 and 72–77.

48. Michel Chion, "The Impossible Embodiment," in Žižek, *Everything You Ever Wanted to Know about Lacan*, 195–207.

49. Žižek, " 'In His Bold Gaze,' " 234.

50. Chion, "The Impossible Embodiment," 197, 203.

51. See Fuss, *Identification Papers*, 58. On female Oedipality, see Sigmund Freud, "Female Sexuality" (1931), *Standard Edition* 21:230. I discuss the dominant psychoanalytic association of lesbian sexuality with preoedipality here not to suggest that lesbianism *is* essentially preoedipal, but in order to examine the consequences of this myth or fantasy for lesbian figures in James's and Hawthorne's texts.

52. Samuel Weber, *Return to Freud: Jacques Lacan's Dislocation of Psychoanalysis*, trans. Michael Levine (New York: Cambridge University Press, 1991), 131.

53. Jacques Lacan, *Feminine Sexuality*, ed. Juliet Mitchell and Jacqueline Rose, trans. Jacqueline Rose (New York: W. W. Norton, 1982), 80, 96.

54. Jacques Lacan, *The Seminar of Jacques Lacan: Book 3*, ed. Jacques-Alain Miller, trans. Russell Grigg (New York: W. W. Norton, 1993), 13.

55. Chion, "The Impossible Embodiment," 204.

56. Paul de Man, *Allegories of Reading: Figural Language in Rousseau, Nietzsche, Rilke, and Proust* (New Haven: Yale University Press, 1979), 205.

57. Bell, *Meaning in Henry James*, 142–43; see also Brodhead, *The School of Hawthorne*, 141.

58. Cited in F. O. Matthiessen, *The James Family: A Group Biography* (New York: Alfred A. Knopf, 1961), 326.

59. James, *Complete Notebooks*, 19.

60. This effect of recognizing lesbian sexuality demonstrates the epistemological formula that Eve Kosofsky Sedgwick persuasively describes in *Epistemology of the Closet* (Berkeley: University of California Press, 1990), 12, 204–5.

61. Cited in Judith Fetterley, *The Resisting Reader: A Feminist Approach to American Fiction* (Bloomington: Indiana University Press, 1978), 104.

62. Joel Pfister, *The Production of Personal Life: Class, Gender, and the Psychological in Hawthorne's Fiction* (Stanford: Stanford University Press, 1991), 71. A later chapter explicitly relates anxieties around Anne Hutchinson to Hawthorne's portrait of Zenobia in *The Blithedale Romance* (86). See also Amy Schrager Lang, *Prophetic Woman: Anne Hutchinson and the Problem of Dissent in the Literature of New England* (Berkeley: University of California Press, 1987).

63. Pfister, *The Production of Personal Life*, 72.

64. Ibid., 96. On Fuller and *The Blithedale Romance*, see also Rieke, "Two Women," 77. As Pfister notes, Sophia Peabody Hawthorne was among Margaret Fuller's female admirers.

65. Lynn Wardley, "Woman's Voice, Democracy's Body, and *The Bostonians*," *ELH* 56 (1989): 639–40.

66. Berlant, *The Anatomy of National Fantasy*, 231 n. 55.

67. Claire Kahane, "*The Bostonians* and the Figure of the Speaking Woman," in *Psychoanalysis and Feminism*, ed. Richard Feldstein and Henry Sussman (New York: Routledge, 1990), 164. A differently inflected version of this essay appears in Kahane, *Passions of the Voice*, 64–79.

68. Brodhead, *The School of Hawthorne*, 149.

69. Fetterley, *The Resisting Reader*, 142. On Basil's separation of sound from sense in Verena's speech, see also Kahane, *Passions of the Voice*, 76; and Carolyn Field Levander, *Voices of the Nation: Women and Public Speech in Nineteenth-Century American Literature and Culture* (New York: Cambridge University Press, 1998), 12–34.

70. Levander, *Voices of the Nation*, 14. While Levander sees the construction of women's public speech in terms of *tone* and not *content* as fundamentally conservative, Wardley argues that the hollow materiality of Verena's speech makes it "the voice of a ventriloqual body" that is "potentially indistinguishable from the alien, the crowd, and a femininity 'odiously perverted,'

possibly subversive" ("Woman's Voice," 647). Kaja Silverman's discussion of the female voice in cinema, which focuses on the "opposition of the maternal voice to the paternal word," indicates the persistence of this structure in twentieth-century ideology (*The Acoustic Mirror*, 75).

71. Jacques Derrida, *Of Grammatology*, trans. Gayatri Chakravorty Spivak (Baltimore: Johns Hopkins University Press, 1974), 35.

72. Ibid., 36.

73. Edelman argues that patriarchal culture "names homosexuality as a secondary, sterile, and parasitic form of social representation that stands in the same relation to heterosexual identity that writing, in the phonocentric metaphysics that Derrida traces throughout Western philosophy from Plato to Freud (and beyond), occupies in relation to speech or voice" (*Homographesis*, 9–10).

74. Wardley provides a slightly different reading of Basil's task, describing it as an attempt to "recover sexual difference" in order to reconstitute the "democratic body" of the nation ("Woman's Voice," 646). Historically, of course, the speech / writing opposition did not mean that women's writing was welcomed as a complement to masculine speech, for the notion of women's writing violated the binary logic that assigned intellectual reproduction to men and biological reproduction to women.

75. de Man, *The Resistance to Theory*, 10.

76. Ibid., 14.

77. On Olive's inability to speak as a hysterical aphasia, see Kahane, "*The Bostonians*," 165.

78. Joseph Litvak, *Caught in the Act: Theatricality in the Nineteenth-Century English Novel* (Berkeley: University of California Press, 1992), 222. Olive, Litvak writes, "marks what remains, on stage and in the text, after the brutal binarisms of heterosexuality have been imposed" (234).

79. Žižek, " 'In His Bold Gaze,' " 242.

80. See Fuss, *Identification Papers*, 62.

81. Kahane, "*The Bostonians*," 165.

2. The Reproduction of Meaning: Language, Oedipality, and *The Awakening*

1. Willa Cather, "Books and Magazines," *Pittsburgh Leader*, July 8, 1899, 6, reprinted in Kate Chopin, *The Awakening*, Norton Critical Edition, ed. Margaret Culley, 2d ed. (New York: W. W. Norton, 1976), 153. While Cather adopts a masculine perspective here, her own authorial "choice of themes" as well as her lesbianism complicate her defense of literary convention. On

Cather as a lesbian writer, see, for example, Naomi Morgenstern, " 'Love Is Home-Sickness': Nostalgia and Lesbian Desire in *Sapphira and the Slave Girl*," *Novel* 29, no. 2 (1996): 184–205; Judith Fetterley, "*My Antonia*, Jim Burden, and the Dilemma of the Lesbian Writer," in *Lesbian Texts and Contexts: Radical Revisions*, ed. Karla Jay and Joanne Glasgow (New York: New York University Press, 1990), 145–63; and Sharon O'Brien, " 'The Thing Not Named': Willa Cather as a Lesbian Writer," *Signs* 9, no. 4 (1984): 576–99.

2. Cather, "Books and Magazines," 154.

3. Chopin, *The Awakening*, 108. All further references will be cited in the text.

4. Margaret Fuller, *Margaret Fuller: American Romantic*, ed. Perry Miller (Garden City, N.Y.: Doubleday, 1963), 30.

5. See Michael Warner, *Letters of the Republic: Publication and the Public Sphere in Eighteenth-Century America* (Cambridge: Harvard University Press, 1990).

6. Ralph Waldo Emerson, "Nature," in *The Collected Works of Ralph Waldo Emerson*, vol. 1, ed. Robert E. Spiller and Alfred R. Ferguson (Cambridge: Harvard University Press, Belknap Press, 1971), 7. All further references will be cited in the text.

7. Harold Bloom, *The Anxiety of Influence* (New York: Oxford University Press, 1973), 8; for Bloom's Oedipal theory of influence, see 10–11.

8. Margaret Fuller, "American Literature: Its Position in the Present Time, and Prospects for the Future," in *Margaret Fuller: American Romantic*, 231. Elaine Showalter discusses the connections among Bloom, Emerson, and Fuller in "Miranda and Cassandra: The Discourse of the Feminist Intellectual," in *Tradition and the Talents of Women*, ed. Florence Howe (Urbana: University of Illinois Press, 1991), 322–23.

9. Jesse F. Battan, "The Word Made Flesh: Language, Authority, and Sexual Desire in Late Nineteenth-Century America," in *American Sexual Politics: Sex, Gender, and Race since the Civil War*, ed. John C. Fout and Maura Shaw Tantillo (Chicago: University of Chicago Press, 1993), 110.

10. Fuller, "American Literature," 232. Stephanie A. Smith offers an antithetical reading of this passage in *Conceived by Liberty: Maternal Figures and Nineteenth-Century American Literature* (Ithaca: Cornell University Press, 1994), 70.

11. See Christina Zwarg, "Emerson as 'Mythologist' in *Memoirs of Margaret Fuller Ossoli*," *Criticism* 31, no. 3 (1989): 229. Mary E. Wood discusses Fuller's place in nineteenth-century sexual ideology in " 'With Ready Eye': Margaret Fuller and Lesbianism in Nineteenth-Century American Literature," *American Literature* 65, no. 1 (1993): 1–18.

12. Christina Zwarg, *Feminist Conversations: Fuller, Emerson, and the Play of Reading* (Ithaca: Cornell University Press, 1995), 30, 63, 256.

13. This argument is indebted to Lee Edelman's discussion of male homosexuality as analogous with the economy of the drives and with the displacements of "pure rhetoric" out of which symbolic discourse and Oedipal object-cathexes emerge. See "Plasticity, Paternity, Perversity: Freud's *Falcon*, Huston's *Freud*," *American Imago* 51, no. 1 (1994): 69–104.

14. Henry James, *The Bostonians* (New York: Bantam, 1984), 8, 290.

15. Jacques Lacan, *Écrits: A Selection*, trans. Alan Sheridan (New York: W. W. Norton, 1977), 167.

16. Emerson, "The American Scholar," in *Collected Works*, 1:66. On Chopin's critique of American individualism, see, for example, Ivy Schweitzer, "Maternal Discourse and the Romance of Self-Possession in Kate Chopin's *The Awakening*," *boundary* 2 17 (1990), 162; and Katherine Kearns, "The Nullification of Edna Pontellier," *American Literature* 63, no. 1 (1991): 62–88.

17. Unsigned review of *The Awakening*, *St. Louis Globe-Democrat*, May 13, 1899, reprinted in Chopin, *The Awakening*, 147; unsigned review of *The Awakening*, *Los Angeles Sunday Times*, June 25, 1899, reprinted in Chopin, *The Awakening*, 152.

18. This discussion replicates the critical debate on Fuller's own role as a unique or representative woman. See Zwarg, *Feminist Conversations*, 10–11.

19. Frances Porcher, review of *The Awakening*, *Mirror*, May 4, 1899, reprinted in Chopin, *The Awakening*, 145; unsigned review of *The Awakening*, *Los Angeles Sunday Times*, June 25, 1899, 12, reprinted in Chopin, *The Awakening*, 152.

20. Jonathan Ned Katz, "The Invention of Heterosexuality," *Socialist Review* 20, no. 1 (1990): 7–34. On the phobic dissemination of the concept of lesbian identity between 1896 and 1916, see Lillian Faderman, *Odd Girls and Twilight Lovers: A History of Lesbian Life in Twentieth-Century America* (New York: Penguin, 1991), 49.

21. Cather, "Books and Magazines," 153. One exception is Elizabeth LeBlanc, whose reading of Edna as a lesbian figure centers on Edna's resistance to, or failure to function within, patriarchal notions of feminine propriety. See "The Metaphorical Lesbian: Edna Pontellier in *The Awakening*," *Tulsa Studies in Women's Literature* 15, no. 2 (1996): 289–307. Other, more oblique discussions of lesbian sexuality in *The Awakening* include Kathryn Lee Seidel, "Art Is an Unnatural Act: Mademoiselle Reisz in *The Awakening*," *Mississippi Quarterly* 46, no. 2 (1993): 199–214; and Kathleen Margaret Lant, "The Siren of Grand Isle: Adele's Role in *The Awakening*," in *Kate Chopin*, ed. Harold Bloom (New York: Chelsea House, 1987), 115–24. It is worth noting that Chopin also addressed the question of lesbian desire in her short story "The Falling in Love of Fedora" (1897).

22. Lillian Faderman, *Surpassing the Love of Men: Romantic Friendship and Love between Women from the Renaissance to the Present* (New York: William Morrow, 1981), 239–53; and Faderman, *Odd Girls*, 34–61.

23. Katz, "The Invention of Heterosexuality," 14–16.

24. While Wolff does not address lesbian sexuality as such, her argument usefully contextualizes the question of lesbian definition by showing one sense in which object-choice yielded to other concerns—such as the *aim* of maternity—as a marker of female sexual propriety and deviance in the late nineteenth century. See "Un-Utterable Longing: The Discourse of Feminine Sexuality in *The Awakening*," *Studies in American Fiction* 24, no. 1 (1996): 3–22.

25. See Smith-Rosenberg, *Disorderly Conduct*, 278–79.

26. These models of lesbianism in *The Awakening* resemble what Edelman, writing on male homosexuality, has described as the production of sexual "identity" through the misreading of metonymy as metaphor. While cultural notions of lesbianism are not generally symmetrical with those of gay male sexuality, the elaboration of lesbianism as an identity category around the turn of the century relied upon the model of male homosexuality, with its attention to bodily signs and its chiastic rhetoric of "inversion." See *Homographesis: Essays in Gay Literary and Cultural Theory* (New York: Routledge, 1994), 8.

27. I quote here from Kearns, "The Nullification of Edna Pontellier"; and Schweitzer, "Maternal Discourse"; but versions of this rhetoric can also be found in Lant, "The Siren of Grand Isle"; Elaine Showalter, "Tradition and the Female Talent," in *New Essays on The Awakening*, ed. Wendy Martin (New York: Cambridge University Press, 1988), 46; and Carole Stone, "The Female Artist in Kate Chopin's *The Awakening*: Birth and Creativity," *Women's Studies* 13 (1986): 23–32. For further discussion of readers' responses to Reisz, see Seidel, "Art Is an Unnatural Act," 199–200.

28. Jane Gallop notes in another context that "peculiar" means *both* "characteristic" and "strange"—a doubling that economically describes the notion of femininity as pathological in patriarchal discourse. See *Reading Lacan* (Ithaca: Cornell University Press, 1985), 49.

29. Sigmund Freud, "Female Sexuality" (1931), *Standard Edition* 21:230.

30. Diana Fuss, *Identification Papers* (New York: Routledge, 1995), 66–67.

31. Sigmund Freud, "Family Romances" (1909), *Standard Edition*, 9:237; and "Some Psychological Consequences of the Anatomical Distinction between the Sexes" (1925), *Standard Edition*, 19:257.

32. Patricia Meyer Spacks, *The Female Imagination* (New York: Knopf, 1975), 75. On narcissism in *The Awakening*, see, for example, Cynthia Griffin Wolff, "Thanatos and Eros: Kate Chopin's *The Awakening*," *American Quarterly* 25 (1973): 459; Lawrence Thornton, "*The Awakening*: A Political Ro-

mance," *American Literature* 52, no. 1 (1980), 52; and Mylène Dressler, "Edna under the Sun: Throwing Light on the Subject of *The Awakening*," *Arizona Quarterly* 48, no. 3 (1992): 68. On views of narcissism in Victorian sexology, see Seidel, "Art Is an Unnatural Act," 214.

33. Bloom, introduction to *Kate Chopin*, 2.

34. Walt Whitman, *Leaves of Grass* (New York: Bantam, 1983), 200–205. Further discussion of Whitman and Chopin can be found in Sandra Gilbert, "The Second Coming of Aphrodite: Kate Chopin's Fantasy of Desire," *Kenyon Review* 5 (1983): 60; and Bloom's introduction to *Kate Chopin*, 3.

35. On the abyss as an "indefinitely multiplied structure" of representation, see Jacques Derrida, *Of Grammatology*, trans. Gayatri Chakravorty Spivak (Baltimore: Johns Hopkins University Press, 1974), 163.

36. Freud, "Female Sexuality," *Standard Edition* 21:230.

37. For a related discussion of sexuality and narrative in Hemingway's *Sun Also Rises*, see chapter 3 of this book. A number of recent texts have addressed narrative, sexuality, and gender; among these are Judith Roof, *Come As You Are: Sexuality and Narrative* (New York: Columbia University Press, 1996); Marilyn R. Farwell, *Heterosexual Plots and Lesbian Narratives* (New York: New York University Press, 1996); the "Sexuality and Narrative" double issue of *Modern Fiction Studies* 41, nos. 3–4 (1995); Paul Morrison, "End Pleasure," *GLQ* 1 (1993): 53–78; Joseph Allen Boone, *Tradition Counter Tradition: Love and the Form of Fiction* (Chicago: University of Chicago Press, 1987); and Teresa de Lauretis, *Alice Doesn't: Feminism, Semiotics, Cinema* (Bloomington: Indiana University Press, 1984), 103–57.

38. Notions of preoedipality, regression, and escape from language have played a large part in readings of *The Awakening*: see in particular Schweitzer, "Maternal Discourse," 185; and Seidel, "Art Is an Unnatural Act," 206. On Edna's regression, see Wolff, "Thanatos and Eros," 471; Stone, "The Female Artist," 24; C. J. Wershoven, "*The Awakening* and *The House of Mirth*: Studies of Arrested Development," *American Literary Realism* 19, no. 3 (1987): 27–41; and James Justus, "The Unawakening of Edna Pontellier," *Southern Literary Journal* 10, no. 2 (1978): 118. Dressler, however, stresses the impossibility of escape from representation in her reading of *The Awakening*, "Edna under the Sun"; and Patricia S. Yeager convincingly posits feminine speech as an "unspeakable" excess *within* the masculine symbolic in "'A Language Which Nobody Understood': Emancipatory Strategies in *The Awakening*," *Novel* 20 (1987): 197–219.

39. Fuss, *Identification Papers*, 73.

40. Eve Kosofsky Sedgwick, *Tendencies* (Durham: Duke University Press, 1993), 51.

41. Jane Gallop, *The Daughter's Seduction: Feminism and Psychoanalysis* (Ithaca: Cornell University Press, 1982), 45. On desire as displacement, see also Jacques Lacan, "Sexuality in the Defiles of the Signifier," in *The Four*

Fundamental Concepts of Psycho-Analysis, ed. Jacques-Alain Miller, trans. Alan Sheridan (New York: W. W. Norton, 1981), 154.

42. Slavoj Žižek, *Looking Awry: An Introduction to Jacques Lacan through Popular Culture* (Cambridge: MIT Press, 1991), 7.

43. Justus, "The Unawakening," 117.

44. Freud, "Female Sexuality," *Standard Edition* 21:231.

45. Sigmund Freud, "The Passing of the Oedipus-Complex" (1924), reprinted in *Sexuality and the Psychology of Love*, ed. Philip Rieff (New York: Collier, 1963), 181. I cite this translation of the essay rather than that of the *Standard Edition* because it more clearly indicates the metaphoric aspect of female sexual development. James Strachey renders this passage as "she slips—along the line of a symbolic equation, one might say—from the penis to a baby" (*Standard Edition* 19:178–79).

46. Edelman, "Plasticity," 73. On the phallus as transcendental signifier, see Lacan, *Écrits*, 285, and *The Seminar of Jacques Lacan: Book 3*, ed. Jacques-Alain Miller, trans. Russell Grigg (New York: W. W. Norton, 1993), 189.

47. Edelman, "Plasticity," 96.

48. Sigmund Freud, *The Interpretation of Dreams* (1900), *Standard Edition* 5:562–63. On the double sense of "transference" in Freud, see Lacan, *Écrits*, 170. Joyce Dyer notes the historical connection between Freud's text and Chopin's in *The Awakening: A Novel of Beginnings* (New York: Twayne, 1993), 114.

49. On metaphor as "carrying over," see Jean Laplanche, *Life and Death in Psychoanalysis*, trans. Jeffrey Mehlman (Baltimore: Johns Hopkins University Press, 1976), 138.

50. Samuel Weber, *Return to Freud: Jacques Lacan's Dislocation of Psychoanalysis*, trans. Michael Levine (New York: Cambridge University Press, 1991), 179–80.

51. Gallop, *The Daughter's Seduction*, 45.

52. Roman Jakobson, "Two Aspects of Language and Two Types of Aphasic Disturbances," in *Selected Writings*, vol. 2 (The Hague: Mouton, 1971), 255–56, cited in Gallop, *Reading Lacan*, 126.

53. This is Jane Gallop's translation of a passage from Lacan's *Le Séminaire III: Les Psychoses* (Paris: Seuil, 1981), 266, in *Reading Lacan*, 126. For the more common translation of this passage, see *The Seminar of Jacques Lacan: Book 3*, 228.

54. On regionalism and synecdoche, see the introduction to *U.S. Local Color Writers, 1880–1920: An Anthology*, ed. Elizabeth Ammons and Valerie Rohy (New York: Viking / Penguin, 1998), xxv.

55. Emerson, "Nature," 20.

56. Chopin, "The Awakening," *Book News* (July 1899), reprinted in Chopin, *The Awakening*, 159.

57. James, *The Bostonians*, 249.

58. Emerson, "Self-Reliance," in *Collected Works* 2:27.

59. Derrida, *Of Grammatology*, 147.

3. Modernist Perversity: The Repetition of Desire in *The Sun Also Rises*

1. Ernest Hemingway, *A Moveable Feast* (London: Grafton Books, 1977), 17. Christopher J. Knight discusses Hemingway's and other modernist writers' notions of originality and imitation in *The Patient Particulars: American Modernism and the Technique of Originality* (Lewisburg: Bucknell University Press, 1995), 138.

2. Ernest Hemingway, *The Sun Also Rises* (New York: Collier, 1986), 64. All further references will be cited in the text.

3. Hemingway's remark on "The Sea Change," published in a 1959 essay, is cited in Robert E. Fleming, "Perversion and the Writer in 'The Sea Change,' " in *New Critical Approaches to The Sun Also Rises*, ed. Jackson J. Benson (Durham: Duke University Press, 1990), 349–50.

4. See, for example, James R. Mellow, *Hemingway: A Life without Consequences* (Boston: Houghton Mifflin, 1992), 104, 166–68, 231, 294; and Mark Spilka, *Hemingway's Quarrel with Androgyny* (Lincoln: University of Nebraska Press, 1990), 297. In a study published after this book was completed, Carl P. Eby offers more complex readings of lesbian sexuality in Hemingway's life and texts; see *Hemingway's Fetishism: Psychoanalysis and the Mirror of Manhood* (Albany: SUNY Press, 1999).

5. On Pilar and female sexuality in *For Whom the Bell Tolls*, see Nancy R. Comley and Robert Scholes, *Hemingway's Genders: Rereading the Hemingway Text* (New Haven: Yale University Press, 1994), 46–50. On similarities between *The Garden of Eden* and "The Sea Change," see Comley and Scholes, *Hemingway's Genders*, 87–93; and Spilka, *Hemingway's Quarrel with Androgyny*, 204, 294–98.

6. Ezra Pound, *Cantos LII–LXXI* (Norfolk, Conn.: New Directions, 1940), 11.

7. Ernest Hemingway, *The Garden of Eden* (New York: Collier, 1986), 108.

8. Leslie Fiedler, "The Death of the Old Men," reprinted in *Critical Essays on American Modernism*, ed. Michael J. Hoffman and Patrick D. Murphy (New York: G. K. Hall, 1992), 93.

9. For a differently focused discussion of Hemingway, repetition, and lesbianism, see Marjorie Perloff, " 'Ninety Percent Rotarian': Gertrude Stein's Hemingway," *American Literature* 62 (1990): 668–83.

10. See Wendy Martin, "Brett Ashley as New Woman in *The Sun Also Rises*," in *New Essays on "The Sun Also Rises*," ed. Linda Wagner-Martin (New York: Cambridge University Press, 1987), 65–82; and Delbert E. Wylder, "The Two Faces of Brett: The New Woman in *The Sun Also Rises*," *Kentucky Philological Review* (1980): 27–33.

11. Burton Rascoe, "Diversity in the Younger Set," *New York Sun*, Nov. 6, 1929, 10, reprinted in *Ernest Hemingway: The Critical Reception*, ed. Robert O. Stephens (New York: Burt Franklin, 1977), 35.

12. Ernest Hemingway, "The Sea Change," in *Winner Take Nothing* (New York: Charles Scribner's Sons, 1970), 39, and *The Garden of Eden*, 14–15. Further references will be cited in the text.

13. On Catherine's similarity to Brett Ashley, see Robert B. Jones, "Mimesis and Metafiction in Hemingway's *The Garden of Eden*," *Hemingway Review*, Fall 1987, 4.

14. Carroll Smith-Rosenberg, *Disorderly Conduct: Visions of Gender in Victorian America* (New York: Oxford University Press, 1986), 265.

15. Cited in Smith-Rosenberg, *Disorderly Conduct*, 270–71. Krafft-Ebing's *Psychopathia Sexualis* was originally published in Europe in 1886; a translation appeared in the United States in 1908. On the "mannish lesbian" in sexological theory and lesbian self-representation, see also Mandy Merck, *Perversions: Deviant Readings* (New York: Routledge, 1993), 86–100.

16. Smith-Rosenberg, *Disorderly Conduct*, 278–79.

17. Sigmund Freud, "The Psychogenesis of a Case of Homosexuality in a Woman" (1920), *Standard Edition* 18:158.

18. Ernest Hemingway, "The Unpublished Opening of *The Sun Also Rises*" (1925), reprinted in *Major Literary Characters: Brett Ashley*, ed. Harold Bloom (New York: Chelsea House, 1991), 5.

19. Leslie Fiedler, *Love and Death in the American Novel*, rev. ed. (New York: Stein and Day, 1966), 319–20; Alan Tate, "Hard-Boiled," review of *The Sun Also Rises*, *The Nation* 123 (15 December 1926): 642–44, reprinted in Stephens, *Ernest Hemingway*, 43. Theodore Bardake, "Hemingway's Women: 1950," in *Ernest Hemingway: The Man and His Work*, ed. John K. M. McCaffery (Cleveland: World Publishing, 1950), 342–44. See also Comley and Scholes on Brett and deviant sexuality (*Hemingway's Genders*, 43).

20. Recent discussions of male homo- and heterosexuality in *The Sun Also Rises*, in addition to Spilka's *Hemingway's Quarrel with Androgyny*, include Ira Elliott, "Performance Art: Jake Barnes and 'Masculine' Signification in *The Sun Also Rises*," *American Literature* 67 (1995): 77–94; and Wolfgang E. H. Rudat, "Hemingway on Sexual Otherness: What's Really Funny in *The Sun Also Rises*," in *Hemingway Repossessed*, ed. Kenneth Rosen (Westport, Conn.: Greenwood, 1994), 169–79. In *Hemingway's Genders*, Comley and

Scholes offer astute but separate readings of gay male sexuality and lesbianism in Hemingway's writing.

21. Eve Kosofsky Sedgwick discusses the cultural policing of male homosocial and homosexual relations in her introduction to *Between Men: English Literature and Male Homosocial Desire* (New York: Columbia University Press, 1985), 1–20.

22. Replicating Hemingway's displacement of masculine anxieties onto women, one strand of the criticism compares Jake's sexuality to lesbianism, with somewhat awkward results. Rudat suggests that "Jake presumably has tried to assume a lesbian's role, that is, Jake-the-male presumably has tried to play the role of a female homosexual" ("Hemingway on Sexual Otherness," 176), while Kenneth Lynn bafflingly proposes that Jake is "like a lesbian" because "he cannot penetrate his loved one's body with his own." See *Hemingway* (New York: Fawcett Columbine, 1987), 323.

23. Robert Cohn loves Brett as well, but not in the same way. Rather than acknowledging her masculine qualities, he takes a sentimentalized view, imagining her as "absolutely fine and straight" (38).

24. In an early draft of "The Sea Change," Phil asks the bartender, "What do the punks drink, James. What can you recommend to a recent convert? . . . Take a look at me and mix whatever you like." See Comley and Scholes, *Hemingway's Genders*, 88; and Fleming, "Perversion and the Writer," 348.

25. Comley and Scholes, *Hemingway's Genders*, 92–93.

26. This line describing the lost generation of *The Sun Also Rises* appears in Hemingway's original first chapter of the novel; see "The Unpublished Opening," 6.

27. "Seeking Sensations," unsigned review of *The Sun Also Rises*, *Springfield Republican*, Nov. 28, 1926, 7F, reprinted in Stephens, *Ernest Hemingway*, 40. Lawrence S. Morris, "Warfare in Man and among Men," review of *The Sun Also Rises*, *New Republic* 49 (Dec. 22, 1926): 142–43, reprinted in Stephens, *Ernest Hemingway*, 44. "Study in Futility," unsigned review of *The Sun Also Rises*, *Cincinnati Enquirer*, Oct. 5, 1926, 5, reprinted in Stephens, *Ernest Hemingway*, 31.

28. Conrad Aiken, "Expatriates," review of *The Sun Also Rises*, *New York Herald Tribune Books*, (Oct. 31, 1926), vii–4, reprinted in Stephens, *Ernest Hemingway*, 33. "Sad Young Man," unsigned review of *The Sun Also Rises*, *Time* 8 (Nov. 1, 1926), 48, reprinted in *Critical Essays on Ernest Hemingway's The Sun Also Rises*, ed. James Nagel (New York: G. K. Hall, 1995), 37.

29. Sigmund Freud, "The Uncanny" (1919), *Standard Edition* 17:237–38. Further references will be cited in the text.

30. Sigmund Freud, *Beyond the Pleasure Principle* (1920), *Standard Edition* 18:22.

31. Judith Butler, *Bodies That Matter: On the Discursive Limits of "Sex"* (New York: Routledge, 1993), 12. Further references will be cited in the text.

32. Krafft-Ebing, *Psychopathia Sexualis*, 351; cited in Smith-Rosenberg, *Disorderly Conduct*, 271.

33. Havelock Ellis, "Sexual Inversion in Women," *Alienist and Neurologist* 16 (1895): 155–56, cited in Smith-Rosenberg, *Disorderly Conduct*, 79.

34. Diana Fuss, *Identification Papers* (New York: Routledge, 1995), 63–67.

35. In her reading of "The Psychogenesis of a Case of Homosexuality in a Woman," Fuss argues that lesbianism cannot properly constitute a repetition-compulsion, since the girl's preoedipal relation to the mother cannot be construed as "lesbian" or even as an object-choice (*Identification Papers*, 58–59).

36. This oscillation marks one difference between lesbian and gay male sexuality; in the twentieth-century Western imagination, at least, gay male sexuality seldom appears without the implication of sexual identity.

37. Neil Hertz, "Freud and the Sandman," in *The End of the Line: Essays on Psychoanalysis and the Sublime* (New York: Columbia University Press, 1985), 102.

38. Jonathan Culler, *On Deconstruction: Theory and Criticism after Structuralism* (Ithaca: Cornell University Press, 1982), 264.

39. Jacques Lacan, *The Seminar of Jacques Lacan: Book 3*, ed. Jacques-Alain Miller, trans. Russell Grigg (New York: W. W. Norton, 1993), 242.

40. Samuel Weber, *Return to Freud: Jacques Lacan's Dislocation of Psychoanalysis*, trans. Michael Levine (New York: Cambridge University Press, 1991), 5.

41. Linda Wagner-Martin discusses Hemingway and modernist ambivalence in her introduction to *New Essays on "The Sun Also Rises,"* 2.

42. Hertz, "Freud and the Sandman," 121. On figurality and repetition, see also Paul de Man, *Allegories of Reading: Figural Language in Rousseau, Nietzsche, Rilke, and Proust* (New Haven: Yale University Press, 1979), 114–15.

43. Cassandra Laity discusses the efforts of "virile" modernism like that of Pound and Eliot to disavow the feminine and feminizing romanticism associated with earlier women writers. See "H.D. and A. C. Swinburne: Decadence and Women's Poetic Modernism," in Hoffman and Murphy, *Critical Essays on American Modernism*, 212–13.

44. T. S. Eliot, *Selected Essays* (New York: Harcourt Brace Jovanovich, 1975), 38, 43. On Hemingway's animosity toward Eliot, see Perloff, " 'Ninety Percent Rotarian,' " 673; on his rivalry with other literary predecessors, see Mellow, *Hemingway*, 562.

45. Paul Morrison, "End Pleasure," *GLQ* 1 (1993): 69.

46. de Man, *Allegories of Reading*, 15.

47. Eve Kosofsky Sedgwick, *Epistemology of the Closet* (Berkeley: University of California Press, 1990), 166.

48. See Rudyard Kipling, *Rudyard Kipling's Verse* (New York: Doubleday, Page, 1940), 440–41.

49. The passage Phil attempts to quote from Pope's *Essay on Man* reads:
Vice is a monster of so frightful mien,
As to be hated needs but to be seen;
Yet seen too oft, familiar with her face,
We first endure, then pity, then embrace.
See Alexander Pope, *The Poems of Alexander Pope*, ed. John Butt (New York: Routledge, 1993), 3:81–82. Hemingway will elaborate Pope's notion of "vice" in the language of *The Tempest*: "Vice is a very strange thing," Phil muses, evoking Shakespeare's "sea-change."

50. In *The Hind and the Panther* Dryden writes, "For truth has such a face and such a mien / As to be loved needs only to be seen." John Dryden, *The Works of John Dryden: Poems, 1685–1692*, ed. H. T. Swedenberg Jr. (Berkeley: University of California Press, 1969), 3:124.

51. Hemingway, *A Moveable Feast*, 21. On Hemingway's anxieties about the "overly discursive," see Elliott, "Performance Art," 88.

52. Gertrude Stein, "Miss Furr and Miss Skeene" (1922), in *Selected Writings of Gertrude Stein*, ed. Carl Van Vechten (New York: Vintage Books, 1990), 568. Perloff discusses this story in " 'Ninety Percent Rotarian,' " 682–83.

53. Gertrude Stein, "Composition as Explanation" (1926), in *Selected Writings*, 516.

54. Hemingway, *A Moveable Feast*, 17.

55. "Marital Tragedy," unsigned review of *The Sun Also Rises*, *New York Times Book Review*, Oct. 31, 1926, 7, reprinted in Nagel, *Critical Essays*, 36.

56. Morrison, "End Pleasure," 69. Morrison's essay demonstrates the usefulness of Freudian concepts to gay and lesbian theory despite its explicitly critical attitude toward psychoanalysis. Psychoanalysis is not merely, as Morrison writes, "the most prestigious of technologies for self-fashioning and self-knowledge" (55); it is also a discourse that even (one might say, especially) in its failures exposes to critical scrutiny the logic by which straight culture "knows" and disciplines sexuality.

57. Ibid., 55. Although Morrison emphasizes the specific question of gay male sexuality in relation to narratives of the AIDS epidemic, he suggests that Freud's notion of homosexuality as a failure of teleology applies to lesbian sexuality as well. The Dora case, for example, is in Morrison's reading a text in which "same-sex desire remains the most inert of facts, utterly devoid of narrative life or potential" (63).

58. Judith Roof, *Come As You Are: Sexuality and Narrative* (New York: Columbia University Press, 1996), 17. Roof argues in more general terms that "the reciprocal relation between narrative and sexuality produces stories where homosexualities can only occupy certain positions or play certain roles metonymically linked to negative values within a reproductive aegis" (xxvii). On repetition and narrative form, see also Peter Brooks, "Freud's Masterplot," in *Reading for the Plot: Design and Invention in Narrative* (New York: Knopf, 1984), 90–112.

59. Hemingway, *A Moveable Feast*, 28.

60. Ibid., 29.

4. Oral Narratives: "Race" and Sexuality in *Their Eyes Were Watching God*

1. Toni Morrison, "Unspeakable Things Unspoken: The Afro-American Presence in American Literature," *Michigan Quarterly Review* 28 (1989): 3, 11.

2. Henry Louis Gates Jr., *The Signifying Monkey: A Theory of African-American Literary Criticism* (New York: Oxford University Press, 1988), 181.

3. Zora Neale Hurston, *Their Eyes Were Watching God* (Chicago: University of Illinois Press, 1978), 31–32. Further references will be cited in the text.

4. Readings that consider lesbian sexuality in *Their Eyes Were Watching God* include Carla Kaplan, "The Erotics of Talk: 'That Oldest Human Longing' in *Their Eyes Were Watching God*," *American Literature* 67 (1995): 115–42; Jane Gallop, *Around 1981: Academic Feminist Literary Theory* (New York: Routledge, 1992), 154–55; Molly Hite, "Romance, Marginality, and Matrilineage: *The Color Purple* and *Their Eyes Were Watching God*," *Novel* 22 (1989): 431–53; Marjorie Pryse, "Zora Neale Hurston, Alice Walker, and the 'Ancient Power' of Black Women," introduction to *Conjuring: Black Women, Fiction, and Literary Tradition* (Bloomington: Indiana University Press, 1985), 18; and Lorraine Bethel, " 'This Infinity of Conscious Pain': Zora Neale Hurston and the Black Female Literary Tradition," in *All the Women Are White, All the Blacks Are Men, but Some of Us Are Brave*, ed. Gloria Hull and Barbara Smith, et al. (Old Westbury, N.Y.: Feminist Press, 1982), 176–88.

5. Jacques Derrida, *Of Grammatology*, trans. Gayatri Chakravorty Spivak (Baltimore: Johns Hopkins University Press, 1974), 35.

6. Hortense Spillers, "The Permanent Obliquity of an In(pha)llibly Straight," in *Changing Our Own Words: Essays on Criticism, Theory, and Writ-*

ing by Black Women, ed. Cheryl Wall (New Brunswick: Rutgers University Press, 1989), 128–29.

7. Jean Walton, "Re-Placing Race in (White) Psychoanalytic Discourse: Founding Narratives of Feminism," in *Female Subjects in Black and White: Race, Psychoanalysis, Feminism*, ed. Elizabeth Abel, Barbara Christian, and Helene Moglen (Berkeley: University of California Press, 1997), 223–51.

8. Barbara Johnson, *The Feminist Difference: Literature, Psychoanalysis, Race, and Gender* (Cambridge: Harvard University Press, 1998), 11.

9. Hortense J. Spillers, " 'All the Things You Could Be by Now, If Sigmund Freud's Wife Was Your Mother': Psychoanalysis and Race," in Abel, et al., *Female Subjects in Black and White*, 139, 136.

10. Frederick Douglass, *Narrative of the Life of An American Slave* (1845), reprinted in *The Oxford Frederick Douglass Reader*, ed. William L. Andrews (New York: Oxford University Press, 1996), 32.

11. Frantz Fanon, *Black Skin, White Masks* (New York: Grove Press, 1967), 110.

12. Ibid., 116. On Fanon and the black body as signifier or "material supplement," see Lee Edelman, *Homographesis: Essays in Gay Literary and Cultural Theory* (New York: Routledge, 1994), 46–47.

13. On women "being" or embodying the phallus, see Jacques Lacan, *Feminine Sexuality*, ed. Juliet Mitchell and Jacqueline Rose, trans. Jacqueline Rose (New York: W. W. Norton, 1982), 84.

14. Zora Neale Hurston, *I Love Myself When I Am Laughing . . .* , ed. Alice Walker (Old Westbury, N.Y.: Feminist Press, 1979), 170.

15. Lauren Berlant, "National Brands / National Body: *Imitation of Life*," in *Comparative American Identities: Race, Sex, and Nationality in the Modern Text*, ed. Hortense Spillers (New York: Routledge, 1991), 113.

16. Richard Dyer, "White," in *The Matter of Images: Essays on Representations* (London: Routledge, 1993), 141–43 passim. On whiteness as a fantasy that is incommensurate with the "white" body, see also Walter Benn Michaels, "The Souls of White Folk," in *Literature and the Body: Essays on Populations and Persons*, ed. Elaine Scarry (Baltimore: Johns Hopkins University Press, 1988), 190.

17. Lacan, *Feminine Sexuality*, 82, 79.

18. Jacqueline Rose, introduction to Lacan, *Feminine Sexuality*, 42–43.

19. Samuel Weber, *Return to Freud: Jacques Lacan's Dislocation of Psychoanalysis*, trans. Michael Levine (New York: Cambridge University Press, 1991), 146. On the phallus as transcendental signifier, see also Slavoj Žižek, *The Sublime Object of Ideology* (New York: Verso, 1989), 223–24; Jacques Lacan, *Écrits: A Selection*, trans. Alan Sheridan (New York: W. W. Norton, 1977), 285, and *The Seminar of Jacques Lacan: Book 3*, ed. Jacques-Alain Miller, trans. Russell Grigg (New York: W. W. Norton, 1993), 189.

20. Barbara Johnson identifies a similar critique of phallic authority in Toni Morrison's *Sula*, arguing that Morrison "deconstruct[s] the phallus as law, patriarchy, and cultural ground, while appreciating the penis for the trivial but exciting pleasures and fantasies it can provide for the female characters in the novel. Morrison reverses the Lacanian elevation of the phallus into the signifier of signifiers by restoring the penis to its status as an organ." See " 'Aesthetic' and 'Rapport' in Toni Morrison's *Sula*," in *The Feminist Difference*, 79.

21. Zora Neale Hurston, *Moses, Man of the Mountain* (New York: Harper, 1991), 235.

22. Priscilla Wald, "Becoming 'Colored': The Self-Authorized Language of Difference in Zora Neale Hurston," *American Literary History* 2 (1990): 81–82.

23. See Edelman on the "recognition" of identity as its social production (*Homographesis*, 14–17).

24. Zora Neale Hurston, "How It Feels to Be Colored Me," in *I Love Myself When I Am Laughing*, 153.

25. On "race" as a trope, see Henry Louis Gates Jr., "Writing 'Race' and the Difference It Makes," introduction to "*Race*," *Writing, and Difference*, ed. Henry Louis Gates Jr. (Chicago: University of Chicago Press, 1986), 5–6. On the name "Alphabet" in *Their Eyes Were Watching God*, see Houston Baker Jr., *Blues, Ideology, and Afro-American Literature: A Vernacular Theory* (Chicago: University of Chicago Press, 1984), 37.

26. Barbara Johnson, "Thresholds of Difference: Structures of Address in Zora Neale Hurston," in *A World of Difference* (Baltimore: Johns Hopkins University Press, 1987), 175.

27. In a collaborative reading of *Their Eyes Were Watching God*, Gates and Johnson describe free indirect discourse as a "paradoxically *written* manifestation of the aspiration to the *oral*." See "A Black and Idiomatic Free Indirect Discourse," in *Zora Neale Hurston's Their Eyes Were Watching God*, ed. Harold Bloom (New York: Chelsea House, 1987), 75.

28. Derrida, *Of Grammatology*, 35.

29. Ibid., 38. Freud's *Moses and Monotheism* (1939), which appeared in the same year as Hurston's *Moses, Man of the Mountain*, links the Mosaic prohibition of graven images to the invention of an alphabet and the "dematerializing" of the deity (*Standard Edition* 23:112–15). Kaja Silverman discusses the speaking subject in classic cinema as an "unseen enunciator," which, like the phallus, exceeds its material embodiment in *The Acoustic Mirror: The Female Voice in Psychoanalysis and Cinema* (Bloomington: Indiana University Press, 1988), 30.

30. Gates, "Writing 'Race' and the Difference It Makes," 9. Gates offers a more detailed commentary on Derrida's account of speech and writing in

Figures in Black: Words, Signs, and the "Racial" Self (New York: Oxford University Press, 1987), 106–7.

31. Gates, "Writing 'Race,' " 11.

32. On the use of dialect in *Their Eyes Were Watching God*, see, for example, Michael North, *The Dialect of Modernism: Race, Language, and Twentieth-Century Literature* (New York: Oxford University Press, 1994), 125–39.

33. Silverman, *The Acoustic Mirror*, 39.

34. Hazel Carby, introduction to Frances E. W. Harper, *Iola Leroy* (Boston: Beacon Press, 1987), ix.

35. On the trial scene as a figure for the cultural challenges to black women's *writing*, see Mae Henderson, "Speaking in Tongues: Dialogics, Dialectics, and the Black Woman Writer's Literary Tradition," in Wall, *Changing Our Own Words*, 21.

36. Robert Hemenway, *Zora Neale Hurston: A Literary Biography* (Urbana: University of Illinois Press, 1977), 231.

37. Richard Wright, review of *Their Eyes Were Watching God* and *These Low Grounds*, *New Masses*, Oct. 5, 1937, reprinted in *Zora Neale Hurston: Critical Perspectives Past and Present*, ed. Henry Louis Gates Jr. and K. A. Appiah (New York: Amistad, 1993), 17. Hemenway discusses Sterling Brown's and Richard Wright's objections to the politics of *Mules and Men* and *Their Eyes Were Watching God* (*Zora Neale Hurston*, 218–20 and 241–42).

38. On the notion of the pear tree as "organic"—a reading that effectively naturalizes the heterosexual "marriage" this trope conjures—see Cheryl Wall, "Zora Neale Hurston: Changing Her Own Words," in Gates and Appiah, *Zora Neale Hurston: Critical Perspectives*, 89. Hemenway's biography of Hurston heavily stresses the notion of "organic union" and "the natural process," taking heterosexuality as "natural" and seemingly inevitable in the pear tree passage and in Janie's relationship with Tea Cake (*Zora Neale Hurston*, 233–35). Claudia Tate's reading of *Their Eyes Were Watching God* offers a useful correction to this view by considering the changing meaning of marriage as a cultural institution in African American history. See *Domestic Allegories of Political Desire: The Black Heroine's Text at the Turn of the Century* (New York: Oxford University Press, 1992), 75–76. For a reading of the novel as a criticism of heterosexual love, see Ann duCille, *The Coupling Convention: Sex, Text, and Tradition in Black Women's Fiction* (New York: Oxford University Press, 1993), 110–23.

39. Baker, *Blues, Ideology, and Afro-American Literature*, 57. Other readers who assert the dominance of questions of language, identity, or economics over romantic love include Missy Dehn Kubitschek, " 'Tuh de Horizon and Back': The Female Quest in *Their Eyes Were Watching God*," *Black American Literature Forum* 17 (1983): 109–15; Gates and Johnson, "A Black and Idiomatic Free Indirect Discourse," 33; Mary Helen Washington, "Zora Neale

Hurston: A Woman Half in Shadow," in Hurston, *I Love Myself When I Am Laughing*, 15.

40. Judith Butler, *Gender Trouble: Feminism and the Subversion of Identity* (New York: Routledge, 1990), 70. Butler locates the genesis of gender identity in the melancholic incorporation of the same-sex parent, as "a form of forgetfulness" that elides the possibility of homosexual object-choice (71).

41. Sigmund Freud, "Female Sexuality" (1931), *Standard Edition* 21:230.

42. Sigmund Freud, "The Psychogenesis of a Case of Homosexuality in a Woman" (1920), *Standard Edition* 18:156. On lesbianism as mother-love, see also "A Case of Paranoia Running Counter to the Psychoanalytical Theory of the Disease" (1915), *Standard Edition* 14:261–72.

43. Zora Neale Hurston, *Dust Tracks on a Road: An Autobiography*, ed. Robert Hemenway, 2d ed. (Chicago: University of Illinois Press, 1984), 260.

44. Sigmund Freud, "The Uncanny" (1919), *Standard Edition* 17:241. Freud reiterates that the prehistory of civilization and the prehistory of the individual psyche are closely connected; indeed, uncanny effects can arise "when infantile complexes which have been repressed are once more revived by some impression, or when primitive beliefs which have been surmounted seem once more to be confirmed" (249).

45. Sigmund Freud, "The Question of Lay Analysis," *Standard Edition* 20:212. Mary Ann Doane offers a valuable reading of this passage in *Femmes Fatales: Feminism, Film Theory, Psychoanalysis* (New York: Routledge, 1991), 210–12. Freud frequently repeats the analogy between "primitive" cultures and psychic formations; in *Three Essays on the Theory of Sexuality* (1905), for example, he notes that childhood appears to the adult as "something like a prehistoric epoch" (*Standard Edition* 7:176).

46. Diana Fuss, *Identification Papers* (New York: Routledge, 1995), 86.

47. Freud, *Three Essays, Standard Edition* 7:222, and *General Theory of the Neuroses* (1917), *Standard Edition* 16:314, cited in Fuss, *Identification Papers*, 85. On orality as "primitive," see *Introductory Lectures on Psycho-Analysis* (1916–17), *Standard Edition* 16:328.

48. See Fuss, *Identification Papers*, 159.

49. Freud, *Three Essays, Standard Edition* 7:145–46.

50. Fuss, *Identification Papers*, 58.

51. Sigmund Freud, *Fragment of an Analysis of a Case of Hysteria* (1905), *Standard Edition* 7:52. On hysteria and the displacement of erotic meaning onto "oral and anal orifices," see *Three Essays, Standard Edition* 7:169, and *Introductory Lectures, Standard Edition* 16:308. Parveen Adams discusses orality and the Dora case in "Per Os(cillation)," in *Male Trouble*, ed. Constance Penley and Sharon Willis (Minneapolis: University of Minnesota Press, 1993), 3–25.

52. Johnson, "Metaphor, Metonymy, and Voice," in *A World of Difference*, 171. Gates offers his full definition of free indirect discourse in *The Signify-*

ing Monkey, 207–15. See also Gates and Johnson, "A Black and Idiomatic Free Indirect Discourse." For a dissenting view of free indirect discourse and Janie's attempt at self-expression, see Susan Sniader Lanser, *Fictions of Authority: Women Writers and Narrative Voice* (Ithaca: Cornell University Press, 1992), 201–6.

53. Kaplan has suggested that Hurston figures the "double voice" of free indirect discourse as a "lesbian" relation between Janie and Phoeby ("The Erotics of Talk," 17). On Janie and Phoeby as figures for Hurston and Janie, respectively, see John F. Callahan, " 'Mah Tongue Is in Mah Friend's Mouf': The Rhetoric of Intimacy and Immensity in *Their Eyes Were Watching God*," in Bloom, *Zora Neale Hurston's Their Eyes Were Watching God*, 87–113.

54. Jonathan Culler, *On Deconstruction: Theory and Criticism after Structuralism* (Ithaca: Cornell University Press, 1982), 198. Derrida discusses invagination in "Living On: Border Lines," in *Deconstruction and Criticism*, ed. Harold Bloom et al. (New York: Seabury, 1979), 75–175; and "The Parergon," *October* 9 (1979): 3–40. Hite proposes a connection between *Their Eyes Were Watching God* and Derrida's notion of the *parergon*, a disappearing frame or margin ("Romance, Marginality, and Matrilineage," 446), suggesting that the frame story in Hurston's text supplants the ostensibly central heterosexual plot. While Hite's reading is persuasive, my concerns focus on the ways Hurston's heterosexual plot is inseparable from, and dependent on, its "lesbian" frame.

55. Bethel, " 'This Infinity of Conscious Pain'," 187; and Hite, "Romance, Marginality, and Matrilineage,"445–47. See also Gallop, *Around 1981*, 147–48.

56. Kaplan, "The Erotics of Talk," 116.

5. Love's Substitutions: Elizabeth Bishop and the Lie of Language

1. Irigaray has suggested that melancholia is the normative state of femininity and the prescribed foundation of feminine gender identity. In this view the girl must incorporate her mother as an object of identification whose loss and whose very existence have been "forgotten," as in *Their Eyes Were Watching God*, but whose meaning is then literalized on and in the feminine body. See Luce Irigaray, *Speculum of the Other Woman*, trans. Gillian C. Gill (Ithaca: Cornell University Press, 1985), 66–70. Judith Butler discusses melancholia as the foundation of gender for both sexes in *Gender Trouble: Feminism and the Subversion of Identity* (New York: Routledge, 1990), 57–72.

2. Where the primal attachment to the mother is concerned, the binary system of identification and desire divides femininity and lesbianism into

mutually exclusive categories. In the psychoanalytic account of feminine sexuality, to desire the mother is to be a lesbian; to identify with her is to be a (heterosexual) woman. As Fuss has argued, however, this arbitrary separation of desire and identification is unsustainable; indeed, lesbian desire and feminine gender identification can resemble and feed on each other. See *Identification Papers* (New York: Routledge, 1995), 123. Acknowledging the competing discourses of various forms of identification, Fuss offers a valuable account of identification as a field of contradictory impulses and structures. She differs from other writers on identification and melancholia by taking identification, in its broadest terms, as a *combination* of the effects that Nicolas Abraham and Maria Torok, for example, associate separately with mourning (metaphor, transference, displacement) and melancholia (incorporation, oral-cannibalistic impulses, sadism). By positing identification, including that of melancholic incorporation, as fundamentally metaphorical rather than anti-metaphorical (37–38), Fuss's argument tends to collapse the difference between mourning and melancholia—an effect that is both problematic and provocative in view of Bishop's similar gesture.

3. I use "Elizabeth" to differentiate the child protagonist of the stories from Bishop as author.

4. Elizabeth Bishop, *The Collected Prose*, ed. Robert Giroux (New York: Farrar Straus and Giroux, 1984), 16. Further references will be cited in the text.

5. Freud names this logic of retroactive experience *Nachträglichkeit*, the deferred action produced by a trauma—paradigmatically, the primal scene—whose displaced effects surface later in life. Jean Laplanche offers a useful discussion of trauma and deferred effects in *Life and Death in Psychoanalysis*, trans. Jeffrey Mehlman (Baltimore: Johns Hopkins University Press, 1976), 41–44.

6. Jane Gallop, "Keys to Dora," in *In Dora's Case: Freud—Hysteria—Feminism*, 2d ed., ed. Charles Bernheimer and Clare Kahane (New York: Columbia University Press, 1990), 208.

7. The memoir's title hints at Elizabeth's placement within the register of social class, borrowing the title of Aesop's fable to name Elizabeth as the modest "country mouse," not the privileged city one.

8. Elizabeth Bishop, *The Complete Poems, 1927–1979* (New York: Farrar Straus and Giroux, 1979), 70.

9. Sigmund Freud, *Beyond the Pleasure Principle* (1920), *Standard Edition* 18:14–16.

10. Samuel Weber, *Return to Freud: Jacques Lacan's Dislocation of Psychoanalysis*, trans. Michael Levine (New York: Cambridge University Press, 1991), 132.

11. Elizabeth Bishop to Robert Lowell, April 4, 1962, cited in Joanne Feit Diehl, *Elizabeth Bishop and Marianne Moore: The Psychodynamics of Cre-*

ativity (Princeton: Princeton University Press, 1993), 53. Bishop often discussed her poems' descriptive accuracy; see, for example, George Starbuck, "The Work! A Conversation with Elizabeth Bishop," *Ploughshares* 3 (1977): 312–30.

12. Lee Edelman describes Bishop's recourse to "the solid ground of literality—a literality that Bishop repeatedly identifies as 'truth,' " going on to suggest that in Bishop's poems "truth comes into alignment with trope, literal and figurative effectively change places." Bishop's poetry, he suggests, acknowledges the vicissitudes of representation and subjectivity "that make direct contact with any literality—with any 'truth'—an impossibility" ("The Geography of Gender," 179–80).

13. Lorrie Goldensohn, *Elizabeth Bishop: The Biography of a Poetry* (New York: Columbia University Press, 1992), 119.

14. Diehl, *Elizabeth Bishop and Marianne Moore*, 41.

15. Bonnie Costello, *Elizabeth Bishop: Questions of Mastery* (Cambridge: Harvard University Press, 1991), 9, 11.

16. Goldensohn, *Elizabeth Bishop*, 68–69. Although at one point Goldensohn aligns lesbian desire with "hidden allegory," in contrast to the "firm literality" of Bishop's poetry, her argument ultimately construes lesbian sexuality in a literal way (62). Brett Millier discusses Bishop's lesbianism in similar terms in her biography, *Elizabeth Bishop: Life and the Memory of It* (Berkeley: University of California Press, 1993). Other discussions of Bishop and lesbian sexuality include David R. Jarraway, " 'O Canada!': The Spectral Lesbian Poetics of Elizabeth Bishop," *PMLA* 113, no. 2 (1998): 243–57; Margaret Dickie, *Stein, Bishop and Rich: Lyrics of Love, War, and Place* (Chapel Hill: University of North Carolina Press, 1997), 82–103; Gary Fountain, " 'Closets, Closets, and More Closets!': Elizabeth Bishop's Lesbianism," in *Queer Representations: Reading Lives, Reading Cultures*, ed. Martin Duberman (New York: New York University Press, 1997), 247–57; Marilyn May Lombardi, *The Body and the Song: Elizabeth Bishop's Poetics* (Carbondale: Southern Illinois University Press, 1995), and "The Closet of Breath: Elizabeth Bishop, Her Body and Her Art," *Twentieth Century Literature* 38, no. 2 (1992): 152–75; Victoria Harrison, *Elizabeth Bishop's Poetics of Intimacy* (New York: Cambridge University Press, 1993); and Jeredith Merrin, "Elizabeth Bishop: Gaiety, Gayness, and Change," in *Elizabeth Bishop: The Geography of Gender*, ed. Marilyn May Lombardi (Charlottesville: University Press of Virginia, 1993), 153–72.

17. Havelock Ellis, *Studies in the Psychology of Sex: Sexual Inversion* (1897), cited in Lillian Faderman, *Surpassing the Love of Men: Romantic Friendship and Love between Women from the Renaissance to the Present* (New York: William Morrow, 1981), 243.

18. Cited in Diehl, *Elizabeth Bishop and Marianne Moore*, 53–54. Diehl offers a strong reading of the way "facts" and self-deception change places in

this passage. Of course, this deconstructive understanding of truth and false-hood goes against the grain of the lesbian criticism that has posited lying as a synonym for closetedness. In her essay "Women and Honor: Some Notes on Lying," for example, Adrienne Rich regards truth-telling as politically essential (*On Lies, Secrets, and Silence: Selected Prose, 1966–1978* [New York: W. W. Norton, 1979], 185–194). See also Catharine Stimpson, "Gertrude Stein and the Lesbian Lie," in *American Women's Autobiography: Fea(s)ts of Memory*, ed. Margo Culley (Madison: University of Wisconsin Press, 1992), 152–66.

19. Millier, *Elizabeth Bishop*, 11. In 1916 Gertrude Bulmer Bishop was "diagnosed as permanently insane" and hospitalized in a public sanatorium in Nova Scotia. She died in 1934 without seeing Elizabeth again.

20. Lombardi reads this passage as a reflection on the "family voice" (*The Body and the Song*, 22), while Millier presents the lie as an example of repression (*Elizabeth Bishop*, 21–22).

21. Sigmund Freud, "Female Sexuality" (1931), *Standard Edition* 21:228.

22. Sigmund Freud, "Mourning and Melancholia" (1917), *Standard Edition*, 14:247–48. If melancholia is a response to an unacknowledged loss, Elizabeth's loss of her mother may be unnameable because it does *not* take the form of death—because, that is, the shame of her mother's madness, like homosexuality in the public sphere, functions as a prohibition of speech.

23. On hysterical symptoms as versions of melancholic symptoms, see Irigaray, *Speculum*, 70–71.

24. Abraham and Torok suggest that mourning or *introjection* is the foundation of speech and signification, through the loss of the mother, which creates an empty space figured by the empty mouth from which speech will emerge when "words replace the mother's presence." See "Mourning *or* Melancholia: Introjection *versus* Incorporation," in *The Shell and the Kernel*, vol. 1, trans. and ed. Nicholas T. Rand (Chicago: University of Chicago Press, 1994), 127–28. See also Butler, *Gender Trouble*, 68.

25. Monique Wittig, *The Straight Mind and Other Essays* (Boston: Beacon Press, 1992), 32. The question of what distinguishes "lesbian" from "woman" is a recurrent concern in lesbian and feminist criticism. One instructive case study is Diana Fuss's exchange with Molly Anne Rothenberg and Joseph Valente; see Fuss's "Look Who's Talking, or If Looks Could Kill," *Critical Inquiry* 22 (1996): 383–92; and Rothenberg and Valente's "Fashionable Theory and Fashion-able Women: Returning Fuss's Homospectatorial Look," *Critical Inquiry* 22 (1996): 372–82. Fuss's original essay, "Fashion and the Homospectatorial Look," appears in *Critical Inquiry* 18 (1992): 713–37. For their part, some lesbian critics have sought to define lesbian specificity as distinct from "woman" and lesbian theory as distinct from feminist theory. See, for example, Teresa de Lauretis, *The Practice of Love: Lesbian Sexuality and Perverse Desire* (Bloomington: Indiana University Press,

1994), 47–51; and Cheshire Calhoun, "The Gender Closet: Lesbian Disappearance under the Sign 'Women,' " in *Lesbian Subjects: A Feminist Studies Reader*, ed. Martha Vicinus (Bloomington: Indiana University Press, 1996), 209–32.

26. Ernest Jones, *The Life and Work of Sigmund Freud* (New York: Basic Books, 1955), 2:279; and Sigmund Freud, "The Psychogenesis of a Case of Homosexuality in a Woman" (1920), *Standard Edition* 18:147. Further references to Freud's essay are cited in the text. On Freud's representation of lesbianism in "A Case of Homosexuality in a Woman," see also Mary Jacobus, "Russian Tactics: Freud's 'Case of Homosexuality in a Woman,' " *GLQ* 2, nos. 1–2 (1995): 65–79; Mandy Merck, *Perversions: Deviant Readings* (New York: Routledge, 1993), 13–32; Judith Roof, "Freud Reads Lesbians: The Male Homosexual Imperative," *Arizona Quarterly* 46, no. 1 (1990): 17–26; and Luce Irigaray, *This Sex Which Is Not One*, trans. Catherine Porter (Ithaca: Cornell University Press, 1985).

27. Joan Riviere, "Womanliness as a Masquerade," in *Formations of Fantasy*, ed. Victor Burgin, James Donald, and Cora Kaplan (London: Methuen, 1986), 43. Stephen Heath offers a useful gloss of Riviere: "In the masquerade the woman mimics an authentic—genuine—womanliness but then authentic womanliness is such a mimicry, *is* the masquerade." See "Joan Riviere and the Masquerade," in Burgin, Donald, and Kaplan, *Formations of Fantasy*, 49.

28. Heath, "Joan Riviere and the Masquerade," 53, 50.

29. To invoke figural language in this way may seem to hold out the possibility of a language that might be anything other than figural and to conjure a fantasy of literal meaning, of what Bishop calls "facts" or "truth." Although all language is in a powerful sense "figural language," I want to preserve for the moment the fantasmatic distinction between literality and figurality in order to trace its structuring role in notions of lesbian desire.

30. Jacques Lacan, *Écrits: A Selection*, trans. Alan Sheridan (New York: W. W. Norton, 1977), 284.

31. Jacques Lacan, *The Four Fundamental Concepts of Psychoanalysis*, ed. Jacques-Alain Miller, trans. Alan Sheridan (New York: W. W. Norton, 1981), 37–38. Lacan discusses lying and truthful speech in relation to the real in *The Seminar of Jacques Lacan: Book 1*, ed. Jacques-Alain Miller, trans. John Forrester (New York: W. W. Norton, 1991), 228–29.

32. Paul de Man, *Allegories of Reading: Figural Language in Rousseau, Nietzsche, Rilke, and Proust* (New Haven: Yale University Press, 1979), 112, 111.

33. Elizabeth Bishop to Robert Lowell, 1954, cited in Goldensohn, *Elizabeth Bishop*, 228; Lacan, "Seminar on 'The Purloined Letter,' " trans. Jeffrey Mehlman, in *The Purloined Poe: Lacan, Derrida, and Psychoanalytic Reading*, ed.

John Muller and William J. Richardson (Baltimore: Johns Hopkins University Press, 1988), 53.

34. Wallace Stevens, *Opus Posthumous*, ed. Samuel French Morse (New York: Alfred A. Knopf, 1957), 162.

35. See Eve Kosofsky Sedgwick, *Epistemology of the Closet* (Berkeley: University of California Press, 1990), 147–54.

36. Jane Tompkins, "Sentimental Power: *Uncle Tom's Cabin* and the Politics of Literary History," in *The New Feminist Criticism: Essays on Women, Literature and Theory*, ed. Elaine Showalter (New York: Pantheon, 1985), 82. Goldensohn also discusses modernism and Bishop's resistance to sentimentality (*Elizabeth Bishop*, 70).

37. For Bishop the modernist model of literary authority presents a double bind. Readers who celebrate the "truthfulness" of her poems most often acknowledge not her grasp of metaphysical truth, but her accurate description of observed detail, returning Bishop to a devalued, "feminine" position.

38. Tompkins, "Sentimental Power," 83. As Sedgwick has noted, even the denunciation of sentimentality involves the observer in a sentimental relation (*Epistemology of the Closet*, 143–50), and "The Country Mouse" is not lacking in sentimental spectacle. Elizabeth's disavowal of her "hideous" lie is at least as self-pitying, as melodramatic in its way, as the would-be orphan's version of her family history. Her rejection of sentimentality also follows a narrative moment intimately concerned with tears. Describing Elizabeth's nights of flashlight games and crying, Bishop quotes Louise Bogan: "At midnight tears / Run into your ears" (31). The tears evoke the nineteenth-century sentimental novel even as the strategy of quotation distances Bishop from the uncomfortable spectacle thus presented. With a citation of another female poet, albeit a modernist one, this rhetorical sleight of hand allows Bishop both to deny and to engage with the hallmark of "feminine" writing, to "blink" that rhetoric "off and on" as Elizabeth does with her flashlight and her tears.

39. Although "Gwendolyn" was written before "The Country Mouse" and seems to correspond to an earlier moment in Bishop's childhood—most likely the summer before her move to Worcester—I want to resist the teleological impulse that would organize the stories in chronological order. Rather than a developmental sequence, "Gwendolyn" and "The Country Mouse" constitute two literary versions of the same story that present alternative ways of working through issues of mother-love, mourning, desire, and femininity. For a biographical account of Bishop's time in Nova Scotia and her move to Worcester, see Millier, *Elizabeth Bishop*, 19.

40. C. K. Doreski offers a quite different reading of "Gwendolyn," discussing metaphor in relation to Elizabeth's self-knowledge, in *Elizabeth*

Bishop: The Restraints of Language (New York: Oxford University Press, 1993), 73–76.

41. Harriet Beecher Stowe, *Uncle Tom's Cabin* (New York: W. W. Norton, 1994), 126–27. On the nineteenth-century sentimental figure of "the Child Angel," see Tompkins, "Sentimental Power," 86.

42. On playing with dolls as "evidence of the exclusiveness of [the girl's] attachment to her mother," see Freud, "Female Sexuality," *Standard Edition* 21:237.

43. See Fuss, *Identification Papers*, 21–56.

44. Sigmund Freud, "Mourning and Melancholia" (1917), *Standard Edition* 14:249–50. In "Female Sexuality" Freud notes that the girl's aggression against her mother, a kind of "death-wish" like Elizabeth's lie, can take the form of oral fantasies: "the child wants to eat up its mother from whom it has had its nourishment" (*Standard Edition* 21:237).

45. Marianne Moore to Elizabeth Bishop, October 16, 1940 (Vassar College collection), cited in David Kalstone, *Becoming a Poet*, ed. Robert Hemenway (New York: Farrar Straus and Giroux, 1989), 80. In "Efforts of Affection" Bishop recalls that Moore objected to words like "spit" in poetry (*The Collected Prose*, 130).

46. Stowe, *Uncle Tom's Cabin*, 126.

47. Like Elizabeth's cannibalistic fantasy, this forgetfulness recalls melancholia. Here, however, in the service of a different relation, it signals not a maternal identification but a phobic response to a socially proscribed desire. On forgetting and melancholia, see Butler, *Gender Trouble*, 70–71.

48. Abraham and Torok, "Mourning *or* Melancholia," 132. Incorporation is "antimetaphorical," they argue, not only in "reverting to the literal meanings of words" but also in "using them in such a way—whether in speech or deed—that their very capacity for figurative representation is destroyed" (132).

49. Slavoj Žižek, *Looking Awry: An Introduction to Jacques Lacan through Popular Culture* (Cambridge: MIT Press, 1991), 30.

50. Jarraway, " 'O Canada!' " 247. It is unclear in Jarraway's argument how an "empowered subjectivity" can exist outside the symbolic, which in Lacanian terms is not only the locus of social power but also the very foundation of subjectivity. Jarraway's notion of the real as a space of political opportunity, however, is echoed in Lynda Hart's account of lesbianism and the Lacanian real. Having argued that patriarchal culture consigns lesbians to the space of the real, Hart suggests that the real is not simply that which symbolization excludes, but rather "that which *evades* the frame of representation and its (en)closures. The 'Real,' in my reading, is precisely the possibilities of the imaginary that are located at the very limits of representation. Or, what representation fails to limit. This is a location where very productive feminist work does—and must, I think—take place." The notoriously

contradictory nature of the real cannot fully account for the slippage here between agency and passivity, between liminality ("at the very limits") and exteriority ("that which *evades* the frame"), between the real as a fantasmatic effect and its interpellation as a "real"—that is, more or less concrete—site of feminist intervention. See *Between the Body and the Flesh: Performing Sadomasochism* (New York: ColumbiaUniversity Press, 1998), 67.

51. Jarraway, " 'O Canada!' " 247.

52. Terry Castle, *The Apparitional Lesbian: Female Homosexuality and Modern Culture* (New York: Columbia University Press, 1993), 19, 11, 7. In her essay "The Psychomorphology of the Clitoris," Valerie Traub responds to Castle's argument (*GLQ* 2 [1995]: 81–113).

53. Foucault's claim is that the construction of sexuality as "the outer limit of every social discourse, something akin to a secret whose discovery is imperative, a thing abusively reduced to silence, and at the same time difficult and necessary, dangerous and precious to divulge" is the mechanism by which sexuality, in all its forms, is rendered available to social discipline. See *The History of Sexuality: An Introduction* (New York: Vintage, 1990), 34–35. Annamarie Jagose offers a useful critique of the repressive hypothesis in lesbian criticism in her introduction to *Lesbian Utopics* (New York: Routledge, 1994), 3–8.

54. For Lacan, as Samuel Weber has noted, "desire is always a desire for something else" (*Return to Freud*, 127), and this restless movement of desire toward the eternal "something else" depends on metaphorical substitution.

55. Tompkins, "Sentimental Power," 85.

56. Sedgwick identifies vicariousness as a defining quality of sentimentality: "the prurient; the morbid; the wishful; the snobbish; the knowing; the arch" are all "subcategories of the sentimental, to the extent that each involves a covert reason for, or extent or direction of, identification through a spectatorial route" (*Epistemology of the Closet*, 51). Hemingway's *Sun Also Rises*, with a typical ambivalence about the literary, describes Jake's activity of reading as a vicarious experience: "I would remember it somewhere, and afterward it would seem as though it had really happened to me" (*The Sun Also Rises* [New York: Collier, 1986], 149).

Conclusion

1. Jacques Lacan, *Feminine Sexuality*, ed. Juliet Mitchell and Jacqueline Rose, trans. Jacqueline Rose (New York: W. W. Norton, 1982), 144.

2. Michèle Montrelay, "Inquiry into Femininity," *m / f* 1 (1978): 89. Cited in Mary Anne Doane, *Femmes Fatales: Feminism, Film Theory, Psychoanalysis* (New York: Routledge, 1991), 103.

3. Bonnie Zimmerman, "What Has Never Been: An Overview of Lesbian Feminist Literary Criticism," reprinted in *The New Feminist Criticism: Essays on Women, Literature, and Theory*, ed. Elaine Showalter (New York: Pantheon, 1985), 200–224. In one sense the story of nineteenth- and early-twentieth-century American literature represents another search for "what has never been." Simultaneously laboring to invent and to reinvent itself, the literature of this era reflects the anxious project of *producing* national identity. In 1901, for example, Frank Norris claimed that "the United States of America has never been able to boast of a school of fiction distinctively its own," calling for the production of a national literature. See "An American School of Fiction?" in *The Responsibilities of the Novelist* (New York: Greenwood, 1968), 193.

4. Ernest Hemingway, *The Garden of Eden* (New York: Collier, 1986), 224.

5. The notion of lesbian "reality" as threatened by discourse often feeds the resistance to theory in lesbian criticism. In their introduction to a 1993 volume, for example, Susan J. Wolfe and Julia Penelope posit not only patriarchal discourse but also language itself—epitomized by the post-structuralist proponents of "mere textuality"—as a threat to lesbian identity. While their association of post-structuralist theory with "mere" language might seem to designate "theory" as inconsequential, Wolfe and Penelope attribute to "mere textuality" the power to disturb the ontological security of "reality" and to "threaten the erasure of real (or, as the postmodernists would say, 'material') Lesbians." See *Sexual Practice, Textual Theory*, ed. Susan J. Wolfe and Julia Penelope (Cambridge: Blackwell, 1993), 2–6 passim.

6. Eve Kosofsky Sedgwick, *Epistemology of the Closet* (Berkeley: University of California Press, 1990), 204.

i n d e x

Abjection, 3, 22, 25, 73, 126
Abraham, Nicolas, 128, 138, 176–77
  n. 2, 179 n. 24, 182 n. 48
Abyss, 55–56, 59, 64, 75
Acousmatic voice, 29–30, 37, 113
Aiken, Conrad, 74
Allegory, 5, 13–15, 19–20, 31–32, 49,
  62, 139, 178 n. 16
American literature, 5–6, 14, 16, 94;
  and lesbian criticism, 148–49; and
  nationalism, 44–48, 62–64, 132, 184
  n. 3
"American Literature" (Fuller), 45–48
Arlen, Michael, 68, 75
Arnold, Ruth, 66
Awakening, The (Chopin), 42–52,
  55–65, 75, 86, 118, 130–31, 144–45

Baker, Houston A., Jr., 107
Bardake, Theodore, 71
Battan, Jesse F., 46
Berlant, Lauren, 5, 34, 99, 156 n. 25
Bethel, Lorraine, 116
Bishop, Elizabeth, 117–28, 131–45,
  148, 177 n. 7, 178 n. 12, 181 nn.
  38–39; critical reception of,
  123–24, 139–40, 181 n. 37; as les-
  bian, 119, 124, 178 n. 16; letters of,

123–24, 131; poetry of, 122,
  124–25
Blithedale Romance, The (Hawthorne),
  13, 15–22, 25–34, 37–38, 41, 43, 71,
  101, 105, 112–13
Bloom, Harold, 44–45, 55
Body: and disembodiment, 28–29, 37,
  139, 173 n. 29; lesbian, 37–38,
  52–53, 139, 154 n. 27; maternal,
  33–34, 110; and "race," 94, 98–106;
  and speech, 29, 33–38, 94, 105–6,
  159–60 n. 70
Bogan, Louise, 181 n. 38
Bostonians, The (James), 13–16, 20,
  26–27, 31–41, 48, 64, 82, 105, 116,
  121
Brodhead, Richard, 19, 34
Brook Farm, 19, 32
Butler, Judith, 2–3, 22, 67–68, 77, 80,
  89, 108, 152 n. 7, 175 n. 40

Carby, Hazel, 105
Castle, Terry, 1, 23, 139–40, 151 n. 3
Castration, 22, 28, 30–31, 53, 59, 109,
  112, 148
Cather, Willa, 6, 42–43, 50, 160–61
  n. 1
Chion, Michel, 28–29, 37

Chopin, Kate, 42–52, 55–65, 75, 86, 118–19, 130–31, 144–45, 162 n. 21
Citation, 67–68, 77–80, 88–89
Cixous, Helénè, 152 n. 9
Class, social, 7, 51, 69–70, 107, 122, 125, 177 n. 7
"Composition as Explanation" (Stein), 84
Costello, Bonnie, 124
Cott, Nancy, 8
"Country Mouse, The" (Bishop), 118–28, 131–33, 137–38, 142, 177 n. 7, 181 nn. 38–39
Criminal Law Amendment Act, 23
"Crusoe in England" (Bishop), 124
Culler, Jonathan, 79, 89, 114

"Dark continent," 111
de Lauretis, Teresa, 2, 179–80 n. 25
de Man, Paul, 3–4, 31, 37–38, 81, 130–31, 156 n. 28
Deconstruction, 3–4, 55, 94
Derrida, Jacques, 35, 64, 94, 103–4, 114
Dialect, 104–5
Diehl, Joanne Feit, 123–24
Diggs, Marylynne, 8
Displacement, 47–48, 58–61, 140–44, 151–52 n. 4; of desire, 54, 56–61, 75–76, 126–28, 133, 137–38; in language, 53–54, 60, 62–64, 76, 83, 118–19, 131, 133, 162 n. 13; and racism, 96–97. See also Transference
Dolls, 120, 133–34, 141–43, 182 n. 42
Dora case, 37, 112, 121, 170 n. 57
Douglass, Frederick, 97
Dryden, John, 83, 89
Dust Tracks on a Road (Hurston), 110
Dyer, Richard, 99

Edelman, Lee, 59–60, 157 nn. 32–33, 160 n. 73, 162 n. 13, 163 n. 26, 172 n. 12, 178 n. 12
Eliot, T. S., 80–81
Ellis, Havelock, 14, 51, 69–70, 78, 124, 128, 130
Emerson, Ralph Waldo, 5, 43–50, 53, 62–64, 148

Essence: and essentialism, 4, 147; lesbian, 9–10, 14, 50, 124, 140, 145; vs. materiality, 17, 37

Family, 25, 60, 63–64, 95, 142; and reproduction, 5, 45–47, 57, 87; as trope of nation, 5, 30
Family romance, 44–45, 54
Fanon, Frantz, 98
Father, 44, 53, 57–59, 97, 126–27
Femininity, 32–36, 45–47, 58, 72, 105–19, 176 n. 1; and lesbian sexuality, 9, 17–18, 32–33, 41, 50–53, 68–71, 118, 128–30, 137, 145–46, 176–77 n. 2, 179 n. 25; and little-girlness, 118–22, 125, 132–36, 140–43. See also Women
Feminism, 33–34, 47–49, 69, 78, 105; and feminist criticism, 49, 95, 179 n. 25
Fetterley, Judith, 32, 34
Fiedler, Leslie, 67, 71
Figural language, 3, 180 n. 29; and displacement/transference, 48, 60–62, 131; and lesbian sexuality, 2, 5, 89, 130–32, 138–40, 147, 149; and lying, 130–31; and repetition, 79–82, 84; as substitutive, 118, 140, 151–52 n. 4 See also Language; Metaphor
Fort-da, 122–23, 126, 142
Foucault, Michel, 10, 151–52 n. 4, 154 nn. 26–27, 183 n. 53
Free indirect discourse, 103, 114, 173 n. 27
Freud, Sigmund, 28–30, 37, 86, 112, 127–28, 135, 170 n. 57, 177 n. 5, 182 n. 44; on displacement and transference, 47–48, 58–62; on the "family romance," 44–45, 54; on femininity, 40–41, 53–54, 56, 110–11; on the fort-da game, 122–23, 126, 142; on lesbian sexuality, 40–41, 57, 69–70, 109, 111–12, 126, 128–31, 137; and "race," 94–96, 110–11, 175 n. 44; on the uncanny, 67–68, 75–79, 88–89, 110

Fuller, Margaret, 33, 43–48, 162 n. 18
Fuss, Diana, 2, 53, 57–58, 78, 111–12,
  134, 169 n. 35, 176–77 n. 2, 179 n.
  25
Future, 5, 53–54, 60–62, 65, 79,
  87–89, 148

Gallop, Jane, 58, 62, 121, 163 n. 28
Garden Of Eden, The (Hemingway),
  66–68, 71, 73–74, 76, 84, 88, 149
Gates, Henry Louis, Jr., 92–94,
  103–4, 114, 173 n. 27
Gay male sexuality, 20, 35, 81–82, 89,
  91, 111; compared to lesbian sexuality, 18, 22–24, 51–52, 59–60,
  71–74, 163 n. 26, 170 n. 57
Goldensohn, Lorrie, 123–24, 178 n.
  16
"Gwendolyn" (Bishop), 118–19,
  132–43, 181 n. 39

Harlem Renaissance, 7
Harper, Frances E. W., 105
Hart, Lynda, 3, 23–24, 152 n. 8, 157
  n. 37, 182–83 n. 50
Hawthorne (James), 13–14, 19
Hawthorne, Nathaniel, 13–22, 25–34,
  37–38, 41, 43, 71, 101, 105,
  112–13, 119
Heath, Stephen, 129–30, 180 n. 27
Hemenway, Robert, 106, 174 n. 38
Hemingway, Ernest, 65–76, 82–90,
  112, 119, 132, 168 n. 24; critical reception of, 66–67, 72, 74–75, 84,
  168 n. 22; and literary style, 67,
  81–82, 85–86, 90, 149, 183 n. 56;
  and "lost generation," 65, 74–75,
  87–88; as modernist, 65, 67, 71–74,
  79–86, 89
Hemingway, Pauline Pfeiffer, 66
Hemingway, Ruth Hall, 66
Hertz, Neil, 79–80
Heterosexuality, 3, 25–27, 31, 40–41,
  52–53, 93, 152 n. 7, 174 n. 38; historical constructions of, 50–51, 69;
  feminine, 17, 53–54, 56, 58, 102,
  106–13, 136–39; masculine, 72–73,
  78–79; and narrative, 85–89,

115–17, 142, 176 n. 54; and the
  real, 22–24, 26, 30–31; and reproduction, 43–47, 59, 63–64, 88–89;
  as trope, 29–30, 37, 42–46. *See also*
  Marriage; Reproduction
Hite, Molly, 116, 176 n. 54
Homophobia, 52, 72–73, 126, 140,
  144–46, 150; and lesbian representation, 1, 10–12, 144–45
Homosexuality, 17–18, 22–23, 40–41,
  111–12, 129; historical constructions of, 8, 51–52, 71;
  and representation, 2–3, 35, 81–82,
  85–86, 152 n. 7, 157 n. 32, 160 n.
  73, 170 n. 57, 171 n. 58. *See also*
  Gay male sexuality; Lesbian
"How It Feels to Be Colored Me"
  (Hurston), 103, 120
Hurston, Zora Neale, 91–120, 128,
  135, 174 n. 38, 176 n. 54
Hutchinson, Anne, 33
Hysteria, 112, 121, 128

Idolatry, 17–18, 31, 94, 101–2, 104,
  110
Identification, 102, 122, 133–34,
  137–38; and desire, 31, 117–19,
  127–28, 140–42, 176–77 n. 2;
  melancholic, 117–18, 127–28, 135,
  138, 176 n. 1
Imaginary, the, 29–30, 112–13
Impossibility, 29–31, 91–92; in
  Bishop, 137–39, 143; lesbian, 1–4,
  15, 24–25, 91, 149–50, 151 nn. 2–3;
  and the real, 15, 22–26, 38–39,
  139–40
"In the Waiting Room" (Bishop), 125
Incorporation, 117, 135, 138–39, 175 n.
  40, 176 n. 1, 176–77 n. 2, 182 n. 48
Individualism, 49, 63–64
"Insomnia" (Bishop), 122
Invagination, 114–15
Inversion, sexual, 8, 14, 70–71, 74, 78,
  111, 122, 124, 163 n. 26
Irigaray, Luce, 176 n. 1

Jagose, Annamarie, 10, 154 n. 26, 183
  n. 53

Jakobson, Roman, 62
James, Henry, 13–16, 19–20, 26–27, 31–41, 48, 64, 82, 105, 116, 119, 121
James, William, 32
Jarraway, David R., 139–40, 182 n. 50
Johnson, Barbara, 95, 103, 114, 173 n. 20, 173 n. 27
Johnson, Edward, 33
Jones, Ernest, 129
Justus, James, 59

Kahane, Claire, 34, 41
Kaplan, Carla, 116, 176 n. 53
Katz, Jonathan Ned, 51
Kipling, Rudyard, 82–83, 97
Krafft-Ebing, Richard von, 14, 69–70, 78
Kristeva, Julia, 3

Lacan, Jacques, 30, 62, 79, 99, 145, 151–52 n. 4, 183 n. 54; on the real, 15, 21–22; on displacement, 47–48, 58; on lying, 130–31
"Ladies, The" (Kipling), 82–83
Language, 31, 112, 133, 151–52 n. 4; corruption of, 5–6, 17, 45–48, 62–63, 80–81, 148–49; and gay male sexuality, 22–23, 35, 59–60; and lesbian sexuality, 1–5, 23–24, 38, 46–48, 57–67, 89, 124–28, 139–41, 143, 147–50, 184 n. 5; "lie of," 118, 130–31, 138, 141, 143; women's, 33–38, 119–22 See also Figural language; Representation; Speech
Law, 20, 22–23, 67–68, 77–80, 88–89, 113
Lefcowitz, Allan B. and Barbara F., 19
Lesbian: in American culture, 7–9, 14, 51–53, 69–70; Bishop as, 119, 124, 178 n. 16; definitions of, 7–10, 146–47; "mannish," 1, 7, 69–70, 78
Lesbian criticism, 119, 139–40, 146–50, 179–80 n. 25, 184 n. 5
Levander, Carolyn Field, 35, 159–60 n. 70
Literariness, 37, 68, 74, 81–84, 89–90, 149

Litvak, Joseph, 40, 160 n. 78
Local color, 62
"Lost generation," 65, 74–75, 87–88
Lowell, Robert, 123–24, 131
Lying, 123–31, 142; and lesbian sexuality, 126, 128–30; and "lie of language," 118, 130–31, 138, 141, 143

Making of Americans, The (Stein), 84
Marriage, 16, 113, 116, 174 n. 38; and narrative, 42, 57, 87, 107–8, 142; resistance to, 9, 25, 56–57, 69; as trope, 29, 37, 45–46, 148
Masculinity, 44–45, 52, 72–73, 78–79, 82–85, 88–89, 105; in women, 66, 68–71, 82, 168 n. 23
Materiality, 17, 35–38, 103–4, 114, 116, 118; in lesbian theory, 147, 149, 184 n. 5; and "race," 92, 94–95, 98–101, 104–6; and women, 46–47, 99–101, 105–6
Melancholia, 117–18, 127–28, 135, 138–39, 176–77 n. 2, 179 n. 22, 182 n. 47
Metalepsis, 77, 80, 112, 115
Metaphor, 3, 31, 80, 130–31, 182 n. 48; and lesbian sexuality, 48, 52, 143–46, 163 n. 26; as substitution, 122–23, 127, 137, 140–44, 183 n. 54; and transference, 60–63, 118, 140. See also Figural language
Metonymy, 8, 14, 47, 52, 62, 163 n. 26
"Minister's Black Veil, The" (Hawthorne), 21
"Miss Furr and Miss Skeene" (Stein), 84
Modernism, 65, 67, 71–4, 79–86, 89, 131–32, 148
Montrelay, Michèle, 145
Moore, Marianne, 124, 135, 182 n. 45
"Morbidity," 16, 43, 48–49, 62–64, 82, 138, 143, 155 n. 13; in The Bostonians, 13, 20, 31, 48
Morris, Lawrence S., 74
Morrison, Paul, 81, 85–86, 170 nn. 56–57
Morrison, Toni, 91–92, 94, 173 n. 20
Moses, Man of the Mountain (Hurston), 102, 173 n. 29

Mother, 30, 53–54, 57–59, 70, 94, 109–13, 131–32, 169 n. 35, 182 n. 44; body of, 33–34, 110; identification with, 121–22, 176 n. 1, 176–77 n. 2; loss of, 109–12, 117–19, 122–28, 135, 137–38, 142, 179 n. 22, 179 n. 24; and motherhood, 8–9, 25, 51, 69, 115, 134; voice of, 28, 110–13, 115, 158 n. 46, 159–60 n. 70

Mourning, 118, 127–28, 132, 135, 137, 142–43, 176–77 n. 2, 179 n. 24

Moveable Feast, A (Hemingway), 83–84, 87

Narcissism, 43, 49, 52, 54–55, 82. *See also* Solipsism

Narrative, 15, 18–20, 112, 170 n. 57, 171 n. 58; closure of, 40–41, 56–57, 65, 85–88, 144; and marriage plot, 42, 56–57, 87, 107–8, 142; Oedipal, 41, 47, 54, 64; oral, 92–94, 113–16

Nationality and nationalism, 14, 30–31, 147–48; and American literature, 44–48, 62–64, 184 n. 3; and family, 5, 30; and "race," 98–99; and women, 33–34, 121

"Nature" (Emerson), 44–45, 47–48

New Woman, 7, 51, 66, 68–71, 73, 76, 86, 145

Nietzsche, Friedrich, 129

Norris, Frank, 184 n. 3

Object-choice, 8–9, 43, 51, 53–56, 58–60, 70, 111, 145–46

Oedipality, 25, 57–65, 162 n. 13; female, 29–31, 52–54, 126–27, 137–38, 142–44; as metaphor for literature, 44–48, 63–64; and narrative, 41, 47, 57, 115. *See also* Preoedipality

Of Mules and Men (Hurston), 92

Orality, 110–16, 118; and oral narrative, 92–95, 113–16, 148

"Out of the Cradle Endlessly Rocking" (Whitman), 55

Patriarchy, 3–4, 15, 22, 24–25, 31, 77–79; and racism, 94–102, 104–5

Peabody, Elizabeth, 32

Penelope, Julia, 184 n. 5

Pfister, Joel, 33

Phallus, 31, 53, 94, 98–101, 114–15, 173 n. 20

Pope, Alexander, 83, 89, 170 n. 49

Pound, Ezra, 67

Preoedipality, 9, 29–30, 53, 57–58, 94, 109–12, 115, 158 n. 46, 158 n. 51, 169 n. 35. *See also* Oedipality

"Primitive," the, 94, 110–113

Psychoanalysis: and gay/lesbian criticism, 149, 170 n. 56; and "race," 95–96. *See also* Freud, Sigmund; Lacan, Jacques

"Psychogenesis of a Case of Homosexuality in a Woman" (Freud), 57, 109, 112, 128–31, 137, 169 n. 35

"Race," 91–106, 110–11, 113–16, 172 n. 16; and psychoanalysis, 95–96

Racism, 94–102, 104–5, 113, 115

"Rappacini's Daughter" (Hawthorne), 33

Real, the, 22–27, 38–41, 119, 149, 157 n. 32; and impossibility, 15, 22–26, 38–39, 139–40; politics of, 22, 139–40, 182–83 n. 50; and "prohibition of the impossible," 26, 38–39; as resistance to symbolization, 15–16, 21–24, 139, 156 n. 28; as trauma, 22–25, 29–31, 112–13

Realism, literary, 7, 10, 13–15, 19–20, 31–32, 62, 67, 123, 148

Repetition, 65–68, 72, 74–90, 111–12, 148, 169 n. 35

Representation, 55–64, 77–80, 97, 114, 122–23, 125–28, 138–43, 147–50, 151 n. 3, 151–52 n. 4, 160 n. 73; of lesbian figures, 2–5, 21–24, 73, 99, 130–31, 149, 152 n. 8; and the real, 15, 21–23, 40, 138–41, 182–83 n. 50; and/as reproduction, 43–48, 62–64; resistance to, 21–24, 40, 91, 156 n. 28; and the type, 13–14, 31–32; and women, 130, 145. *See also* Language

Representative Men (Emerson), 49

Repressive hypothesis, 139, 183 n. 53
Reproduction, 9, 25, 51, 53–54, 145,
    148, 160 n. 74; and narrative,
    87–89, 115; and/as representation,
    43–48, 62–64
Rich, Adrienne, 154 n. 24, 178–79
    n. 18
Romance, 7, 10, 14–15, 19
Romantic friendship, 7–9, 51, 136
Roof, Judith, 2–3, 23–25, 86, 151 n. 2,
    157–58 n. 41, 171 n. 58
"Roosters" (Bishop), 135
Rose, Jacqueline, 99

Saussure, Ferdinand de, 104
"Sea Change, The" (Hemingway),
    66–68, 73–74, 83, 88–89, 168 n. 24
Sedgwick, Eve Kosofsky, 58, 82, 150,
    181 n. 38, 183 n. 56
Seidel, Kathryn Lee, 52
"Self-Reliance" (Emerson), 43–45, 49,
    64
Sentimentality, 67, 80, 82, 131–32,
    142–43, 148, 181 n. 38, 183 n. 56
Separate spheres, 8, 33, 36, 69
Sexology, 1, 3, 7–8, 14, 22, 46, 51,
    69–71. See also Ellis, Havelock;
    Krafft-Ebing, Richard von
Shakespeare, William, 88
Shelley, Mary, 46
Signifier, 59–61, 97, 123, 131, 137;
    phallus and whiteness as, 99–101,
    173 n. 20; and signified, 17, 38,
    61–62
Silverman, Kaja, 105, 158 n. 46,
    159–60 n. 70, 173 n. 29
Smith-Rosenberg, Carroll, 1, 8–9
Solipsism, 43, 45, 55, 82. See also Narcissism
Spacks, Patricia Meyer, 55
Speech, 84, 97–98, 100, 121, 179 n.
    24; women's, 27–28, 33–41, 92–95,
    110–16, 145, 159–60 n. 70, 160 n.
    74; compared to writing, 35–36, 41,
    94–95, 103–6, 114, 160 n. 73. See
    also Orality; Voice
Spillers, Hortense, 95–96
Stein, Gertrude, 65, 67, 75, 83–84, 87
Stevens, Wallace, 131

Stowe, Harriet Beecher, 134–35, 142
Style, literary, 42, 67, 81–82, 85–86,
    90, 132, 148
Subjectivity, 126–27, 130–31, 150,
    151–52 n. 4; female, 108, 112, 120,
    139–41, 182–83 n. 50; male, 20,
    71–73; and "race," 92, 96, 98, 102–3
Sun Also Rises, The (Hemingway),
    65–76, 82–90, 112, 168 n. 23, 183
    n. 56
Supplement, 64, 172 n. 12
Symbolic order, 58–60, 63, 77–79;
    and the preoedipal, 29–30, 57,
    112–13; and the real, 15–16, 21–24,
    30, 39–41, 113, 139–41

Tate, Alan, 71
Tate, Claudia, 174 n. 38
Teleology, narrative, 65, 86, 112, 170
    n. 57; of sexual development, 17,
    30, 41, 54, 65, 79, 110
Tempest, The (Shakespeare), 88
Their Eyes Were Watching God
    (Hurston), 91–118, 128, 135, 174 n.
    38
Theory, resistance to, 149, 184 n. 5
Tompkins, Jane, 132, 142
Torok, Maria, 128, 138, 176–77 n. 2,
    179 n. 24, 182 n. 48
Transcendental signifier, 99–101
Transference, 41, 47–48, 56–64,
    126–28, 131, 137, 151–52 n. 4; and
    metaphor, 60–63, 118, 140. See also
    Displacement
Traub, Valerie, 10
Truth, 123–25, 130–31, 141, 150, 178
    n. 12, 180 n. 29, 181 n. 37
Types and typology, 13–15, 17, 19–21,
    27; of women and lesbians, 31–32,
    49–50, 52, 69–71, 145

Uncanny, the, 67, 74–80, 88–89, 110,
    139, 175 n. 44
Unconscious, the, 61, 75–76, 110,
    130, 151–52 n. 4

Vicinus, Martha, 8
Voice, 55, 98, 100, 121; female, 15,
    27–30, 33–41, 105; of mother, 94,

110–16; and racialized body, 92, 105–6. *See also* Speech

Wald, Priscilla, 103
Wall, Cheryl, 107
Walton, Jean, 95
Wardley, Lynn, 33–34, 159–60 n. 70, 160 n. 74
Warner, Michael, 44
Weber, Samuel, 30, 61, 79–80, 99–100, 122–23, 183 n. 54
Westphal, Karl von, 14
"What White Publishers Won't Print" (Hurston), 98–99
Whipple, E. P., 16
Whiteness, 94, 98–102, 114, 172 n. 16
Whitman, Walt, 55
Wittig, Monique, 24, 128
Women, 7–9, 49–52, 100; African American, 92, 96–98, 105–6, 113–15; as feminists, 33–34, 47, 49–51; and lesbians, 9, 17–18, 32–33, 41, 50–53, 68–71, 118, 128–30, 137, 145–46, 176–77 n. 2, 179 n. 25; masculinization of, 66, 68–71, 82, 168 n. 23; in psychoanalytic theory, 17, 40–41, 53–56, 94, 111, 117; and speech, 27–28, 34–36, 159–60 n. 70; as writers, 42–43, 132, 148, 160 n. 74. *See also* Femininity.
Wright, Richard, 106–7
Wright, Walter F., 32
Writing, compared to speech, 35–36, 41, 94–95, 103–6, 114, 160 nn. 73–74

Zimmerman, Bonnie, 148
Žižek, Slavoj, 3–4, 15, 21–24, 26, 29–30, 40, 58–59, 139–40
Zwarg, Christina, 47